C000173528

The Mortimers, Lords of the March

The Mortimers, Lords of the March

by
Charles Hopkinson & Martin Speight

LOGASTON PRESS

LOGASTON PRESS
Little Logaston, Logaston,
Woonton, Almeley, Herefordshire HR3 6QH

First published by Logaston Press 2002
Reprinted 2011
Copyright © text: Charles Hopkinson & Martin Speight 2011
Copyright © illustrations as per Acknowledgments

All rights reserved. No part of this publication
may be reproduced, stored in a retrieval system,
or transmitted, in any form or by any means,
electronic, mechanical, photocopying, recording
or otherwise, without the prior permission,
in writing of the publisher

ISBN 978 1873827 53 6

Set in Times by Logaston Press
and printed in India by
Imprint Digital Ltd

*Front cover illustration: Roger (IV) greeting Isabella,
wife of Edward II, in front of Hereford in 1326 with the younger
Despencer being led off for execution by the gateway into the city
after his and Edward II's capture at Neath
(British Library MS Roy 15 E IV f 316v)*

'In short, the very name of Mortimer implies turbulent restlessness and never-sated ambition, alternate honour and disgrace, the greatest ascendancy succeeded by the most utter ruin'
R.W. Eyton (1815-1881), historian of Shropshire

Contents

Acknowledgments

In writing this book we gladly acknowledge our debt to the published work of past and present historians, especially Professor Rees Davies whose publications have shed so much light on dark corners of the history of the March of Wales. In addition B.P. Evans's unpublished thesis, 'The Family of Mortimer', has been of particular value.

We would like to record our gratitude to the organisations and individuals who have in one way or another encouraged and assisted us. The staffs of the Herefordshire Record Office, Hereford Library, Shropshire Records and Research Centre, Birmingham Central Library, The National Library of Wales and the National Monuments Record (Wales) have been unfailingly helpful. Michael Faraday, Tony Fleming, Sue Hubbard, Richard Stone and Jim Tonkin have helped and advised us in different ways. Some of the material in this book first appeared in the *Transactions of The Woolhope Naturalists' Field Club*.

Several organisations and individuals have given permission to use illustrations, and we would like to thank the following, who retain copyright in each case: The British Library pp.118 (MS Roy 18 E.II f 226v), 120 (MS Roy 18 E.II f 401v); 126 (MS Julius E IV Art VI fo 19v); Brian Byron pp.193 and 195; Mr. and Mrs. Challis p.37; Dúchas, The Heritage Service, Dublin p.80; Mrs. Gillian Hodges p.206 (both); National Trust Photo Library pp.189 (both); Chris Musson and CPAT p.139; Keith Parker p.40; Public Record Office pp.147 and 148; The Radnorshire Society pp.181 and 185; Royal Commission on the Ancient and Historical Monuments of Wales (RCAHMW) pp.10, 26, 169, 170 and 187; Society of Antiquaries, London p.205; Martin Speight pp.70 and 131; Gareth Thomas of the Cat's Whiskers Studio, Ludlow pp.83 and 84; Ann E. Thompson p.190; Woodmansterne Publications Ltd. p.100; Logaston Press pp.3, 11, 22, 23, 34, 41, 42, 47, 48, 49, 51, 55 (both), 59, 66, 67, 68 (both), 71, 74, 88, 93, 123, 127, 143, 144, 159, 160, 167, 168, 171, 172, 174, 175, 176 (both), 182, and with thanks to Mr. and Mrs. Challis for providing assistance and access pp. 194, 197 and 198.

Andy Johnson of Logaston Press who commissioned this book has prepared the maps, genealogical tables and illustrations. His support, knowledge of history and editorial rigour in weaving into a single strand the contributions of two authors has been of inestimable value.

Finally, we are indebted to our families who have had for many months to live, as it were, with the Mortimers as lodgers; without their support this book would never have seen the light of day.

Foreword

Some 150 years ago the Herefordshire historian C.J. Robinson wrote that 'It would require an entire volume to detail the fortunes of the house of Mortimer and to show the influence which successive members of it exerted upon the affairs of the kingdom'. This book sets out to do not only this, but also to describe the political backcloths in medieval Wales against which the Mortimers established themselves as the longest living and perhaps the most formidable of the marcher families, as well as the government of their vast estates, their castles and prominent branches of the family.

The Mortimers were one of the greatest dynasties of medieval England and their careers were intimately bound up with English, Welsh and Irish history. Of Norman origin and coming to England at the time of the Norman Conquest or shortly afterwards, they were firmly established at Domesday as lords of Wigmore in Herefordshire. For nearly 350 years the family's fluctuating fortunes brought them wealth and influence as well as humiliation and disgrace as they carved out for themselves empires in Wales and Ireland, and jockeyed for status in England. After about 1200 they were seldom far from the centre of government and at times exerted great influence on the course of events. One of them became a close friend and loyal servant of King Edward I, his grandson made himself earl of March and virtual dictator of England, and at the end of the 14th century a descendant was named heir presumptive to the throne. The male line failed in 1425 and the Mortimer interests passed by the female line to Richard, duke of York, whose son and heir, Edward, was crowned king of England in 1461.

There is now little evidence of the Mortimers' once pervasive presence in England, Wales and Ireland. Names of towns and villages have survived, indicating that they were once the family's estates; there is the site of the battle of Mortimers Cross, the remains of Wigmore Abbey, and above all the ruins of their many castles — physical reminders of the Middle Ages and the power and wealth that the Mortimers once wielded in the kingdom.

In this reprint of 2011, the opportunity has been taken to correct a handful of errors.

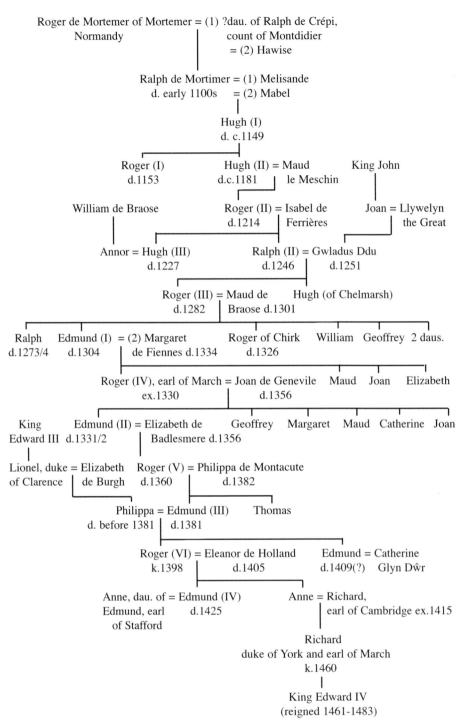

Select Family Tree of the Mortimers
An alternative descent would omit Roger (I) and Hugh (II) and suggest that
it was Hugh (I) who died c.1181 (see page 31)

CHAPTER I

Norman Origins & English Opportunities

> An interesting class of men …who were not of any particular importance
> in Normandy, but who became so in England; whose fortunes were made
> by the Conquest.[1]

In 1054, when Orderic Vitalis tells us that a Roger de Mortemer[2] held a castle
at Mortemer in the Duchy of Normandy, no Norman, let alone the embat-
tled duke fighting for his life in a civil war, could surely have imagined that
within just 16 years they would have completed the military conquest of one
of the major states of western Europe. The irruption of the Normans onto the
European scene — in the Mediterranean as well as in the north-west of the
Continent — is a striking phenomenon of European history, and the Mortimers
are exemplars of a restless and acquisitive society which mastered England, but
which within a few generations had been assimilated into a new racially mixed
aristocracy within the kingdom.

The Duchy of Normandy into which Roger de Mortemer was born, tradition
has it before 990, was a recent creation; it was in or about 911 that the emperor
Charles III had recognized Rolf (Rollo), a Viking who hailed from Norway
or Denmark, as the ruler of territory in France bordering the lower reaches of
the river Seine. For many years this region had been subjected to Viking raids
evolving into more permanent Scandinavian occupation, and Charles's confirmation of Rolf's status would have been little more than acceptance of a *fait
accompli*. It is clear, however, that Charles claimed overlordship of the new
province and this was to develop into the vassalage of its rulers to the kings of
France. This relationship, sometimes recognized by the Norman rulers when it
suited their purposes, sometimes not, would play a major part in the political
survival of Roger de Mortemer's contemporary, Duke William II — William
the Conqueror.

By the mid-930s the dynasty which Rolf had founded had expanded the
borders of the lands that its members ruled to much the same limits as the mid-

1

11th-century duchy that Roger de Mortemer knew, and by his time the 'counts' of the 10th century were now more often referred to as 'dukes'. Over the years Scandinavian influence within the duchy had been steadily eroded as its aristocracy absorbed Latin and Christian culture — although as late as 1014 Duke Richard II had welcomed to his capital of Rouen a heathen Scandinavian army which had wrought havoc in parts of north-western France. Aristocratic turmoil and civil war were regular occurrences in 10th- and 11th-century Normandy, and the accession of Duke William II in 1035, illegitimate and only about seven years old, was the occasion of a new outbreak of violence as the great families of the duchy fought for power.

For 25 years William and his supporters struggled for survival in more or less continuous civil war within Normandy and in the face of threats and on occasion invasion by their neighbours. Stepping-stones in William's struggle for political survival occurred in 1047, when the French king, his overlord, came to his rescue by defeating his enemies at the battle of Val-ès-Dunes, and in 1054 when the Normans effectively destroyed a threat from the French king, Henry, and from Geoffrey of Anjou by winning the battle of Mortemer. It was not, however, until 1060, with the deaths of King Henry and Count Geoffrey, that political and military pressure on Normandy eased. Only six years later William was in a position to launch an attack on the kingdom of England.

The crisis for William which was resolved by the Norman victory at Mortemer was a turning point in his fortunes, and arguably he was never again to be faced by quite such a potential disaster. It is in Orderic Vitalis's mention of this battle, and in the events surrounding it, that we have the first firm reference to Roger de Mortemer, ancestor of the Mortimers of Wigmore.

Early in 1054 a coalition led by King Henry and Geoffrey of Anjou with support from disaffected elements within Normandy mounted a two-pronged attack on the duchy. To the south of the Seine Duke William confronted the French king's army advancing through the *comté* of Évreux. To the north of the Seine, in Upper Normandy, a second Norman force, under the command of Robert, count of Eu, William of Warenne, Roger de Mortemer and other barons, and largely drawn from their estates in the region, opposed a French army under Count Odo of Blois and other magnates. At the battle of Mortemer, near the castle, the French army was comprehensively defeated and such was the disaster that the French king abandoned his invasion of the duchy. Roger de Mortemer was by this time clearly a person of some standing — at least in Upper Normandy — in the burgeoning new aristocracy grouped around Duke William as he slowly managed to assert his authority and reward his supporters.

The genealogy of the 11th-century Mortimers is far from certain.[3] There is evidence, which is sometimes contradictory and which has therefore by no means met with universal acceptance, that Roger was born prior to 990, the son of Hugh, bishop of Coutances, while his mother was an unnamed niece or sister of Gunnor, the wife of Duke Richard I (942-996). Furthermore it has been claimed that Roger's mother was a sister of Herfast, the grandfather of William FitzOsbern, later the first Norman earl of Hereford. Roger seems also to have been a kinsman of William of Warenne, a fast-rising family in 11th-century Normandy destined to become earls of Surrey after the conquest of England. If, as has been postulated, Roger was born prior to 990 and he appears to have survived to witness a charter *c*.1080, he must have lived to a suspiciously great age. The identification of him as Bishop Hugh's son, for linking his mother to the ducal house and for his relationship to the FitzOsberns and the Warennes is unlikely ever to be confirmed, but in any event in the compact Norman aristocracy blood relationships, regular and irregular, would have been widespread.

Mortemer Castle today — part of the keep remains on a large thickly wooded motte surrounded by a deep, dry moat

It is clear, however, from Orderic Vitalis's account of the times, that in 1054 Roger held the castle of Mortemer, near Neufchâtel-en-Bray about 30 miles north-east of Rouen. He had married the daughter[4] of Ralph de Crépi, count of Montdidier, Amiens and Valois, and did homage to the count for lands outside Normandy brought to him by his wife. Count Ralph was a leader of the French army which was defeated at Mortemer and Roger de Mortemer therefore found himself holding his father-in-law and liege lord as prisoner in his castle. Roger released Ralph as he had done homage to him, but without the duke's, his superior lord's, authority. For Duke William this unauthorised release of an important prisoner was a grave trespass upon his prerogative and, in the words which Orderic Vitalis put into Duke William's mouth in the latter's death-bed speech:

> I banished Roger from Normandy for this offence, but became recon-
> ciled with him soon afterwards and restored the rest of his honour to him.
> I withheld from him, however, the castle of Mortemer in which he had
> preserved my enemy … and gave it to his kinsman William of Warenne,
> a loyal knight.[5]

Years later, in 1086, William as king of England was to remind the baronage of their obligations to him when he made 'all the people occupying land who were of any account over all England, no matter whose vassals they might be', swear loyalty to him 'against all other men'.[6]

William's treatment of Roger de Mortemer was typical of his methods of maintaining discipline amongst his baronage by rewarding loyalty at the expense of those whom he considered had crossed him. The bridling of the aristocracy in Normandy, and later his maintenance of baronial discipline in England, were not the least of William's achievements. As Orderic explained, again putting words into William's mouth:

> If the Normans are disciplined under a just and firm rule they are men
> of great valour, who press invincibly to the fore in arduous undertakings
> and, proving their strength, fight resolutely to overcome all enemies. But

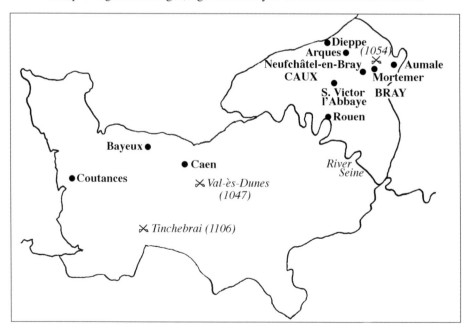

Normandy, showing places mentioned in the text

4

without such rule they tear each other to pieces and destroy themselves, for they hanker after rebellion, cherish sedition, and are ready for any treachery. So they need to be restrained by the severe penalties of law, and forced by the curb of discipline to keep to the path of justice. If they are allowed to go wherever they choose, as an untamed ass does, both they and their ruler must expect grave disorder and poverty. I have learnt this by now through repeated experience.[7]

William's 'just and firm rule' would not always be achieved by his successors as kings of England, and in its absence the medieval English baronage would, just as in William's reign, take advantage of any royal weakness or injustice.

After the restoration of his lands Roger de Mortemer moved his seat to St. Victor-en-Caux (now St. Victor-l'Abbaye) some 15 miles north of Rouen, and St. Victor remained the seat of the Mortimers in Normandy, where they held estates in the bailiwicks of Caux and Bray, until the duchy was lost to France in 1204.

Roger is recorded as being a benefactor of, and perhaps the founder of, the abbey of St. Victor-en-Caux as a priory of the abbey of Saint-Ouen in Rouen. It had taken many years to rebuild ecclesiastic vitality in the duchy after the depredations of the Vikings in the 9th and early 10th centuries, but by the year 1000 a reconstruction of the Norman Church and a strong resurgence of monasticism was taking place, galvanised by able and influential bishops under the patronage of the Norman dukes. Duke William continued this tradition of monastic patronage and the new nobility of Normandy followed his example in founding and endowing religious houses; in due course they were to take with them to England the custom of making such benefactions. Motives, other than piety, were mixed and strings might well be attached to endowments. For the duke these institutions, which formed a loose but coherent power-block, brought a degree of political stability to the duchy, and in any case he was inclined to treat them almost as if they were part of his demesne; for members of the aristocracy there were financial motives as well as the matter of prestige; lords might, for instance, convert newly acquired estates into cash by receiving regular payments, or they could obtain credit, from religious houses in exchange for endowments. Thriving abbeys and monasteries which attracted pilgrims and traders would also augment the income that magnates obtained from their estates.

Roger was one of the Norman barons who were required to contribute ships for Duke William's fleet for the invasion of England in 1066, although doubt has been cast on the accuracy of this record. As Roger's son by a reputed second marriage, Ralph, was likely to have been under age, indeed perhaps had not been born, at the time of the battle of Hastings. The Wigmore chronicler's assertion[8] that he was present at the battle and distinguished himself in the fighting is highly suspect; chroniclers and genealogists have always been tempted to

The Norman invasion fleet as depicted in the Bayeux Tapestry

endow families — so often their patrons — with unjustified military glory and prestige and the Wigmore chronicler was no exception: 'my family came over with the Conqueror' is only too often an example of wishful thinking.

Nothing more is heard of Roger de Mortemer after his witnessing a charter in Normandy *c.*1080, but Ralph came to England, whether or not he fought at Hastings, and by 1086 was firmly established as a tenant-in-chief in William of Normandy's kingdom. How he obtained this status is not altogether clear. It is very possible that he was associated with William FitzOsbern, created earl of Hereford in 1067, and, as the Wigmore chronicler records, distinguished himself two years later in suppressing the rebellion of an Anglo-Saxon magnate, Edric the Wild. Edric had taken up arms against the Normans in Herefordshire and Shropshire and had joined forces with two Welsh princes. The rebels threatened Hereford, burned Shrewsbury and the rising spread northwards into Cheshire and Staffordshire. King William temporarily abandoned personal control of his campaign in the north-east of England to deal with the rising, and appears to have done so with his usual ruthless military efficiency before returning to the north a few weeks later to launch his infamous harrying of Yorkshire. Perhaps at this time Ralph had come to William's notice and in this context Ralph certainly held estates in 1086 which had once belonged to Edric. When William FitzOsbern was killed in battle in Flanders in 1071, he was succeeded as the second earl by his son, Roger, who unsuccessfully rebelled in 1075; it is apparent from King William's favour to Ralph Mortimer that he was not party to the rebellion, and may indeed have been one of the lords whom the *Anglo-Saxon Chronicle* records were involved in its suppression. Certainly Ralph received a number of the estates which Earl Roger of Hereford had forfeited, very probably soon after the rebellion when the king did not appoint a successor to the earldom.

The major figure in the central sector of the Anglo-Welsh borderlands after FitzOsbern's death was Roger of Montgomery, another of King William's trusted lieutenants whom he had created earl of Shrewsbury in 1071 or possibly 1074. As Earl Roger of Shrewsbury's vassal and seemingly related to him, Ralph was allied to one of the most powerful barons in the kingdom; he was probably the earl's seneschal or steward, his right-hand man of business, and held his Shropshire estates through this service.

Domesday Book records that Ralph Mortimer held land and property in 12 English counties, mainly in Herefordshire and Shropshire, with several manors 'waste in the Welsh March' — no doubt districts devastated in turn by Anglo-Welsh violence prior to the Conquest, in Edric the Wild's rebellion and during Roger of Montgomery's campaigns. The most substantial estates were in Herefordshire and Shropshire, and the Domesday surveyors were clearly not always sure in which county an estate lay. The list of holdings in Herefordshire is headed by Wigmore Castle which had been built by William FitzOsbern, and the honour of Wigmore was to become the core of the Mortimer dominions and the castle the family's principal seat — or *caput* — until the 14th century when it was superseded by Ludlow Castle. In addition to the castle at Wigmore, there was by the time of Domesday a borough there worth £7 which had probably been established at much the same time as the castle. Its prosperity was largely linked to the castle and the economic activity that this engendered, so, when the castle was increasingly neglected in the 14th century, the borough's economic activity and prosperity dwindled. Even so, in 1425 it had at least seven shops. The English estates outside Herefordshire and Shropshire lay in Hampshire (in addition to numerous manors and four houses in Southampton, the abbey of St. Victor-en-Caux also held land in the county), Berkshire, Leicestershire, Lincolnshire, Oxfordshire, Somerset, Warwickshire, Wiltshire, Worcestershire and Yorkshire. That Ralph held some estates in Shropshire as a tenant-in-chief and others as a vassal of Earl Roger, probably as the earl's steward, can be explained by William FitzOsbern having established himself in parts of southern Shropshire before Roger was granted the county, and that the king granted these lands to Ralph sometime after their forfeiture in 1075.

William the Conqueror, king of England and duke of Normandy, died in 1087, and was succeeded in accordance with his wishes by his eldest son, Robert, as duke of Normandy, and by his second surviving son, William, as king of England. The succession of William II — William Rufus — was unpopular with many of the baronage; there was sympathy for Robert, who had received only the dukedom, and perhaps more to the point the barons knew of the easy-going Robert's political ineptitude and would have preferred the milder regime which he would offer, rather than the Conqueror-style discipline they could anticipate from his brother. It was soon plain that William was intent on restoring undivided control of the kingdom and dukedom, and it would be under his sole rule. The consequent rivalry between William and Robert put Normans such as Ralph Mortimer who held lands in both Normandy and England in a difficult position, as they would inevitably break their allegiance to one or the other of their liege lords.

Before William could set about achieving his ambition, however, he had to deal with a rebellion in England. The focus of the baronial opposition in the spring and summer of 1088 was in south-east England where Duke Robert was expected to land with an army in support of the rebels. Roger, earl of Shrewsbury, appears to have sat on the wall in his castle at Arundel, awaiting events and unwilling overtly to join the rebels. Meanwhile other barons rebelled, including a group in Herefordshire and Shropshire with Ralph Mortimer among their number. Ralph's feudal relationship with Earl Roger — his status in Shropshire is perhaps suggested by Florence of Worcester, where he is listed amongst the rebels immediately before 'the vassals of Earl Roger'[9] — make it likely that he was Roger's lieutenant in the west. Ralph, furthermore, seems to have been in Normandy early in 1088 as, in March, he witnessed a charter in favour of the abbey of Jumièges in the company of Duke Robert who could have taken the opportunity to sound him out as to where his loyalties lay. In south-east England the rebellion quickly collapsed in the face of the king's vigorous campaign and the failure of significant military support from Normandy; nor, after some initial successes did the dissident barons' cause fare better elsewhere. The rebels of Herefordshire and Shropshire, with Ralph Mortimer as one of their leaders, were routed with the native English *fyrd* playing a prominent part in their defeat, and the rebellion in the west petered out. The king treated the rebels leniently, he needed their support and there is no evidence of the western rebels being punished; Earl Roger and Ralph were forgiven and soon drawn into King William's designs on his brother's dukedom.

In 1095 the king had to deal with a further rebellion in which Hugh de Montgomery, the second earl of Shrewsbury who had succeeded his father the previous year, was implicated. On this occasion there is no suggestion that Ralph Mortimer was involved; he may have managed to distance himself from the rebellion or perhaps he was in Normandy. This time King William's vengeance ensured that he was not again troubled by rebellious magnates in England. The king may have 'reproached Hugh, earl of Shrewsbury, privately, and shrewdly took him back into his favour for three thousand pounds',[10] but another rebel, William of Eu who had taken part in the rebellion of 1088, was blinded and castrated and his steward hanged after being whipped outside every church in Salisbury.

During the Conqueror's reign, the Normans had made significant inroads into southern and northern Wales, but in central Wales raids mounted by Earl Roger of Shrewsbury had not been followed up by more permanent occupation, probably because military resources were needed to deal with a resurgent Powys under Gruffydd ap Cynan. As a vassal of Earl Roger, Ralph may well have been involved in Roger's raids into Wales during the 1070s and *c*.1081. The last decade of the 11th century, however, saw a much more aggressive attitude towards Wales on the part of the Norman lords with lands in the borderlands when a Welsh chronicle related with some exaggeration, 'the French seized all the lands of the Britons'.[11] These conquests and colonisations of parts of Wales were private enterprise ventures on the part of individual lords which developed into the marcher lordships that dominated so much of Wales in the Middle Ages. Earl Roger pushed far into Ceredigion and then into Dyfed to set up what would become the lordship of Pembroke. Ralph Mortimer may well have been involved in this campaign and in the free-for-all along the Anglo-Welsh frontier; the Welsh *cantref* of Maelienydd, adjoining the Mortimer estates in Herefordshire and Shropshire, would have been a natural choice for Ralph's annexation of territory on his own account, probably in the early 1090s when other border lords in the region were acquiring Brycheiniog (Brecon), Buellt (Builth) and Elfael.

The Wigmore chronicler is probably correct in crediting Ralph with the conquest of Maelienydd and in any event it had fallen to the Mortimers by the mid-1130s. Maelienydd had once been part of the kingdom of Powys but, after the collapse of Gruffydd ap Llywelyn's empire when he was killed in 1063, it seems to have been ruled by local chieftains. It was an upland region with little scope for economic exploitation by its new lords, but by this relatively unrewarding conquest Ralph had made clear his determination that the Mortimers were not to be left out of the border barons' race to carve out for themselves territories and spheres of influence in Wales. Even though Maelienydd was the centric lordship in Wales of the Mortimers, their control was to remain precarious with it reverting to Welsh rule on a number of occasions before the final collapse of Welsh independence in the last quarter of the 13th century. It is likely that Ralph built the castle of Cymaron to secure control of his new lands; this castle, on the site of the *cantref's* old Welsh court, became the major fortress of the lordship until it was replaced, probably in the 13th century, by Cefnllys; it did, however, remain the centre of Maelienydd's judicature.

Norman inroads into Wales at the end of the 11th century met with setbacks. A widespread uprising broke out in 1094 and in many districts, very probably in Maelienydd if it was already in Ralph's hands, the Welsh regained temporary control of their lands. The lords were unable to cope with the crisis and the king had to come to their rescue — a pattern which would be repeated on a number of occasions in the following centuries; Norman control over their lordships in Wales, other than in the remoter parts of the north and west, was re-established but it was often tenuous. Maelienydd seems to have been Ralph Mortimer's only significant acquisition of Welsh territory.

The site of Cymaron Castle, indicated by a line of earthworks encircling some farm buildings

In the 1090s and in the first few years of the next century Ralph's attention and resources seem increasingly to have been engaged in events in Normandy and the quarrels between on the one hand Kings William II and Henry I, and on the other Duke Robert to whom the Conqueror had bequeathed Normandy. For the barons of Ralph's generation, Normandy was 'home'. Although they might have gained honours and status in England and were winning for themselves lordships in Wales, their roots in Normandy and the prosperity of their fiefs there meant that they were by sentiment and self-interest deeply concerned with events in the duchy, particularly now that the kingdom and duchy were no longer subject to one authority. Normandy was as important as England to the early Norman kings and aristocracy, but the descendants of the first genera-tion of Norman barons in England were to become increasingly ambivalent in their attitude to the duchy until, in 1204, they were forced to choose between England and Normandy, a choice dependent upon which side of the Channel their more important interests lay.

After the death of William the Conqueror Normandy slipped rapidly into anarchy as his son, Robert, proved a disastrously incompetent ruler. William II of England exploited the situation by meddling in the duchy's affairs in pursuit of his ambition to reunite the sovereignty of England and Normandy. In 1089 he established a bridgehead in eastern Normandy by suborning certain lords and in the following year fomented an unsuccessful rebellion in Rouen. As for Ralph Mortimer, he may have been in Normandy in the spring of 1088, when as we have seen he could have done homage to Duke Robert for his lands in the

The site of Cymaron Castle from the north-east.
The motte rises behind and to the left of the farmhouse

duchy, but if so he soon changed sides as Orderic lists him as one of the barons who supported William in his quarrel with the duke. Ralph's estates lay within the king's sphere of influence in the duchy, and he was probably among the barons who, Orderic records, put their castles in a state of defence and garrisoned them at the king's expense. Again, when William crossed to Normandy in 1091, it is likely that Ralph was at the king's headquarters at Eu when many barons submitted to him.

Since the rebellion of 1088 Ralph had clearly been William II's man in both England and Normandy; but in the duchy, in the confusion of treaties and wars between the two brothers, there is a hint that he did not sever all connections with Duke Robert. At some time between 1091 and 1095 he was at Lisieux, witnessing with the duke a charter again in favour of Jumièges Abbey; this may have occurred during the uneasy peace between the king and the duke of 1091-3 and does not necessarily indicate any disloyalty to the king.

After the death of King William in 1100, Orderic Vitalis mentions Ralph in a list of magnates who, probably in 1104, accompanied King Henry I to Normandy, but little credence can be placed on the Wigmore chronicler's account of Ralph's prominent part in the battle of Tinchebrai in 1106, when the writer gives his death as having taken place six years previously; further, Orderic does not mention him in his account of the battle. Henry I's victory over Duke Robert at Tinchebrai was the culminating point in the struggle for Normandy and now, after 19 years, the king of England was once more duke of Normandy; like the battle of Hastings, Tinchebrai was a touchstone of prestige amongst the Normans, a battle with which the aristocracy wished to be associated if they possibly could be.

Ralph had kept his distance from the rebellion of Robert, the third earl of Shrewsbury, and other barons in 1102 — an unsuccessful conspiracy in alliance with Duke Robert of Normandy to unseat King Henry; indeed he had benefited from the earl's disgrace, as the king's decision not to appoint a successor to this powerful magnate had removed one of the contestants for power along the Welsh border and in central Wales. One would assume that Ralph's affairs there and in England, as a loyal supporter of Henry I, had prospered, but there is no record of him, or indeed sound evidence for the existence in England of a Mortimer, during the 25 years between 1115 and 1140 — no mention in charters, no record of a presence at great events nor in the chronicles, places where one would expect to find some reference. A possible explanation for this hiatus in the records is that Ralph and, or, his heir in some way fell foul of King Henry and that the Mortimer lands in England and Wales were confiscated. There are, however, no sound grounds for such an explanation, except a possible alliance between Ralph and the chronically rebellious Stephen of Aumale through the marriage of Ralph's daughter to Stephen.[12] Stephen was William the Conqueror's nephew; he had been implicated in the 1095 revolt as a possible replacement for William II, and in the reign of Henry I had been involved in unsuccessful baronial rebellions in Normandy which had been supported by Louis VI of France. His castle at Aumale, about nine miles east of Mortemer, was one of the great border fortresses of Normandy.

The date of Ralph's death is not known. He can be assumed to be the Ralph noted in the Lindsey Survey of c.1115 as holding land in Lincolnshire, an estate which he had held in 1086; it also seems that he had died or resigned his honours before 1137 when, it can be deduced from the archbishop of Rouen's confirmation of the estates of the abbey of St. Victor, that the Mortimer lands in Normandy were held by Hugh, his son and heir by either his first wife Melisande or second wife Mabel. When Hugh received his inheritance he became a substantial landholder in both Normandy and England, and in Wales there might be opportunities to augment the foothold won by his father.

CHAPTER II

Wales & the Marcher Lordships

Although the Normans took some five years to conquer England it was to take the Anglo-Normans 200 years to subjugate Wales. During this period the parts of Wales under Anglo-Norman control came to be known as *marchia Wallie* — the March of Wales — whilst independent Wales governed by its native rulers was known as *Wallia* or *pura Wallia*. With the ebb and flow of conquest and the periodic recovery of their lands by the Welsh, the boundaries of the March were constantly changing; the medieval 'March' as a geographical term therefore had a very different meaning to the modern 'March' which is used to describe the Anglo-Welsh border counties.

The Mortimers were to amass lands in England, Wales and Ireland, but it was in Wales that their fortunes were based and it was from their resources in the March of Wales that they exercised power and influence in England. Holding lands in Wales as marcher lords they were members of a select group of barons owing allegiance as tenants-in-chief to the king but ruling their lordships with a degree of independence unobtainable by most of the king's subjects. The origins of this constitutional anomaly lay in William the Conqueror's arrangements for the settlement and defence of the Anglo-Welsh border.

For many years prior to the Norman Conquest Anglo-Saxon kings had claimed lordship over Wales and this loose relationship had been widely accepted by the Welsh princes; Earl Harold's devastating campaign of 1063 had forcibly reminded the Welsh of the military strength of their English neighbours. As king of England, William the Conqueror inherited this claim to Wales but, faced with problems in England and Normandy for some years after the battle of Hastings, he had little inclination to involve himself directly in Wales. He did, however, make arrangements for the defence of the frontier, indeterminate as it was, and for the introduction of Norman administration to the English borderlands, a remote area where his representatives would have to have more freedom of action than elsewhere in the kingdom.

Three of the king's trusted lieutenants were given responsibility for the region: William FitzOsbern was created earl of Hereford in the south; Roger de Montgomery was created earl of Shrewsbury and Hugh d'Avranches earl of Chester with authority for the central and northern sectors respectively. The three earls appear to have been given widespread powers within their earldoms, untrammelled by the king, but what, if any, instructions they were given with regard to military adventures in Wales is not known; it seems likely, however, that they were advised that they could annex lands in Wales on their own account, but must not involve King William whose primary interests lay elsewhere. In the early 12th century Henry I, in what is probably an example of the kind of licence that King William granted explicitly or implicitly to his border earls, authorised one of his barons to conquer part of Wales:

> King Henry sent a messenger to Gilbert FitzRichard, who was a mighty, powerful man and a friend of the king, and eminent in his deeds. And he came forthwith to the king. And the king said to him: 'Thou wert always asking of me a portion of Wales. Now I will give thee the land of Cadwgan ap Bleddyn. Go and take possession of it.' And he accepted it gladly from the king. And he gathered a host and came to Ceredigion and took possession of it and made two castles in it.[1]

Certainly the earls rapidly and individually moved aggressively against the eastern districts of Wales, with Earl Roger also launching raids deep into the interior, and thus began the piecemeal, private enterprise colonisation of the country. The king's solution to the problem of the border with Wales worked whilst his appointees were men with whom he had a personal bond and whom he could trust; but when the earldoms with all their prerogatives passed by inheritance to the earls' successors, there would be distinct dangers for the Crown as was evident as early as 1075 when William FitzOsbern's son, Roger, the second earl of Hereford, rebelled.

Wales was very different to England, politically as well as geographically. Although its inhabitants acknowledged a common Welsh identity, it was a country of many sovereign states with the mountainous terrain governing their borders and hindering relationships with their neighbours. These petty principalities — perhaps as many as 18 of them in the 11th century — were often at each others' throats, as Giraldus Cambrensis, a great-grandson of a Welsh prince described:

> This nation is, above all others, addicted to the digging up of boundary ditches, removing the limits, transgressing landmarks, and extending their territory by every possible means. So great is their disposition towards this common violence … hence arise suits and contentions, murders and conflagrations, and frequent fratricides.[2]

A source of perennial political weakness were the rules of inheritance where land was divided equally between all the sons which militated against any constitutional centralisation. A politically fractured Wales made it much easier for the marcher lords to conquer the country piece by piece and conduct a policy of divide and rule; on the other hand the usual lack of a Welsh national leader made it more difficult to conduct diplomatic negotiations. To what extent individual conquests in Wales were actually licensed is not clear but many were probably not expressly authorised by the king. From time to time during the Middle Ages, however, a Welsh prince was able to win control over other principalities, form alliances and exert capable leadership over large tracts of Wales; the Welsh would then prove formidable adversaries to the marcher lords. Such Welsh unity was, however, fleeting; it did not long survive the departure of a national leader and the principalities soon reverted to their customary political isolation and bickering. When there were leaders such as Rhys ap Gruffydd in the 12th century, and Llywelyn ap Iorwerth and Llywelyn ap Gruffydd in the 13th, an uneasy *modus vivendi* between the Welsh and the English would be established after military successes had enabled the Welsh to recover some, and on occasion almost all, of their lands.

If independent Wales was politically fragmented, so in one sense was the March. The lords may have on the surface presented a coherent power bloc, but the pattern of lordship and power in the March, with the marchers' individual political agendas and rivalries, would often change. Death and lack of a direct line of male heirs, marriage, wardship, and the creation of new lordships by, and forfeiture of them to, the king all influenced the evolution of the March.

For 200 years after the Norman Conquest the total subjugation of even a disunited Wales was beyond the military capacity of England, so often preoccupied, as it was, with events elsewhere. It was Edward I's single-minded concentration of the kingdom's resources and the shrewd use of his armies — and his navy to supply them — that brought Welsh independence to an end in the last quarter of the 13th century when Wales was united with England in 1284 by the Statute of Rhuddlan. What had been independent Wales now became Crown lands which in 1301 were granted by Edward I to his son Edward of Caernarvon to comprise the Principality; the 40 or so marcher lordships, comprising over half the country, were not disturbed and were to remain in existence until 1536.

How the marcher lords acquired their special constitutional status in Wales has been the subject of debate. It is argued on the one hand that they simply acquired the regal powers of the Welsh rulers they dispossessed. The basic units of Welsh territory and administration within a *gwlad* (in general, an identifiable administrative region or one subject to a single ruler) were the *cantrefi* consisting of two or more *cymydau* which can be very loosely equated to the English Hundreds. By annexing a relatively small *cantref* or *cymyd*, with its *llys* or administrative court, an invading lord stepped into the shoes of the local Welsh ruler — either king, prince or lord, synonymous terms in Welsh law and custom. The marcher lords were therefore, by right of conquest, sovereign over their Welsh lordships, just as if one Welsh prince had defeated another and annexed his territory.

On the other hand it is argued that the lords' powers were openly or tacitly granted by the king as rewards for carrying out their conquests on, it could be said, the Crown's behalf. The March of Wales was not, however, a homogenous region, subject to a systematic and uniform style of conquest and administration. It was through varying individual circumstances that the lords of the March won the prerogatives which in due course coalesced into their rights or privileges as a group and which came to be recognised by 13th-century lawyers.

Whilst the king acknowledged that his writ did not run in the March, in the last resort he reserved his authority over the lords as tenants-in-chief, for instance in the case of disputed titles to lordships. What the lords considered to be their rights, the king considered as privileges, and the extent to which the king could interfere constitutionally in the affairs of the marcher lordships was to prove a running sore between strong and ambitious kings and the marchers. The position was further complicated by the fact that the marcher lords also held lands in England by normal feudal tenure; indeed, by 1307 seven out of the ten English earls held lands in England as well as Wales. In England they were constrained in their actions, in Wales with their independent jurisdictions they could do much as they liked. In 1199 William de Braose declared that 'neither king, sheriff nor justice had any right to enter his liberty', and John Fitzalan, lord of Oswestry and Clun greeted a royal writ in 1269 with the observation that 'in the part of the March where he now resided he was obliged to do nothing at the king's mandate and nothing would he do'.[3] As late as 1465 when Edward IV granted the lordship of Raglan to William Herbert, he gave him 'all royal courts and other jurisdictions, powers and authorities as in any other royal lordship in Wales or the marches of Wales with all fines, amercements, issues and profits from the same before their stewards at Raglan, with power of oyer and terminer, an authentic seal for commissions, writs and warrants, and power of appointing justices to hold cessions in eyre and other cessions and courts'.[4] The inference is that these rights were held by all marcher lords. A specific instance of the marchers' autonomy related to castle-building; the earls of Hereford would have had, at least in theory, to obtain a licence to build a castle in Herefordshire; in their marcher lordship of Brecon they could have built a castle without reference to the Crown.

The marcher lords were pragmatic individualists in a world where military power was the ultimate sanction. Common interests — towards the Welsh and towards the king and his policies in the March — usually overruled quarrels among themselves, but they seldom formed large cohesive political groupings; when they did, as during the Barons' War of the 1260s, their military muscle could be crucial. Kings, then, did well to consider carefully the consequences of their policies for the political situation in the March and in England, as well as for their personal concerns as they also held their own lands in the March alongside the baronial lordships. In their relations with independent Wales, kings also shared interests with the marcher lords and would pursue an aggressive Welsh policy on their own account. Early in the 12th century, for instance, Henry I, in the anguished words of a Welsh chronicler, 'against whom no one could be of avail save God himself',[5] founded the royal lordship of Carmarthen.

The bedrock of the marcher lords' authority and independence of action in their lordships was the law and their right to exercise justice. The Law, or Custom, of the March, was an amalgam of Norman, English and Welsh law and custom, and by the beginning of the 13th century it had come to be recognised in England as the way that the March was ruled. It was enshrined in Magna Carta: 'And if a dispute arises over this [the dispossession of lands], then let it be decided in the March by the judgement of their peers — for holdings in England according to the law of England, for holdings in Wales according to the law of Wales, and for holdings in the March according to the law of the March'. The Law of the March evolved and differed in the various lordships but, whilst kings might claim ultimate authority over and above it as Edward I successfully did in 1291, its common principles identified the March as a specific administrative region and governed its administration.

One of the pivotal prerogatives enjoyed by the marchers was the right to wage war, or 'private war' as it is sometimes known; in England this was a right strictly reserved to the king. It was this which enabled the marcher lords to wage war against the Welsh or one another at their sole discretion, and an example of this involving Ralph Mortimer (II), his Welsh enemies and his feudal relationship with King Henry III occurred in 1240-41.

For the previous 150 years Wales had been subjected to periodic attack and colonisation by the marcher lords. In the face of Welsh resistance and counter-attacks the lords' conquests were far from permanent; their lands increased and decreased in area, but by 1200 much of eastern, southern and south-western Wales was under English control. Within a few years, however, Llywelyn ap Iorwerth — Llywelyn the Great — had with his allies recovered much of the March for the Welsh, including the Mortimer lordships of Maelienydd and Gwerthrynion. In 1234 the Treaty of Middle brought about an uneasy peace between Henry III, the marcher lords and Llywelyn. On Llywelyn's death in April 1240 the king refused to recognize his heir's, David's, right to his father's conquests; Henry appears to have authorised the marchers' recovery of their lands in Wales as, soon after Llywelyn died, he ordered the sheriff of Herefordshire to transfer possession of Maelienydd to Ralph Mortimer. During the following summer of 1241 Ralph recovered the lordship by force and agreed a truce with the local Welsh rulers. Earlier that year, however, they had met Henry III at Worcester when presumably they pressed their claim to Maelienydd. After the Welsh had formally submitted to the king he confirmed that their oaths of fidelity would not be negated by any hostilities between them and Ralph Mortimer after their truce had expired. The king had in effect endorsed the right of lords, Welsh and English, to wage war amongst themselves in Wales; Ralph might be a subject of the king, at war with the Welsh, but that did not necessarily mean it was the king's business, involving his relationship with both Welsh rulers and marcher lords.

Fifty years later Edward I intervened decisively in the March, determined to demonstrate that affairs there *were* his business and that he exercised paramount authority over the marcher lords. After his conquest of Wales and the partition of the country into Crown lands and the March, Edward, with his passion for law and order, would have considered the divided administration of the country, the relative independence of the rulers of much of it and its fragmented judicial system, as an anathema; but the marchers with their jealously guarded immunities were difficult to dislodge, and although Edward from time to time flexed his muscles in his relationship with them he seems to have accepted the political situation in the March — provided his authority as monarch was recognised. He had made this clear as early as 1275 when, in the Statute of Westminster, he declared that he would do right in the March, and anywhere else where his writ did not run, to all complainants. It was some years before he was given an opportunity, in a dispute between two high-profile marcher lords and ironically at the request of one of them, to assert in dramatic fashion royal supremacy in the March.

By 1290 Gilbert de Clare, earl of Gloucester and lord of Glamorgan in the March of Wales, and Humphrey de Bohun, earl of Hereford and lord of Brecon in the March, were at loggerheads, largely over a disputed debt. The bitterness between them was such that when Gilbert built a castle at Morlais (near Merthyr Tydfil), on land alleged by Humphrey to be part of Brecon and not Glamorgan, hostilities between the two earls in accordance with the Law of the March seemed likely. In January 1290 the king issued a proclamation forbidding the two earls to wage war; Gilbert de Clare pointedly ignored the proclamation and Humphrey de Bohun, militarily the weaker of the two, appealed to the king. Appreciating this opportunity to demonstrate his authority, Edward appointed commissioners to enquire into the facts since his proclamation and take evidence from a jury drawn from the March. The marchers now realised the implications of the commissioners' proceedings and the Pandora's Box that Humphrey de Bohun had unwittingly opened when he had referred the dispute to the king, and made excuses for not serving on the jury. The commissioners accepted that Edmund I Mortimer's lands were too far away from Brecon, where the enquiry was being conducted, for him to have had time to arrange for any of his tenants to attend, and that, as Roger Mortimer of Chirk held lands from Humphrey, he, too, should be excused attendance.

The marcher lords as a whole contended that matters affecting the March should be settled according to the Law of the March and recalled the clause in Magna Carta to that effect. The commissioners for their part dismissed this argument, observing that marcher lords held their honours under the Crown and that on occasion, and in the public interest, the king was above law and custom — a somewhat startling assertion. A jury was at last sworn, facts established, damages assessed and a report submitted by the commissioners to the king, whilst in the king's name they forbade the renewal of hostilities. The two earls continued their armed squabbling and Humphrey, so far the aggrieved disputant, now foolishly refused to return some of Gilbert's cattle, which the constable of Brecon had found grazing on the land which Humphrey claimed. The constable had forcibly taken possession of them, in the process killing some of Gilbert's men, and Earl Humphrey defied an injunction to return the animals by retaining them as security until it was decided that the land was indeed his. Humphrey should have returned the cattle in exchange for compensation for any keep, damage, etc., the normal practice as it must always have been between neighbours on reasonably good terms in England or, for that matter, in the March. What the two earls could not do in England was resort to armed aggression, and King Edward was determined that they would not do so in the March in contravention of his direct order.

In the autumn of 1291 the two earls, summoned in their capacity as lords of Glamorgan and Brecon, were arraigned before the king and council at Abergavenny, and in the following January before parliament at Westminster. Gilbert de Clare was found guilty of waging war after the king's injunction and Humphrey de Bohun of defying the king by claiming that he was entitled to act in the March of Wales in a way he could not do in England. The two lords were sentenced to imprisonment and forfeiture of their lordships of Glamorgan and Brecon during their lifetimes; but the king soon relented and in place of the sentences fined them. Gilbert and Humphrey were released and their lands restored to them, but they do not seem ever to have paid their heavy fines.

King Edward's masterful management of this affair, and the severe penalties meted out to two prominent marcher lords, must have had a traumatic effect on their fellows. A cherished right and symbol of their status — the right to make war — had been abolished by a royal proclamation. There had been royal intervention in the March before on a number of occasions: Henry II in the second half of the 12th century had been able to dominate the marchers and had obtained assurances from them of military assistance as and when he required it: in 1208 King John had destroyed one of the most important of the marchers, William de Braose, politically — but the king had in this instance moved against an individual and not against the marcher lords as a body. Edward I's intervention in Wales of 1291-2 constituted a precedent and a turning point in the constitutional standing of the marcher lords — and he did not stop at the humiliation of the two earls.

In 1292 he persuaded the marcher lords to pay a tax on their lands in Wales as a contribution towards a subsidy granted to him by parliament two years previously. This was a novel financial imposition although the king promised that it would not create a precedent, and in the event the marcher lordships were to remain outside the orbit of national taxation until their abolition in the 16th century. Writs of *quo warranto* — how can you prove your claim to this right or privilege — were extended to include the marchers. Edmund Mortimer (I) found himself the subject of an investigation into the rights which his father had appropriated in Shropshire in the 1260s and which Edmund had continued to enjoy. He seems to have defended his claims with some success, if not with the panache of the earl of Surrey who dramatically drew a rusty sword in court crying: 'This is my warrant. My ancestors came with William the Bastard and won their lands by the sword; and by the sword I will defend them'.[6] On another occasion the king confiscated Wigmore Castle when Edmund executed an inhabitant of the royal lordship of Montgomery, thereby encroaching on the king's rights, and Edmund was only able to recover it after payment of a fine of 100 marks and providing a straw effigy of the unfortunate man to be hung on the gallows in the town of Montgomery. In 1297 the men of the Mortimer lordship of Maelienydd submitted a list of grievances to the king who seems to have induced Edmund into granting the men of the lordship charters of their liberties — another example of royal interference in the marchers' administrations. The marcher lordships were to exist for more than another two centuries

The outline of Montgomery Castle on the hill overlooking the borough,
from an old postcard

20

but their constitutional status would never again be as secure as it had been before the reign of Edward I. Furthermore, the unification of England and Wales towards the end of the 13th century had rendered obsolete the justification for the very existence of the marcher lordships, namely the conquest of Wales and the suppression of any threat to England.

Although the marchers were conspicuously involved in the civil strife of Edward II's reign, during the rest of the 14th century they were by and large left alone by kings with more pressing problems elsewhere. Edward III needed the support of his barons during the Hundred Years War with France; a number of them held lands in the March and it was from their domains that were recruited many of the Welsh archers and spearmen in the king's armies. King Edward may have been preoccupied with the war but he did not neglect the security of Wales and in 1354, when there was a possibility of a French invasion of Wales, Edward emphasised that the loyalties of the marchers must be to the Crown. Wales and the borderlands were still viewed with suspicion; it was an area where it was difficult to exercise royal supervision and intervene militarily, and there were always doubts as to the loyalty of the independently minded marchers. Throughout the Middle Ages the marcher lordships served as a refuge for rebellious barons and criminals — anyone who wanted to 'disappear'. It was in the Wyre Forest, part of the Mortimer liberty of Cleobury, that dissident barons from England met to discuss their grievances against Edward I in 1297; and it was a region where one chronicler, recording the rebellion against Edward II of 1321-2, noted, 'the barons had their safest refuge, and it was difficult for the king to penetrate it without a strong force'.[7]

The marchers were utterly unable to cope with Owain Glyn Dŵr's rebellion which broke out in 1400. The sheer scale and ferocity of the Welsh attacks overwhelmed both the Principality and the March, and the English campaigns of 1400-3 did little to dent Owain's military and diplomatic successes. It was not until 1405 that the armies of Henry IV and the Prince of Wales began to gain the upper hand, and it was they which finally recovered the marchers' lands which had been lost to the Welsh. Henry IV had major interests in Wales; as Henry Bolingbroke, he had been an important lord in the March holding Brecon and Hay, which he had acquired by marriage to Mary de Bohun, heiress of the earl of Hereford, and Monmouth, Kidwelly and Iscennen in south Wales which he had inherited from his father; his strength in the March had been a major factor in his coup against Richard II.

The commons in England criticized the marcher lords for garrisoning their castles inadequately and failing to raise sufficient troops, and not unnaturally they wanted to know why England should pay for the restoration of the marchers to their lands when these were outside the ambit of the government's administration. These were no doubt fair criticisms, but the administration of the Principality could be accused of similar negligence; it was the fractured nature of English rule in Wales that permitted the early successes of the Welsh. There had been precedents for royal assistance for the marcher lords when they were under pressure — beginning with William Rufus's campaign of 1095, the king had had to come to the rescue of the marchers on a number of occasions — but the abject and very public failure of the marchers to contain Owain Glyn Dŵr's rebellion in their territories inevitably reinforced calls for reform of the governance of the March. This demand for reform faltered in the face of England's preoccupation with the renewal of the war with France in 1415, and this was followed by a growing failure of government generally, culminating in the Wars of the Roses in which Wales was extensively concerned and reform was politically impossible. Yorkist and Lancastrian families in the March provided fighting men from their lordships for the armies of the rival factions and it was Edward, earl of March and Lord Mortimer, who won the throne in 1461 as Edward IV.

After 30 years of intermittent hostilities in the Wars of the Roses, and the accession to the throne of Henry VII in 1485, the political control of the March had been transformed. Many lordships had been forfeited or changed hands, notably the 22 Mortimer lordships which had passed to the Crown in the person of Edward IV; the Crown lordships and the Principality now dominated the political map of Wales. Under Henry VII's firm hand a reinvigorated Council in the Marches, the descendant of Edward IV's Prince's Council which had been

The inner bailey at Ludlow, showing the solar block and Great Hall on the immediate left, erected at the time of Roger (IV) and the Great Chamber block in the middle. Part of the earlier round chapel is on the right

Clifford Castle — the remains of the keep on the motte

formed in 1471, began in the king's name to bring about some uniformity in the government of the various lordships, particularly in the field of the administration of justice. Within an increasingly centralised state the special political arrangements in the March were becoming untenable and the late 15th century and early years of the 16th saw growing royal intervention and influence in the affairs of the March.

The inconsistency and lack of coordination of justice in the lordships had long been a bone of contention between kings and marchers; the latters' jurisdictional independence inhibited the administration of justice and was a major cause of the notorious lawlessness of that part of the kingdom. Without some form of extradition criminals had been able to avoid justice by fleeing from one lordship to another; further, they had claimed immunity in a lordship where they had committed a crime by professing that they were natives of another lordship.[8] Henry IV had tried to limit the first of these abuses, and years later, in 1476, the marchers were summoned to Ludlow to explore ways of addressing the intractable difficulties of administering justice in the March. In 1490 Henry VII agreed amongst other matters to a form of extradition treaty with the steward of the lordships of Clifford, Winforton and Glasbury. A clause in the agreement appears to have allowed 'hot pursuit' in certain circumstances. In practice many of these measures and agreements were ineffective, and in addition to the inefficient administration of the March there was the problem of the defence of the kingdom. Wales was England's weakly bolted backdoor; French troops had landed in Pembrokeshire during Owain Glyn Dŵr's rebellion and again in 1461, and the future Henry VII had landed there in 1485 on his way to winning the throne. Some degree of unified defence of Wales was of major importance to England's security.

Henry VIII's solution to the constitutional anachronism in Wales was not to tinker with it but to abolish the system lock, stock and barrel. The Statute of Rhuddlan of 1284 had united England and Wales which then consisted of the Principality and the March. In 1536 by the 'Act for Laws and Justice to be Ministered in Wales in like Fourme as it is in this Realm', and by further measures over the next few years, the Principality and the March were united as part of the kingdom of England and Wales. The lordships in the March were abolished and, by combining them in groups, new shires were created which would be governed on the English pattern; the 12 Welsh counties made up of the existing ones in the Principality and new ones from the March were to survive more or less intact until the local government reorganisation of the 1970s. The marchers were permitted to retain their lands and their rights of lordship as practised in England, but they lost their special status and immunities. Welshmen became entitled to the same rights as Englishmen and were to be represented in Parliament; some Welsh customs were to be allowed to continue, but English administration and law was to rule Wales with English becoming the official language of both government and the courts.

Henry VIII was as masterful a monarch as Edward I who had once before cut the marcher lords down to size, and the lords appear to have accepted their lot without offering any resistance. Now fewer in number and with most of the lordships in the hands of the Crown, they were largely absentee landlords; their interests in England, vulnerable to royal retaliation, were more valuable to them than their Welsh ones which, since the more profitable days of the 14th century, had collapsed economically during the mayhem of Owain Glyn Dŵr's rebellion and had only partially recovered. The more far-sighted of the marchers would have realised that the system of government of the March of Wales which had lasted for some 400 years had had its day.

Internal Organization

Although historical records of the internal organisation of the lordships in the March are scanty, there are certain aspects of these domains which seem to be common to many of them. They varied immensely in size and in physical character which largely governed their potential for profitable exploitation — their lords' primary aim in winning and administering their conquests. Glamorgan was a large, and much of it agriculturally productive, lordship; Maelienydd, a core lordship of the Mortimers, was much smaller and by contrast an upland and sparsely populated one of less intrinsic value; another lordship of the Mortimers, Clifford, was very small, perhaps 20 square miles in extent, but of strategic importance in the valley of the Wye, a gateway into Wales. Given the often agriculturally inhospitable terrain, many of the marcher lordships were of limited value to their lords compared to their more financially attractive estates in England. When, over the years lords acquired additional lands, they were able to link them in groups for the purpose of administration but amalgamations of their lordships were unusual.

Conquest was followed by settlement and the evolution of 'Englishries' and 'Welshries' — division of the lordships along racial lines. The Welsh would be evicted from the more low-lying and arable districts of the lordships which would become Englishries, organised on the English manorial system. Here the lords established, as rewards for service, their vassals and followers as well as immigrant settlers farming the demesne or paying rent. Lords would take their share of the various profits from these lands and courts as in England. Often with their major interests in England, the marchers would be absentee landlords leaving the administration of their lands in the March to trusted officials; in this respect the Mortimers were atypical in that the cornerstone of their power and prosperity lay in Wales. The Welsh who were evicted from the Englishries settled in the Welshries which consisted of the upland and less productive districts of the lordships where raising cattle and sheep were the principal agricultural enterprises. The Welshries might be more or less self-governing. In the duke of Buckingham's lordship of Huntington in 1500 there was a court for the Englishry and one for the Welshry, and there would be little interference in the Welshry from the lord provided its inhabitants gave no trouble and paid their tributes in kind according to Welsh custom. In the lordship of Hay, in the mid-14th century, while the men of the Englishry paid for their lands with rent and services, the Welshry as a whole gave the lord the traditional tribute of 24 cows every other year although this was soon replaced by payment in money. In the later Middle Ages the gradual abandonment of Welsh laws, customs and systems of land tenure was welcomed in some quarters of Wales, particularly among peasant farmers; in the second half of the 14th century Welshmen in Clwyd were eager to surrender their holdings and receive them back on 'English' terms while others were willing to pay for the privilege of 'English' status. This in particular involved the inheritance law of primogeniture, in contrast to the Welsh system of equal division of inheritance between all a man's sons (gavelkind), as well as superseding the complex Welsh obligations imposed on proprietors restricting their disposal of land. It seems that the clear distinction between Englishries and Welshries was by then breaking down.

Englishries and Welshries can sometimes be identified from old place-names; in the former districts names would be predominately English and in the latter, Welsh. The unattractiveness to settlers of the two Mortimer upland lordships of Gwerthrynion and Cwmwd Deuddwr, north-west of Rhayader,

Cefnllys Castle

is evident from the absence of English placenames. Another feature of the lordships was the establishment of boroughs — often associated with castles and again for commercial exploitation — such as the Mortimer foundation of Newtown. Other boroughs were not so successful. Cefnllys near Llandridnod Wells, which was also established by the Mortimers, failed presumably because of its isolated position remote from major trade routes and its very limited potential for agricultural exploitation; when the once important castle had been down-graded or abandoned its fate was sealed. Similarly the prosperity of the borough at Wigmore languished after the Mortimers moved their seat to Ludlow.

The government of the marcher lordships is poorly recorded; but certainly in the larger and wealthier ones — although there was no uniformity of administration — it must in its final form have been sophisticated and modelled along the lines of that in England. There are documentary references to chanceries, exchequers, treasurers, sheriffs, 'keepers of the peace' (itinerant justices), and *curia* (councils). Some lordships, such as Glamorgan and Pembroke, appear to have been organised much like English shires, but in more sparsely populated lordships, Maelienydd for instance where there does not appear to have been knight service, the Mortimer administration was less English in form.

An exception to the marchers' control of their lordships was the Church and its domains whose bishops as tenants-in-chief were independent of the lords. There had been a great religious revival in Normandy during the first half of the 11th century which was carried to England by the Conquest. The Normans considered the Welsh Church, like the English, backward and needing reform, but they recognized in it an institution they could use in their own interests; political considerations were never far distant when the Norman and English lords interested themselves in religious matters in Wales. The early conquests in Wales were accompanied by expropriation of Church property for the benefit of religious foundations in Normandy and by the appointment of French bishops whose dioceses by the early 12th century had been incorporated into the province of Canterbury. In the Anglo-Welsh borderlands and the March, the abbey at Much Wenlock was refounded c.1080; the Mortimers founded an abbey c.1140 at Shobdon, a predecessor of Wigmore Abbey, and later they were benefactors of the abbey at Cwm Hir in Maelienydd. The native religious houses of Wales were slowly superseded by Anglo-Norman foundations or reformed in the new tradition as religious and cultural control of the Church passed out of Welsh hands. Hardly surprisingly this meddling was a cause of great resentment, with that champion of the Welsh Church, Giraldus Cambrensis, indignantly asking the pope: 'Because I am a Welshman, am I to be debarred from all preferment in Wales?'[9]

The independently minded marchers seem seldom to have acted as a confederate body; they did, however, in 1236 unsuccessfully claim the right in the face of the claim by the barons of the Cinque Ports to bear the canopies over Henry III and his bride at their wedding — an apparently minor privilege but one of constitutional and ritual significance. Their final resort in settling disputes among themselves was military force, but full-blown war was unusual and arrangements were developed among them, and sometimes with their Welsh neighbours, to resolve quarrels which would usually be of a minor nature over such matters as cattle rustling and boundaries. In later years formal agreements and regular discussions between officials of the lordships in 'Days of the March' defused potential trouble and 'Letters of the March' were forms of passports for travellers and merchants passing from one lordship to another. If a traveller was arrested in a lordship other than his own, he could present the letter, which would have been issued by his lord stating that he was a tenant, and request that he be returned to face justice in his own lordship.

The military security of the marcher lordships depended on castles, boroughs and the lords' private armies. Castles were pivotal to the lords' security and their territorial ambitions as well as being status symbols; they served as launching pads for aggression, defensive strong points and bases in which the lords would reside when they were in their lordships and from which their stewards would administer their lands and exercise justice. In the boroughs the burgesses, who often possessed commercial privileges in and around their towns, were expected to man the town defences and protect their lords' interests. The marcher lords inherited from the Welsh princes the obligation of all free men in their lands to serve and fight for them, and Wales in the Middle Ages provided a pool of experienced fighting men upon which kings and marchers could draw. Welsh 'friendlies' constituted an important element of Edward I's forces in the Welsh wars of 1276-77 and 1282-83. Edmund Mortimer (I) sent 600 foot soldiers from his lordships, and his mother a further 300 from her lands, for Edward I's campaign in Scotland of 1298; indeed most of the infantry in the king's army were Welshmen. Welsh archers and infantry distinguished themselves in the Hundred Years War, fighting in discrete units in the English armies under their own officers like Rhys ap Gruffydd who was knighted by Edward III. Roger Mortimer (IV) maintained a retinue or private army of Welsh soldiers during his political ascendancy in the late 1320s, and during the Wars of the Roses the armies of Yorkist and Lancastrian lords in the March played a major part in the fighting.

Like Sir Rhys ap Gruffydd, a number of individual Welshmen achieved rank, office and respect in the king's service and in the March. One such in the 13th century was Hywel ap Meurig whose family had long been associated with the Mortimers. In 1260 he was appointed a negotiator on behalf of the Crown with Llywelyn ap Gruffydd and two years later he was constable of the Mortimer castle of Cefnllys; he served as the king's bailiff in Builth and soon after the end of the Welsh war of 1276-77 was commissioned as a justice in Wales. Hywel ap Meurig and his family prospered as important cogs in the English administration in Wales. Marriage and relationships were other points of contact between the races. Political marriages could be advantageous to both the marchers and the Welsh aristocracy. Giraldus, writing about the marriage in the last years of the 11th century of his grandfather, Gerald of Windsor, to Nest, a Welsh princess, noted that he did it in order to establish himself more securely in Wales. Llywelyn the Great married four of his daughters to marcher lords, one of them was Gwladus Ddu who married Ralph Mortimer (II) in 1230; Edmund Mortimer, uncle to Edmund (IV), married Owain Glyn Dŵr's daughter in 1402 to further his political ambitions.

The English, however, viewed the Welsh collectively with long-established distrust and contempt. Giraldus, proud of his Welsh ancestry, noted Gildas's description of the Welsh in the 6th century:

> This nation conceives it right to commit acts of plunder, theft, and robbery ... When an opportunity of attacking the enemy with advantage occurs, they respect not the leagues of peace and friendship, preferring base lucre to the solemn obligation of oaths and good faith'.[10]

These sentiments were returned by the Welsh with interest and given extra bite by hatred born of foreign domination, resentment at the exploitation of their country and their treatment as second-class citizens. The medieval English suspicion of the Welsh is exemplified by a letter from Edward I's 'Master of the King's works in Wales', Master James, who was in fact a native of Savoy: 'Welshmen are Welshmen, and you need to understand them properly'.[11] For the Welsh their defiance is evident as early as 1098, when the *Brut y Tywysogyon* related that, 'since the men of Gwynedd could not suffer the laws and judgments and violence of the French [Normans] upon them, they rose up against them a second time'.[12] Again, 158 years later, 'the magnates of Wales, despoiled of their liberty and reduced to bondage, came to Llywelyn ap Gruffydd and mournfully made known to him that they preferred to be slain in battle for their liberty than to suffer themselves to be trampled upon in bondage by men alien to them. And Llywelyn was moved at their tears'.[13]

The prosperity of the lordships depended largely on agricultural exports to England, principally cattle and wool, with much of the latter being sent on to the great textile towns of Flanders as part of England's international wool trade. In 1349, 400 cattle were driven from the Bohun lordship of Brecon to Essex for fattening. Twelve years earlier 14 sacks of wool were despatched from the Mortimer lordship of Radnor *en route* to Dordrecht, and in 1340 another 30 sacks were awaiting despatch (each sack weighed 165 kilos). Wool exports to Flanders, a generally thriving business since at least the early 12th century, was a vital constituent of England's trade, and the wool of Wales, though of inferior quality to that of England, was exported via English ports from an early date. This trade, such an important element in the incomes of the marcher lords, was subject to royal regulation and interference for political and financial purposes; the Mortimers' wool awaiting despatch in 1340 was probably held up because of the chaotic conditions in the trade at the time as a result of Edward III's financial machinations in the early stages of the Hundred Years War.

The English exploitation of Wales and export of its wealth, particularly in the 14th century, was a primary cause of intermittent national and regional rebellions. In 1387, for instance, 11 archers escorted a convoy of treasure worth £400 from Wigmore to London — a vast sum, worth perhaps close on a million pounds at the beginning of the 21st century, which had presumably been milked from Wales. A particular cause of Welsh resentment was the status and privileges of the boroughs planted by the English in Wales and which often extended miles beyond the towns' boundaries. A case in point was Newtown, established by Roger Mortimer (III) in the 1270s, which, with its commercial advantages from which Roger would profit, supplanted a nearby Welsh town.

The Welsh would not accept the English as their masters; Henry II asked an old Welshman if his countrymen could resist his military might. The reply amounted to a classic declaration of independence: 'This nation, O King, may often be weakened and in great part destroyed by the power of yourself and of others, but many a time, as it deserves, it will rise triumphant. But never will it be destroyed by the wrath of man, unless the wrath of God be added'.[14]

29

Rebellion would be followed by repression and by racially discriminatory legislation which was particularly severe in the Principality and the March after the suppression of Owain Glyn Dŵr's rebellion. Welsh hatred focussed on the marcher lords as agents of English rule. When Roger Mortimer (IV) and his uncle Roger of Chirk surrendered to Edward II in January 1322 after their unsuccessful rebellion, the Welsh petitioned the king not to show mercy to them. Two hundred years later, in 1521 and in the dying days of the March of Wales as a separate part of the kingdom, the duke of Buckingham asked for a royal licence from Wolsey, the lord chancellor, that he could have an armed guard when he travelled through his lordships, declaring that he did not dare enter his lands in the March without an escort of 300-400 armed men.[15] Active dislike of the English can still be detected in some quarters in Wales; could it be that one element in this is a folk-memory of 450 years of military domination and economic exploitation by the kings and lords of a more powerful neighbour?

CHAPTER III

Lords of the March

The genealogical descent of the Mortimers during the 12th century, like the 11th, is uncertain. A Hugh Mortimer died in 1180-1, but whether this was the Hugh who succeeded Ralph, or was Hugh's son of the same name, has been the subject of debate. On balance it would seem that Hugh [Hugh (I)], who succeeded Ralph, died *c.*1149 and was followed by his son Roger who died in 1153. Roger was then succeeded by his brother Hugh (II), who lived until 1180-81, and it is on these assumptions that this account is based.[1] Whatever the date that Hugh (I) succeeded his father, in England he did not attract attention until the 1140s when he is mentioned in the chronicles of the period and in a grant of King Stephen.

Two events dominated this period: the rebellion of the Welsh which broke out early in 1136 and the civil war in England and Normandy between the adherents of King Stephen and Queen Matilda which followed three years later. With Henry I's active participation and encouragement the Normans had extended their hold on Wales, so that when the king died in 1135 only the remoter parts of the country remained firmly in Welsh hands. Henry I's death and the subsequent dispute about the succession, which developed into a civil war in England in 1139, gave the Welsh the opportunity to intensify their nationwide rebellion which had broken out three years previously; at that time Stephen's claim to the throne had not yet been seriously challenged and it seems to have been a coincidence that the rebellion began in south Wales little more than a week after his coronation. In the next few years many of the Norman lordships fell to the Welsh, with Stephen unable effectively to support his harassed barons, and it must have been at this time that the Mortimers lost Maelienydd when Madog ap Idnerth drove Hugh Mortimer's men out of the lordship and kept control of it until 1144.

The marcher lords became, in general, disillusioned with Stephen's weak policy towards Wales and his inability to sustain his barons. Many of them accepted Matilda as queen in the civil war, but Hugh Mortimer (I) appears to have been an exception with the Normandy factor perhaps weighing heavily with him. The problem for many Norman magnates was that Matilda had married Geoffrey Plantagenet, count of Anjou. The counts had for generations been rivals to the dukes of Normandy and the Norman barons now feared that, as by Norman law Matilda's rights and property would pass to her husband, the duchy would fall to Geoffrey of Anjou — an anathema to the proud Norman baronage. A number of barons in England with lands in Normandy therefore supported Stephen's claim to the dukedom, and by extension to the kingdom of England.

In 1140 King Stephen granted Herefordshire, and perhaps its earldom, to Robert de Beaumont, earl of Leicester, but excluded the lands and obligations of Hugh Mortimer and two other barons from Robert's jurisdiction. The chronicler of Wigmore Abbey tells of Hugh's feuds with Miles, Matilda's nominee as earl of Hereford, Miles's son Roger, and with Joce de Dinan who captured him and imprisoned him in his castle at Ludlow. Whether or not this account of 'private' war between Hugh and his fellow lords is accurate, it vividly portrays the anarchic state of this part of England during the 1140s. Hugh seems to have played little or no part in supporting Stephen on the national stage, his priorities were his interests in the March and in the English border counties where he succeeded in reconquering Maelienydd in 1144 and was able to rebuild his castle of Cymaron. The Welsh chroniclers relate that in 1145-8 he captured and imprisoned the Welsh prince Rhys ap Howel and later had him blinded — he was probably a hostage and suffered for the misdeeds of his countrymen — and he killed the son of the late chief of Maelienydd and the neighbouring *cantref* of Elfael who, no doubt, had been implicated in the revolt a few years previously.

Earlier in the century, across the Channel in Normandy, Henry I had been involved in intermittent warfare in the duchy for most of his reign, and a Mortimer, Ralph of St. Victor, had been one of the magnates who had 'remained loyal to the king in adversity'[2] during the French invasion of 1119. The Mortimer interests in Normandy north of the Seine lay in a strategically important and vulnerable part of the duchy. St. Victor-l'Abbaye was only some 20 miles from the historical frontier of the duchy while, 15 miles to the south, the valley of the Seine constituted one of the major invasion routes into Normandy. The fortunes of St. Victor and its lords during the wars of the 11th and 12th centuries, and in the early years of the 13th, were largely bound up with its geographical position. The Norman victory at the battle of Mortemer in 1054 had been a turning point in the duchy's fortunes; it was in this region that William II had established a foothold in his bid to win the duchy, and it was the last part of Normandy to fall to the Angevins in 1144 and to the French in 1204.

By 1143 Geoffrey of Anjou had won control of Normandy south of the Seine and the next year he subdued the remainder of the duchy. Although there is charter evidence that Hugh Mortimer was in Normandy at some time in the 1140s there is no evidence that he took part in the war with Anjou.

Geoffrey Plantagenet's victory in Normandy and his assumption of the title 'duke' placed those barons who held land in both England and Normandy in a dilemma similar to the one when William II was crowned king of England and his brother became duke of Normandy. Lords with interests in England who continued to support Stephen could hardly expect to retain their honours in Normandy. Those lords whose interests in Normandy were more important than those in England, and who therefore did homage to Geoffrey and by inference to Matilda, jeopardized their English interests in the parts of the kingdom where Stephen's writ ran. Waleran de Beaumont's answer to this difficulty was, apparently, to withdraw from the quandary by joining the Second Crusade, but how Hugh Mortimer or his successor reconciled their divided loyalties and preserved the family's status in both England and Normandy is not clear. Other families were in a similar predicament; the real solution to these divided allegiances lay in the reunification of England and Normandy and this was achieved in 1154 when Geoffrey's and Matilda's son, Henry, who had become duke of Normandy in 1150, was crowned King Henry II of England.

Hugh Mortimer (I) died *c.*1149, by which time the worst of the civil war was over with Stephen gaining the upper hand although in practice large stretches of the kingdom remained under the control of local warlords. He was succeeded by his son, Roger, of whom virtually nothing is known except that in 1138 he had commanded King Stephen's forces at Malmesbury, where Bishop Roger of Salisbury held a castle which he was forced to surrender to the king and charter evidence of 1150. Roger's brother Hugh (Hugh II) inherited the family honours in 1153.

When Henry II succeeded to the throne of England on Stephen's death in 1154, by an agreement between the two, his primary task was to restore order to the kingdom after years of political mayhem and the breakdown of royal authority. Warlords had 'filled the country full of castles. They oppressed the wretched people of the country severely with castle-building. When the castles were built, they filled them with devils and wicked men'.[3] Henry was determined that royal castles which in one way or another had fallen into the hands of various barons were to be surrendered to the Crown, and unlicensed castles, the 'adulterine castles' which had been built in such profusion, must be dismantled. His order was openly defied by a number of magnates, among them Hugh Mortimer who refused to give up the former royal castle of Brug (Bridgnorth).

Brug had been surrendered to King Henry I by Robert de Bellême, third earl of Shrewsbury and the castle's builder, during his rebellion of 1102. Hugh (II) may have based his claim to the castle, if he had one other than by conquest during the Anarchy, on his grandfather's office as steward to the earls of Shrewsbury. After the confiscation of the third earl's lands, Ralph may have had some responsibility for the royal estates in Shropshire which could have been renewed by Henry I or Stephen. This duty may have entitled him to the custody of Brug or, alternatively, Henry I may have appointed Ralph Mortimer or Hugh (I) as Brug's castellan. Whatever the circumstances, Hugh (II)'s stance over Brug was a direct challenge to the authority of the recently crowned Henry II. Perhaps Hugh presumed too much on Henry II's goodwill recalling that, in 1153 when Henry as duke of Normandy and Stephen's heir had promised grants to Ranulph, earl of Chester, Hugh Mortimer's fees in Staffordshire, along with those of other barons, had been excluded. Accustomed to belligerent independence during many years of civil war, Hugh underestimated Henry's determination.

The keep at Bridgnorth Castle (Brug)
— its present angle is the result of slighting
in the Civil War of the 1640s

William, count of Aumale, was the first of the rebellious barons to submit to the king when he surrendered Scarborough Castle, and early in 1155 Roger, earl of Hereford, who had earlier declined to relinquish Gloucester and Hereford Castles, made his peace with the king. King Henry now advanced with an army into the borderlands to recover Brug and discipline Hugh Mortimer who was now more or less isolated in his defiance, with only a few recalcitrant barons elsewhere in the country awaiting the confrontation before deciding how they would act. The king's army wasted Hugh's estates and besieged his castles of Wigmore, Cleobury and Brug — the earthworks to the north-west and south-east of Wigmore Castle may be the remains of siege castles constructed by the king's army — whilst Hugh's forces in their turn pillaged lands in the region. William of Newburgh, among other chroniclers in slightly differing accounts, described the outcome:

> When this man was ordered to rest content with his own lands and to surrender those which he occupied belonging to the Crown, he obstinately refused to do so and prepared to resist with all is might. But subsequent events showed that this arrogance and indignation were greater than his courage ... [the king] obtained its [Brug's] surrender and granted pardon to the earl, whose heart a little before had been like the heart of a lion, but who now became a humble suppliant.[4]

Hugh was forced to submit to the king before a gathering of magnates at Brug. He had to surrender the castle but retained Wigmore, Cleobury and his other honours, and does not seem to have been otherwise penalised. Henry had made his point. With his eye on the restoration of the Crown's authority in Wales, he needed baronial support, particularly from those lords with lands in Wales and along the border, and there was little to be gained in alienating a baron as important in the region as Hugh Mortimer as well as antagonising the baronage in general by over-zealous punishment of one of their number.

Pride, antipathy to the house of Anjou and a possible claim to Brug, will all have played a part in what appears on the face of it to have been Hugh Mortimer's reckless opposition to the king. That he persisted in his defiance in virtual isolation is evidence either of *folie de grandeur* or of the status that the Mortimers had attained by the middle of the 12th century. To William of Newburgh, Hugh was 'a man powerful and of noble birth'; to Robert de Torigny he was arrogant; to Giraldus Cambrensis he was an excellent knight; to the chronicler of Wigmore Abbey he was 'worthy, brave and bold ... of fine bearing, courageous in arms, judicious in speech, wise of counsel ... renowned and feared above all those who were living in England at that time ... the most generous and liberal in his gifts of all those known anywhere in his lifetime'.[5] The last writer's description of this paragon of knightly virtue may safely be disregarded as a hagiography of Wigmore Abbey's founder.

Hugh lived on for 25 or 26 years after the events of 1155, but the records shed little light on his activities. His relationship with Henry II seems to have remained an uneasy one; in 1167 he repeated his defiance of 12 years earlier when he refused the king's command to surrender cattle which he had seized from one of his knights, in return for the knight's surety against any claim that Hugh might have against him. Hugh was fined the considerable sum of £100 but did not pay it, as in 1184, after his death, the £100 was charged against his heir, but was respited until the return of the king from France and there is no record of it ever having been paid. From the lack of documentary evidence Hugh does not appear to have played a major role in the politics of England and Normandy, and in Wales his ambitions were circumscribed by the ascendancy of the formidable Welsh prince, Rhys ap Gruffydd — the Lord Rhys — who came to dominate southern Wales and influenced much of the remainder of the country until nearly the end of the century. Rhys forced the marcher lords once more on to the defensive, regained much territory, and in the early 1170s agreed to a quasi-feudal relationship with Henry II who had finally given up hope of a conquest of the country.

Rhys ap Gruffydd attacked the lordships of Buellt and Brecon, and probably Maelienydd, in 1169. There is no record of the loss of Maelienydd by Hugh Mortimer, but six years later the Welsh prince or chief of Maelienydd, Cadwallon ap Madog, was one of a number of Welsh lords who attended a council at Gloucester which had been summoned to deal with Welsh affairs. Cadwallon purchased the right to his lands by paying the king 1,000 cattle, and in 1188 his son, Maelgwn, ruled Maelienydd whilst acknowledging, with other Welsh princes, Rhys as his overlord. Possibly Hugh or his son managed to hold on to, or recover, their castle of Cymaron which lay only some eight miles from the westernmost of Ralph Mortimer's estates in 1086, and even less from the Braose lordship of Radnor which Rhys had not conquered. As a corollary, the Mortimers may also have maintained or regained control of some of the eastern districts of Maelienydd.

Hugh Mortimer, however, was unable to recover all Maelienydd in the atmosphere of mutual trust which developed between Henry II and Rhys ap Gruffydd who, as his obituarist was to describe him, 'was the head and the shield and the strength of the South and of all Wales and the defence of all the race of the Britons'.[6] Despite this trust at high level, animosity between the Anglo-Normans and the Welsh often ran high and trouble between them was likely to flare up at any time. In one of several recorded instances, in 1179, towards the end of Hugh's life, Cadwallon ap Madog was killed while travelling under the king's safe-conduct. Hugh and his son, Roger, were implicated in the affair and the king's reaction was severe. Roger was imprisoned and his father appears to have had his lands confiscated, circumstances from which the family recovered two or three years later.

Hugh does not seem to have been involved in the great rebellion of 1173-4. Baronial resentment at King Henry's strong government had finally developed into rebellion in England and in parts of his continental empire when the king's oldest surviving son, Henry, publicly damned his father's methods of government and promised their reform. The rebels had the support of King Louis of France — always alert to opportunities of discomforting his rival — but in England the justiciar and his allies soon suppressed the uprising while, across the Channel, King Henry rapidly reasserted his authority and patched up peace with his son Henry and his troublesome brothers, as well as with the French king. The Mortimer estates in Normandy were threatened by the French during their invasions of the duchy and in 1173 a French army came within some 15

*An aerial view from the south of Wigmore Abbey. The present Grange,
which includes the abbot's quarters, is the building below the farm complex.
The south wall of the southern transept of the abbey stands to the right of the
lawned area, the remains of the nave walls being hidden in the undergrowth
to its north. The outlines in the ground further east mark the site of the
abbey's fishponds*

miles of St. Victor l'Abbaye before retiring. The next year Louis advanced
along the same route before being driven back. Roger Mortimer may well have
supported King Henry in the crisis and been rewarded for his loyalty, as in 1174
he received the first of a series of grants from the king when 'there were only
a few barons at that time in England who were not wavering in their allegiance
to the king'.[7]

Hugh (II) is principally remembered for his establishment of Wigmore
Abbey. As already noted, religious benefactions played a prominent role in
Norman politics and culture with the abbey of St. Victor-en-Caux flourishing
under the patronage of the Mortimers. Hugh (I) had enriched the abbey
and confirmed its possessions, while a charter of the archbishop of Rouen

confirmed a gift to the abbey made by Hugh (II); his son, Roger, was also a benefactor. Wigmore Abbey was one of a number of religious houses established in Wales and the border counties by the Normans, of which Wenlock Priory, refounded by Roger de Montgomery c.1080 is perhaps the best known. The Mortimers' first recorded religious benefaction in England or Wales was an Augustinian house which they founded c.1140 at Shobdon in Herefordshire, and this was soon moved to a site in Aymestry and then to Wigmore. The abbey's chronicle records the monks' unhappiness with their latter move:

> Then the abbot and the canons saw that the place where they were to live was too narrow and too squalid to make a dwelling place for them, and above all was very short of water, while the climb to the church was very hard for them ... And when Sir Hugh de Mortimer realized this, he was very pleased, and ordered them to seek throughout his lands for a more suitable place which would be more convenient as a permanent residence for them, and to let him know.[8]

The monks found a site about a mile and a quarter north of the castle and work commenced there in 1172; the church was dedicated seven years later, not long before its founder's death, and Hugh was the first of many lords of Wigmore to be buried in the abbey. Dying, or resigning his honours in late 1180 or in 1181, Hugh was succeeded by his son, Roger, the oldest surviving son of his marriage to Maud, daughter and co-heir of William le Meschin, who at the time seems to have been in prison for his part in the murder of Cadwallon of Maelienydd in 1179.

It was during the latter half of the 12th century that the Mortimers' anomalous status in the English baronage became apparent. In some way Hugh (II) acquired certain privileges which both set him apart from the bulk of the barons and were retained by his descendants. The Victorian historian of Shropshire, R.W. Eyton, discusses the question of how these privileges were obtained and suggests that they were the result of Ralph (I)'s service as steward to the earls of Shrewsbury.[9] They were not lost with the sequestration of the earldom in 1102, became hereditary and may have been confirmed by Henry II in 1155 in a settlement between the king and Hugh Mortimer which followed Hugh's abortive defiance of the king. The Mortimers seem to have enjoyed widespread though not complete immunity from military obligations to the Crown, both in scutage and aids. Another facet of these privileges is the specific omission of Hugh (I)'s and Hugh (II)'s estates from the grants made by King Stephen and Duke Henry which have already been described. In the case of Stephen's grant to Robert de Beaumont, Hugh (I) was indeed a tenant-in-chief, but the king thought it necessary to make clear that Mortimer estates in Herefordshire, which had once been part of the 11th-century earldom of Hereford, were excluded from the grant. Similarly, Duke Henry specifically exempted Hugh (II)'s Staffordshire estates from his promise of a grant to Ranulph, earl of Chester. It may be that this emphasis on the Mortimers' status as tenants-in-chief recognised certain existing privileges — however they had been obtained. In 1155, 1167 and 1179, King Henry was in a strong position to abrogate or curtail these privileges but did not do so and they were to become enshrined in custom.

Hugh (II)'s heir, Roger (II), was soon released from prison and those of his and his father's estates which had been sequestered after the murder of Cadwallon were returned to him. At some time before King Henry's death in 1189 Roger attested one of Henry's charters while the king was in Normandy.

The uneasy peace which had existed between the marcher lords and Welsh princes for nearly two decades came to an end with Henry's death. Rhys ap Gruffydd considered that his relationship with Henry had been a personal one and did not bind him to the king's successor, Richard I, who exhibited little of his father's subtlety in handing Welsh affairs. Whether as a matter of policy or naivety, Richard appears to have refused to travel to Wales to receive Rhys's homage, and the Welsh prince was aggrieved at what he took to be a slight. He foresaw a lack of royal empathy and renewal of Anglo-Norman aggression, and as soon as Richard left England for the Holy Land as a leader of the Third Crusade, he took the offensive and began to raid the remaining Anglo-Norman lordships of south and south-west Wales. In the king's absence abroad until the spring of 1194, and with the conspiracies of his brother, Prince John, who had built up a faction among the English baronage, royal intervention in Wales was hamstrung. John, as lord of Glamorgan, at least part of which had remained in Anglo-Norman control, was closely concerned with Wales and used Welsh politics to destabilise the English administration. Roger Mortimer gravitated towards John's camp and his long and faithful association with John probably dates from this time. At all events, in 1191 as England was slipping into anarchy inspired by John, the justiciar and bishop of Ely, William Longchamp, besieged and captured Wigmore Castle and banished Roger for three years for plotting with the Welsh, a charge which may well have involved conspiring with John. Richard of Devizes tells how Roger's peers deplored his spinelessness when, in spite of his wealth and resources, he had so quickly submitted to the justiciar — a mere priest: but Roger would have remembered the humiliation meted out to his father by Henry II in 1155.

The Emperor Henry VI released King Richard from imprisonment in Germany in February 1194 and, by April, Roger Mortimer was back in England. The next year the king authorised a campaign to reconquer Maelienydd, and Roger Mortimer re-established his lordship and rebuilt Cymaron Castle. In 1196 Rhys ap Gruffydd attacked the lordships of eastern Wales including Radnor whose lord, William de Braose, was campaigning in

The ruins of Abbey Cwmhir

south-west Wales. Roger Mortimer and Hugh de Say of Richard's Castle led an army into Radnor against the Welsh who comprehensively defeated them and who, after burning the town of Radnor, marched south to besiege Painscastle in Elfael, another of William de Braoses' lordships; Roger was fortunate that Rhys's army had followed up its victory at Radnor by attacking Elfael and not by striking north into Maelienydd.

Rhys ap Gruffydd died in 1197 and when the Welsh were defeated in a decisive battle at Painscastle the threat to lordships in south-eastern Wales was lifted. Roger Mortimer, the scourge of the rebellious Welsh as the Wigmore chronicler described him, was now able to consolidate his grip on Maelienydd and apparently push even further westwards; he confirmed the abbey of Cwmhir's possessions and the charter commended to God the souls of his family and the men who had died in the conquest of Maelienydd. This Cistercian abbey, six miles north of Llandrindod Wells, had been founded in 1143, was re-established in 1176 and was pillaged on a number of occasions in the Middle Ages. In the intermittent warfare in the newly conquered territories the Welsh destroyed Roger's castle in Gwerthrynion in 1202, very possibly the one at Rhayader which had been built by Rhys ap Gruffydd 25 years earlier. Any further exploitation by the marcher lords of Welsh weakness in the southern and central parts of the country had now, however, to be largely suspended because of the deteriorating military position in Normandy.

Henry II's Angevin empire in France had passed to Richard I without major loss, but in 1193 Philip II of France invaded Normandy and unsuccessfully besieged Rouen. A truce ceded the castle of Drincourt (Neufchâtel-en-Bray), along with other fortresses, to the French; Drincourt was only eight miles from the Mortimers' seat at St. Victor-l'Abbaye and their estates in Normandy were now in the front line in the struggle for the duchy. The following year King Philip again laid siege to Rouen but Richard, recently freed from imprisonment, landed in Normandy and over the next five years restored and was able to maintain the duchy's integrity. Richard died in 1199 and was succeeded by John, and in the following year the Treaty of Le Goulet brought peace until 1202 when hostilities were renewed. The French rapidly conquered much of north-eastern Normandy, so that the next year St. Victor appears to have lain only just inside the part of the bailiwick of Caux which was still under Norman control. In June 1204 Rouen surrendered to Philip, and Normandy with the exception of the Channel Islands was lost.

Roger Mortimer was one of the lords with lands in Normandy who seems to have supported King John to the bitter end, though in company with other magnates he refused in 1201 to serve in person when the king summoned an army to assemble at Portsmouth for service in France. Roger and others were fined; but in fact, John had probably never meant them all to go to France and the summons to Portsmouth was a ruse to raise money for the hire of mercenaries to campaign in Poitou. William Rufus had done much the same thing in 1094. Roger's fine was remitted, he was with John in Normandy when Philip was stage-managing the break with him in April 1202, and he was also probably with the king in July of the following year while Norman resistance in the duchy crumbled. A William de Mortemer played a conspicuous part in the

The entrance into the outer bailey at Arques, near Dieppe, Normandy

The western facing outer bailey wall at Arques, with the keep in the distance

defence of Normandy under Richard I and John. He was appointed bailiff of Caux in 1203 but, after the fall of Arques, the principal castle of the bailiwick, he made his peace with King Philip.

In 1205 Roger Mortimer landed at Dieppe which does not seem to have been fully under French control until that year. When the newly appointed governor of Arques and bailiff of Caux, John de Rouvray, heard that Roger was organising a resistance movement, he ordered his arrest. In due course Roger was ransomed for 1,000 marks, which was raised by his wife who had obtained a loan of 200 marks from the king and who was permitted to raise the sum by collecting scutage on her husband's vassals. By the summer of 1207 Roger was back in England when he was ordered to give up custody of Knighton and Norton Castles.

There are tantalizingly few details of this incident. At the time John had by no means given up hope of recovering his lands in France. One English army mustered at Dartmouth with Poitou as its destination while another assembled in and around Portsmouth, presumably for an invasion of Normandy. Roger Mortimer could well have been sent to the former duchy to obtain intelligence and organise a fifth column, but any success he had before his capture was to no avail as John abandoned the Portsmouth expedition when faced by what amounted to a mutiny of the baronage.

Anglo-Norman magnates with interests on both sides of the Channel were in a quandary after the fall of Normandy. In October 1204 King John dispossessed those barons who had made their peace with King Philip, while Philip prepared to confiscate the estates in Normandy of those barons who would not do so. A few lords such as William Marshal, earl of Pembroke, who remained loyal to John, succeeded in making arrangements which safeguarded their possessions in Normandy. In April 1204 Earl William gave Philip of France 500 marks on condition that the French king would not take any action against his estates for a year and a day and then, if his lands were still in French hands, he would do homage for them. William Marshal would therefore be Philip of France's man in Normandy, while in England he would be John's man. This was a nice constitutional issue with a furious John more or less accusing the earl of treason, when he declined to join the king in an expedition to France, while William asserted that he had had John's permission to save his estates in Normandy by taking an oath of loyalty to Philip. John, so Earl William's chronicler goes on to record, took counsel with his knights who agreed that William had no valid excuse for not joining the king. One of them, however, observed that if William, with his prestige and reputation for feudal probity, maintained his position, only a judicial duel would prove his guilt or innocence: and with the earl's fearsome record 'in the ring' who would dare volunteer as the king's champion? And there the frustrated king let matters rest, but the incident only increased his paranoiac distrust of the baronage. During his captivity Roger Mortimer may have been offered an opportunity of following the earl's example in making peace with both kings, but if so he refused or was unable to do so and his estates in the duchy were confiscated. In addition to their seat at St. Victor in the bailiwick of Caux, the Mortimers held lands in Bray, including a number of estates of the Warenne Honour of Mortemer. Roger Mortimer's losses in Normandy were serious but not disastrous. His paramount interests lay in England and Wales, and the harrying of eastern Normandy during the recent wars must have drastically reduced the value of his estates and his income from them. Roger would have smarted under his eviction from the family's ancestral home but there would for many years be the chance that Normandy could be recovered; in the meantime there were opportunities to exploit in England and Wales, and now that he enjoyed the king's favour he could concentrate on his affairs on this side of the Channel. Although he held land in at least 13 counties of England, it was in Wales that his interests were centred and where there was scope for their expansion; he could surely never have seriously considered throwing in his lot with Philip of France — unlike his brother-in-law, Henry, lord of Ferrières, who did so and whose lands in England were forfeited as a result.

For most of the first decade of the 13th century King John had successfully kept independent Wales politically divided by cunningly playing off the Welsh princes one against the other and thus taking the pressure off the marcher lords. By 1210, however, two events had radically altered the balance of power in Wales and were limiting the freedom of action of the marchers: the fall of the house of Braose and the rise to power of the Welsh prince Llywelyn ap Iorwerth.

What evidence there is suggests that Roger Mortimer's relationship with William de Braose, lord of Radnor, Buellt and Elfael, all of which which adjoined Maelienydd, was reasonably amicable in the last years of the 12th century and the early years of John's reign. In the crisis of 1196 Roger Mortimer had gone to his neighbour's assistance, both Roger and William had loyally served King John in Normandy, and Roger's son and heir, Hugh, had married William's daughter, Annor. In 1208 John determined to break William de Braose politically. Suspicious by nature, increasingly mistrusting the ambition of his erstwhile favourite whom he had set up as a counterweight to William Marshal, John acted with his customary violence. He hounded William de Braose out of the country and pursued a relentless vendetta against his family. His wife and one of his sons were reputedly starved to death in prison, William died in exile in France in 1211, and his daughter and Hugh Mortimer's wife, Annor, was imprisoned for several years — either as a hostage for her husband's or father-in-law's behaviour or simply because she was a Braose. The king confiscated the Braose estates in England and Wales and gained 20 castles. A number of Roger Mortimer's vassals served in the army which John took to Ireland in 1210 to reinforce his control of the country and to punish those barons who had protected William de Braose when he had fled there. Roger's loyalty to the king may well have been tried; along with other marcher lords, he would hardly have relished John's apparently unjustified and high-handed treatment of a prominent baron. If one of the highest in the land could so easily be destroyed, who might next be subject to John's capricious dislike and suspicion of powerful subjects? But Roger's loyalty does not seem to have faltered in this crisis or indeed in those to come. The enduring bond between King John and the Mortimers, Roger (II) and his son Hugh (III), can probably be explained by their group interest — with perhaps a little encouragement from Roger's daughter-in-law's imprisonment. Most of the marcher lords supported John; he was a marcher lord himself and in addition to his royal rights shared with them a common interest in Wales, and however harsh and arbitrary his rule the marchers could usually rely on his patronage. Certainly one hesitates to credit Roger and Hugh with the feudal rectitude of William Marshal who had fallen foul of John at much the same time as William de Braose, but who considered his oath of allegiance inviolable in spite of the wrongs he had suffered at the king's hands.

The other destabilising factor for Roger and his ambitions in Wales was the crumbling of John's overall policy towards the country. The king had at first approved of, or at least tolerated, the increasing power and influence in Wales of Llywelyn ap Iorwerth — Llywelyn the Great — but in 1210 their friendly relations came to an end. After a devastating campaign in north Wales in 1211,

John, now hamstrung by baronial unrest in England, had to abandon another expedition the following year. So that he could put Llywelyn in his place once and for all, and also so that he could strengthen his deteriorating political position in England, John made his peace with the pope and brought to an end the damaging rupture with Rome, which had its origins in the disputed succession of the archbishop of Canterbury in 1207 when Pope Innocent III had, and it was a precedent, imposed his candidate on the king. Negotiations came to nothing, relations with Rome steadily deteriorated and in 1208 England was placed under an interdict, which meant in effect that church services were suspended with the exception of those of baptism and for the dying. John took reprisals against the Church and its property and the following year he was excommunicated. An impasse persisted, although the Church was in practice able to continue some of its ministry, until 1213 when Roger was one of the 12 barons and three bishops who sponsored John's good faith in his reconciliation with the pope and the archbishop of Canterbury. Discontent amongst the baronage, however, was now widespread, but Roger Mortimer remained firmly in the king's camp until his death in May or June of 1214. Shortly before he died he resigned his honours in favour of his son, Hugh, and he was survived for many years by his wife, Isabel, daughter of Walkelin de Ferrières.

When his father died, Hugh Mortimer (III) was in France with the king who was trying without success to restore his authority in Poitou and other lordships, and who returned to England in the autumn of 1214 to find the baronage seething with discontent. Soon after his arrival John ordered the release from prison of Hugh's wife, Annor. If he calculated that Hugh's loyalty would not waver, he was correct, and years later when Hugh lay mortally ill, his loyalty was formally acknowledged when Henry III permitted him to make his will in recognition of his faithful service to his father and to himself, and in spite of his large debt to the Crown.

Most of the marcher lords rallied around the king when the dissidents showed their hands in the spring of 1215, and Hugh played a part in the political manoeuvring and sabre-rattling which preceded the signing of Magna Carta in June. At the end of April he was at Gloucester with other loyal barons when they were ordered by the king to bring as large an armed force as possible to him at Cirencester where John was identifying his supporters among the baronage and mustering an army. Shortly afterwards Hugh and his fellow lords were each rewarded with a valuable warhorse and Hugh was granted Tetbury and Hampnett in Gloucestershire.

Despite this loyalty, Matthew Paris does not list Hugh in his roll of John's entourage at the signing of Magna Carta. It seems likely that he would have been mentioned if he had been present at Runnymede and one can conjecture that he was absent on the king's business, and no doubt his own, in Wales where the Welsh were taking advantage of the king's and his barons' preoccupation with affairs closer to home. The political and military situation in Wales had deteriorated seriously. Llywelyn ap Iorwerth had allied with the rebels in England, and the Welsh, with Giles and Reginald de Braose (sons of the disgraced William and thus Hugh's brothers-in-law) were revenging themselves on King John by capturing some of the former Braose castles. It is not clear when the Welsh attacked Maelienydd and Gwerthrynion. The family of the Welsh rulers of Maelienydd, who had been ejected in 1196, had been fomenting trouble in the region and at some time during the last years of John's reign or shortly afterwards the Mortimers lost control of the two lordships.

Within a couple of months of the signing of Magna Carta the agreement between King John and the rebels was foundering, and among the military preparations made by both sides Hugh was given the custody of Church Stretton Castle. In the civil war of 1215-16 the king found most of his support in the west of England, while the rebel barons predominated in the east and south-east of the country. The greater part of the fighting took place in the east, but Wales and the borderlands constituted a secondary military theatre as well as a major recruiting ground for John's armies, and it was in this region that Hugh Mortimer seems mainly to have been involved.

In May 1216 the king appointed Hugh as one of his commissioners charged with coming to an agreement with Reginald de Braose who, with Welsh support, had recovered some of his family estates in Brecon, Radnor and elsewhere. Nothing came of the negotiations and at the end of July the king himself arrived with an army in Hereford. John's attempt at peace-talks was no more successful than that of his commissioners and he proceeded to harry the Braose lands before marching north to Shrewsbury. Evidence is lacking but it is very likely that Hugh was with the royal army where his local knowledge of the country and experience of fighting and negotiating with the Welsh would have been valuable to the king.

Hugh continued to receive marks of royal favour in return for his fidelity and he had certainly left Wales and was with the king's army in the east of England in September when John raised the siege of Lincoln. It was there, at the end of the month, that Hugh attested a charter, the last of John's charters listed in the rolls. Three weeks later John was dead and at his wish was buried in 'the church of St. Mary, Worcester [Worcester Cathedral]'.[10] Hugh was among the seemingly few prominent barons who were present at the ceremony but he was not numbered among the 13 executors of John's will. This omission is perhaps an indication of Hugh's status in the baronage; it was naturally inferior to that of the papal legate, bishops and earls, but also to men like the marcher lord, Walter de Lacy, who were also executors.

Henry III was only nine years old when he was crowned in October 1216 and a council with William Marshal as regent, undertook the government of the kingdom. Hugh was a member of the council and associated with its policy

*Bytham Castle, Lincolnshire. The mounds indicate the extent of the motte and
bailey, but the castle was destroyed during the Wars of the Roses*

of reconciliation and restoration of order. Decisions, however, appear to have
been largely taken by an inner circle of King John's executors, although they
would no doubt have sought Hugh's advice when it came to formulating policy
towards Wales and Llywelyn ap Iorwerth.

When the council wanted in January 1217 to stiffen the resistance of royal
castles in the persistent civil war in which a French army was now involved,
Hugh and other loyal barons undertook to ransom all loyalists who were
captured defending the king's castles, and in the same year he was granted
the right to confiscate the lands of those of his vassals who opposed the king.
Although the marcher lords provided strong military support for King Henry,
there is no record of Hugh's part in the fighting before peace was more or less
restored by the Treaty of Kingston in September. Four years later he took part
in the successful siege of Bytham Castle in southern Lincolnshire which was
held by William de Forz who had refused, among other matters, to surrender
his castle in accordance with the treaty.

In Wales, Llywelyn ap Iorwerth's political ascendancy in the country and
his military resources now balanced the forces of King Henry and the marcher
lords. In 1218 Llywelyn had done homage, after a campaign in south Wales,
to the young king in return for Henry's confirmation of his conquests, and
in 1223 Hugh was present at Montgomery when King Henry met the Welsh
prince; earlier that year Hugh had been granted 20 marks to fortify his castle
at Wigmore. Relationships between the marcher lords and the Welsh remained
tense and the stability of the lordships fragile. In 1220, when Henry had
ordered Llywelyn — with little chance of successfully enforcing his order
— to surrender Maelienydd to Henry Audley, who was then to hand it over to

Hugh Mortimer, Llywelyn had demurred. He wrote that he would not insist on his legal rights until Henry became of age, but if Hugh attempted to regain his lordship by force he would be met by force, and there the matter seems to have rested with Hugh continuing to claim Maelienydd while Llywelyn supported the local Welsh rulers. This was but one of a number of recorded disputes between the Mortimers and Llywelyn. The manors of Knighton and Norton, formerly in English hands but now under Welsh control, were also claimed by the Mortimers, but here there may have been some movement in favour of the Mortimers. On the wider stage, when faced by Llywelyn's formidable military power, it was royal policy not to provoke unnecessary confrontations with the Welsh and it was beyond the marchers' capacity to act decisively against the Welsh prince. Not until after Llywelyn's death were the Mortimers able to regain Maelienydd.

The setback to Hugh Mortimer's fortunes in Wales, and his widespread interests in England where he was assessed for scutage in 21 counties, made Hugh more a baron of England, where he was involved in national affairs, and less of a lord of the Welsh March than his father or grandfather. In 1225 he witnessed the reissue of Magna Carta and two years later he died, according to the Wigmore chronicler from injuries he had received in a tournament. In the year of his death and secure in the king's favour, he obtained a renewal of

Looking north-west from the inner bailey at Clun Castle,
where Ralph was appointed custodian in 1231

a grant to hold an annual fair in Cleobury, and was allowed to make his will, despite owing the king £1,015 2s. 3d., a warhorse and two hawks. Having no surviving children he was succeeded by his brother, Ralph. His widow lived on for some years, apparently as a recluse.

Ralph Mortimer (II) had, like his elder brother, remained loyal to King John until the king's death. He had been in royal service in 1216 and the next year he was one of the witnesses of the treaty between England and France which had brought to an end the French intervention in support of the baronial party. His release in 1229 from much of his debt to the Crown, which he had inherited from his brother, shows that he enjoyed the confidence of Henry III. For the rest of his life his interest was focused on Wales, and here he was in the end successful in re-establishing the Mortimers' power and influence.

In 1230 Ralph married Gwladus Ddu, a daughter of Llywelyn the Great and, it is generally accepted, a granddaughter of King John.[11] It seems unlikely that the Mortimers could have sustained their claim of a connection with King John if this was not true, and in any case it was the perception, not necessarily the truth, of Gwladus's ancestry which would be valuable to the family for the next two and a half centuries. When Llywelyn's legitimate line of descent failed, the Mortimers could argue — although seemingly convincing little Welsh or English opinion — that Ralph and Gwladus's descendants were the

The 'Keep', or Great Tower, on the right, is a late addition,
built in the late 13th to early 14th century

49

rightful heirs to his principality; in the late 14th century the descent from King John bolstered the Mortimer claim to the throne, and during the Wars of the Roses the Yorkist cause in Wales was promoted by propagandising Welsh bards recalling the Mortimer connection with Llywelyn the Great.

Marriages between the Anglo-Norman baronage and the Welsh for political reasons were nothing new, but an alliance with a granddaughter of a king of England, albeit via an illegitimate intermediary, who was also the daughter of the Welsh prince recognised as *primus inter pares* among the rulers of Wales constituted a political coup for Ralph: a coup bigger than he could have foreseen at the time. For his part, Llywelyn would have viewed this relationship with a Mortimer, and he married three other daughters to prominent marcher lords, as a means of reducing tension in Wales and hopefully loosening the bonds between Ralph and King Henry in the event of hostilities between the king and himself. If Ralph hoped that the alliance would encourage Llywelyn to return Maelienydd and Gwerthrynion to him he was to be disappointed. Ralph's apparent repossession of Knighton in territory formerly controlled by Llywelyn, and inferred from Ralph's right by a charter of 1230 to hold a fair there, may well have been connected with his marriage in that year; it is, however, possible that the king used the charter to demonstrate his support for Ralph in his disputes with Llywelyn although the prince continued to control the district. Both Llywelyn and Ralph Mortimer found their differences irreconcilable and relations between them continued at a low ebb.

At least some of Ralph's activities during the intermittent and confused warfare between 1228 and 1234 in Wales and the border counties are recorded. The king ordered Ralph and others in the summer of 1228 not to take any hostile action against Llywelyn, while the prince's wife, Joan, the king's half-sister, was travelling to Shrewsbury under safe conduct to meet Henry and might be accompanied by Llywelyn himself. In May 1231, the year of one of Llywelyn's devastating raids through eastern Wales, Ralph was appointed custodian of the honour and castle of Clun, and the same month Henry, preparing a campaign against Llywelyn, ordered Ralph and others to suppress any trade between their lands and the regions of Wales under Llywelyn's control. From the earliest days trade between English and Welsh had often continued, if necessary through the back door, in spite of the fighting. An economic blockade, particularly in food, although it would hurt English traders, was a potent weapon against a country whose agricultural resources, particularly cereals, were limited, but sanction-breaking is notoriously difficult to control and it no doubt continued in spite of royal injunctions. In October 1231, Ralph and other named lords were ordered that, if Llywelyn invaded the king's lands, they were to obey John de Monmouth and accompany him to the threatened district where they were to do all in their power to ensure that the king suffered no loss through their negligence. Three weeks later, Ralph and others were summoned to support Richard, earl of Cornwall, whom the king was sending to the March to bolster the English war effort.

In June 1233, at the beginning of the rebellion of Richard Marshal, earl of Pembroke, and his Welsh and baronial allies, Ralph with other marcher lords surrendered hostages as security for their loyalty to the king during the emergency; five months later Ralph was with King Henry at Hereford, a base from which were launched royal campaigns against the rebels and the Welsh. During these troubled years which wrought havoc in southern and eastern Wales, and to the English borderlands, Ralph was in close contact with King Henry and received a number of grants for his loyalty and services. He was allowed in 1239 to take three bucks and five does from the king's forest of Savernake to stock his park at Stratfield Mortimer in Hampshire.

In 1234 the Treaty of Middle finally brought an uneasy peace which lasted until Llywelyn died in 1240, and for the last six years of his life his domination of Wales and his conquests were not seriously challenged by either the English or by his Welsh rivals.

With the death of Llywelyn the English judged that the time had come to recover the lands which they had lost during the previous 30 years. King Henry meddled in the dissension among the Welsh rulers which faced Llywelyn's son and successor, David, as he strove to maintain his paramountcy in Wales. Finally David rebelled and the king resorted to force of arms with a campaign in north Wales in 1245. Ralph was ordered to harass the Welsh between Brecon and Shrewsbury, and at the onset of the winter of 1245-6 he and other lords were to ensure that no one sold anything, specially food, to the Welsh. In 1246,

Part of the extensive view across the bailey from the motte of Cefnllys Castle, with the rock cut ditch between the motte and the bailey in the foreground

as the English slowly gained the upper hand, David died and his heirs, his nephews, were forced to submit to the king. The Treaty of Woodstock of 1247 confirmed the renewed English domination of Wales and the destruction of Welsh unity which had been built up by Llywelyn the Great, while King Henry reserved for himself and his successors the homages and services of the Welsh princes and nobility. Before then, in 1241 and as is described in chapter II, Ralph Mortimer had regained control of his lands in Maelienydd which 'were being harassed by certain Welsh chiefs of Kerry and Maelienydd in alliance with David',[12] and here Ralph was able to rebuild his castle of Cefnllys.

King Henry also had ambitions to restore English influence and power in France. In the spring of 1242 many of the English barons refused to become involved in the king's scheme to support a rebellion in France. Even so, Henry landed in the district of Saintonge, north of Bordeaux, and in June ordered Ralph to join him as soon as possible in Gascony. In view of the Mortimers' long-established loyalty to the Crown it would not have been surprising had Ralph been one of those barons who did support the king's adventure in France, but Henry's plans came to nothing and the next year he had to make his peace with King Louis of France. Ralph died in 1246, commemorated by the Wigmore chronicler as *bellicosus vir et strenuous* — a warlike and vigorous man — and was succeeded as head of the house of Mortimer by his son, Roger, while Gwladus survived him by five years receiving several favours from the king.

CHAPTER IV

'Long and Praiseworthy Services'[1]

The often shadowy Mortimers of the 11th, 12th and early-13th centuries give way in the person of Roger (III) to a relatively well-documented national figure. Roger's career in the second half of the 13th century was a turning point in the fortunes of the Mortimers, and by the time of his death in 1282 he had become a prominent lord and office-holder in the kingdom. He held widespread estates in England, Wales and Ireland and contemporary records demonstrate his standing and influence as a friend and trusted servant of that able and exacting king, Edward I.

In 13th-century England a baron could obtain power in a number of ways. Land was the measure of wealth and had to be amassed by hook or by crook as the cornerstone of power and political influence. Success as a soldier in one of the king's wars and ability as a wise counsellor and administrator were likely to bring favour, and he who had the ear of the monarch or of his superior lord wielded influence and obtained rewards. Patronage was, as it always has been, a useful tool in the hands of the powerful. Advantageous marriages and alliances with powerful families and factions advanced a baron's status, benefactions to a church or monastery could earn the goodwill of influential ecclesiastics. Military resources enhanced prestige and political fortunes, and strong castles and armed retainers formed effective intimidatory weapons, particularly when the king's rule was weak and 'might' could become 'right'. Civil war and 'private war', which was permitted in Wales by the Custom of the March, as well as manipulation of an ineffectual monarch provided opportunities for ambitious and aggressive barons to build and consolidate their political strength (see also chapter II).

The art of lordship was to manufacture and use opportunities in these fields to advance the family fortunes. Although one would not want to take the analogy too far, medieval lordship was in some ways akin to the direction of a modern commercial company in a private-enterprise economy. The successful magnate organised his estates and strengthened his political position for the benefit not only of himself but also of his family, dependants and vassals—shareholders who would participate in their patron's prosperity. Like any entrepreneur he had to move forward: to stand still led to weakened influence and power vis-à-vis his fellow lords, and might well invite predatory actions from competitors. Luck naturally played a role in a magnate's success or lack of it. In addition to accidents of birth and death, if he backed the winner in feuds, conspiracies and civil wars, his position was improved, but if by ill-luck or misjudgement he backed the loser, the cost had to be met, at the very least in diminished prestige and influence. The greatest danger to a baron lay in his relationship with his patron or overlord who for men of consequence was the king. Arbitrary action or legal process initiated by the monarch could bring down great men, sometimes at a stroke, as happened to William de Braose in 1208 and to the earls of Gloucester and Hereford in 1292.

This, then, was the political environment in which Roger Mortimer (III) won for himself power and influence; being a major baron in medieval England was no profession for the scrupulous and faint-hearted and the Mortimers were to prove adept at it.

Roger was probably born in 1231 and was therefore a minor when his father died. The death of a tenant-in-chief such as Ralph Mortimer (II) involved an often lengthy investigation, particularly to discover whether his heir was a minor, before the heir could enter into his inheritance: the rule of inheritance was primogeniture for heirs and equal division among heiresses. In Roger's case he was granted his patrimony in February 1247, six months after his father's death. He paid a fine of 2000 marks and this no doubt represented not only the normal fine in such circumstances—an inheritance tax—but also a sum to compensate the king for his lost profits from Roger's wardship. The value of wardship lay in the logical concept that a ward could not perform the services by which he held his estates and that profits from them were therefore due to his lord and custodian. It was accepted that when an heir came of age, his estates should be handed over to him in the condition in which they had been received, but there was plenty of scope for profiteering from the management of a ward's affairs and by sale of the wardship.

In 1247 Roger married Maud de Braose, the first of the three great marriages made by the Mortimers which were to bring them immense landed wealth. Maud was a coheiress of William de Braose (captured and hanged by Llywelyn the Great in 1230 for having philandered or worse with his wife) and his wife Eve (d. c.1246). Eve in her turn was a daughter of the redoubtable William Marshal, earl of Pembroke (d.1219), and coheiress with her sisters of his son earl Walter (d.1245). Maud therefore inherited a share of the Braose and Marshal lordships in England and Wales, as well as part of the widespread Marshal lands in Ireland. The division of the Braose estates in particular, however, was a protracted business and indeed was not finally agreed until 1259.

The site of the castle at New Radnor dominates the settlement

The ruins of Narberth Castle

In terms of power politics Roger's marriage was a superlative one. By adding the Braose lordship of Radnor to his existing lordships of Maelienydd and Gwerthrynion, the Mortimer lands now constituted a formidable bloc in the middle March. The Mortimers also gained from Maud's Marshal inheritance the lordships of Narberth and part of St. Clears in south-west Wales as well as other estates, and also the newly established lordship of Dunamase in Ireland, Maud's share of the great lordship of Leinster.

The genesis of the Mortimer estates in Ireland lay in the private enterprise military intervention in 1170 of Richard de Clare ('Strongbow'), earl of Pembroke, at the invitation of Dermot McMurrough, king of Leinster. Strongbow married Dermot's daughter, Eva, and inherited Leinster on the king's death in 1171. He was forced

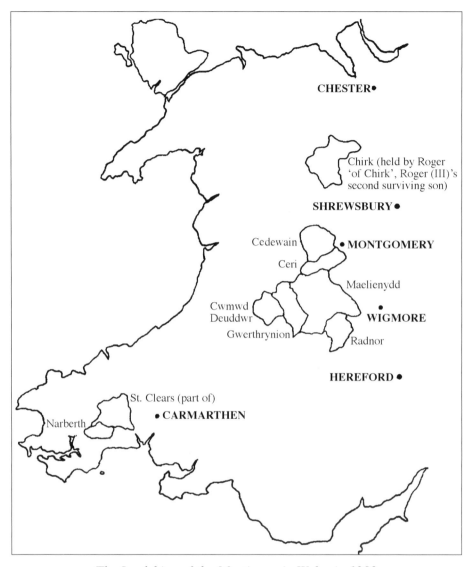

CHESTER●

Chirk (held by Roger
'of Chirk', Roger (III)'s
second surviving son)

SHREWSBURY ●

Cedewain   ●MONTGOMERY

Ceri

Maelienydd

Cwmwd
Deuddwr   ●
                              WIGMORE

Gwerthrynion
              Radnor

HEREFORD ●

St. Clears (part of)

●CARMARTHEN

Narberth

The Lordships of the Mortimers in Wales in 1282

to surrender Leinster to King Henry II, who was determined not to allow the growth of a semi-independent March in Ireland as had happened in Wales, but was confirmed in most of his lordship which, on his death in 1176, passed to his son and then his daughter who married William Marshal. William was created earl of Pembroke in 1199, and at his death in 1219 left five sons none of whom had surviving children. After the deaths of William's sons the Marshal inheritance was divided between his granddaughters including Maud de Braose. Roger Mortimer does not appear to have ever visited Ireland; his interests there were of secondary importance to those in England and Wales and the crises which beset them for most of his life. Edward I, for much the same reason, also displayed relatively little interest in the island, either as prince and lord of Ireland, which was granted to him in 1254, or as king of England. Indeed, after King John's expedition in 1210, nearly 200 years were to pass before another king, Richard II, set foot in Ireland.

Roger first makes an appearance on the national stage in 1253-4 when he, with other English magnates, was with the king in France. A few months earlier he had been knighted before the king had left England for Gascony where Simon de Montfort, earl of Leicester and *custos* of the duchy, had alienated the independently-minded Gascon baronage by his insensitive handing of affairs and where there were fears, which never materialised, of an invasion by Alfonso of Castile. Henry successfully appeased the Gascons and soon focused his attention on an adventure in the kingdom of Sicily, which comprised not only the island but also the mainland south of the papal states and which the pope had offered to Henry's son, Edmund. The snag was that Henry would have to fight for the kingdom and he therefore turned to a determinedly reluctant baronage for support; in its absence and in the face of an obdurate new king of Sicily Henry was forced to climb down in humiliating circumstances.

Discontent in England with the king's administration and policies seems to have been brought to a head by the Sicilian fiasco and led to the growth of a baronial movement for governmental reform in which, for a time, Roger Mortimer was involved. He would have come into contact, in Gascony and in England, with the charismatic arch-reformer, Simon de Montfort, earl of Leicester; in addition most of his fellow marcher lords, together with many of the rest of the baronage, supported reform, so his lapse of loyalty is hardly surprising. Roger was one of the 12 barons chosen by the reformers to work with 12 of the king's party and this committee effected radical changes in the king's administration which, it was intended, would in future be the responsibility of the baronage as well as the king, and which found expression in the Provisions of Oxford of 1258.

The following year Roger accompanied the justiciar when he travelled round the shires adjudicating on complaints and disputes, and he was present at the confirmation of the Treaty of Paris which was to bring peace between England and France for a generation. He was a member of the council and during the king's absence in France was one of the regency council of seven magnates which governed the kingdom. But there was one field where his affairs were not prospering—Wales, where a Welsh prince was intent on abrogating the Treaty of Woodstock of 1247.

Llywelyn ap Gruffydd was a grandson of Llywelyn ap Iorwerth ('the Great') and therefore a cousin of Roger Mortimer (III). In 1255 he had defeated two of his brothers to attain sole power in Gwynedd, and then mobilising his countrymen throughout most of Wales he had the following year launched attacks on the English lordships and initiated a decade of warfare in the March. Preoccupation with politics in England sapped the marcher lords' ability to offer concerted opposition to Llywelyn and the king was almost powerless to assist them. Llywelyn was therefore able to pick off the lordships one by one, and by 1258 was justified in assuming his title of Prince of Wales. In 1256 Llywelyn 'took Gwerthrynion from Roger de Mortimer and held it in his own hand'.[2] In the spring of 1258 the king promised Roger financial assistance in the war and this was followed in the summer by a truce; by now the March had, according to the chronicler Matthew Paris, been reduced to a desert inhabited by none but thieves and outlaws. The truce was renewed the following year with Roger appointed one of the king's commissioners responsible for its supervision. Hostilities, however, began again in 1260 when Llywelyn attacked the lordship of Builth, one of Prince Edward's honours but which was at the time in the custody of Roger Mortimer. A Welsh chronicle describes Llywelyn's campaign:

> One thousand two hundred and sixty was the year of Christ when Llywelyn ap Gruffydd, immediately after Epiphany, went to the land of Builth; and he took that land from Roger de Mortimer, who ruled it at that time, except for the castle [Builth] and the town of Llanfair. And so, after he had traversed all Deheubarth without doing injury to anyone, he returned again. And after that, as men from the castle were opening the gates for the others who were without, behold Llywelyn's men leaping in by night and taking the castle. And so it was taken without so much as an arrow-shot, and such men and horses and arms and equipment as were in it; and it was destroyed to the ground.[3]

Roger was initially blamed for the loss of Builth Castle. He seems to have been accused of failing to exert himself sufficiently in its defence, and although he was formally exonerated Prince Edward appears for a time not to have been fully convinced as he 'exclaimed against the said release'.[4] At the time Roger was constable of Hereford Castle, the base from which any counter-attack up the valley of the Wye would be mounted, and his fellow lords were ordered to assist him in the crisis; but preparations for the relief of Builth, and indeed any campaign against the Welsh, had been overtaken by the developing crisis in England between the king and the reformers.

Henry had decided to try and recover the authority he had lost through the Provisions of Oxford. In July 1260, the month that Builth Castle had fallen, Roger attended a meeting of the council in London—during these years of crisis in the March he does not appear to have taken a great part in the council's proceedings, probably because of his activities in Wales. The king now determined to destroy Simon's influence by bringing him to trial on a hotchpotch of charges, most of them of minor significance. Henry was, however, constrained to drop proceedings in the face of Simon's effective defence that he had only acted for the public good and the king's honour, and with the knowledge of the whole council. Peace was patched up between king and earl and animosity between the factions was temporarily diverted into planning a great campaign in Wales. Wisely, Llywelyn was willing to come to terms and Roger was one of the king's commissioners who negotiated a two-year truce with him.

In 1261-2 King Henry took the offensive against the reformers. While a disillusioned Simon de Montfort retired to France, Roger Mortimer joined most

Builth Castle, captured by Llywelyn ap Gruffydd in 1260 and for whose loss Roger Mortimer (III) was blamed but later exonerated. The castle was reconstructed by King Edward I on the site of the probable late 11th-century stronghold of the Braoses. Work began in May 1277 and the next month writs were sent to 'divers parts of the realm' requisitioning labour to augment the labour force of 19 carpenters and 25 labourers. Later that year the king inspected the works, was satisfied with their progress and granted a bonus to the masons. In August 1282, however, the workforce had to go onto a four-day week 'for lack of funds'. Stone for the castle was brought from Cusop and Clifford, a distance of about 20 miles. Stone for burning into lime and lime itself came from Talgarth, Hay-on-Wye and Radnor (15-18 miles) and lead from Mold in Shropshire (90 miles). Iron and steel would have been brought from Newcastle-under-Lyme (over 80 miles). A Master Henry of Leominster and a Master William of Winchcombe are recorded as master masons employed on the site in 1278 and the castle was substantially complete in about five and a half years

of the baronage in accepting an amnesty and the restoration of royal authority. The predominant concern of the reformers in the baronage had been to oppose the king, and in the case of the marcher lords this had led to neglect of their affairs in Wales. In order to preserve at least a toehold in Wales, some lords had entered into tacit agreements with the Welsh, which in some instances had developed into formal alliances with each side using the other for the same ends, the submission of the king. Roger's fortunes in the March, however, could only flourish at the expense of the Welsh and military and political support was what he needed; this could only come from a strong central authority in the person of the king. More immediately, Roger's growing identification of his interests in Wales with those of Prince Edward, who had eventually accepted Roger's innocence over the loss of Builth Castle and who had himself broken with Simon de Montfort, as well as the quarrel between Simon and the influential marcher lord, Richard de Clare, earl of Gloucester, were all events which would have attracted Roger to the king's camp.

The truce between Henry and Llywelyn was renewed in May 1262, but even so hostilities soon broke out with the Welsh prince complaining that Roger had broken it. The Welsh now took the offensive when:

> … certain people by their own counsel came from Maelienydd and they took the castle [Cefnllys] by treachery, which then belonged to Roger de Mortimer … And they made that known to the Lord Llywelyn's seneschal and constable. And those came in haste and burned it to the ground. And when Roger heard that, he came with many leading men as his supporters in arms. And he stayed within the castle walls for a few days. And the Lord Llywelyn's officers made that known to him. And he gathered a host and came to Maelienydd, and he received the homage of the men of the land, and took two other castles; and he gave Roger and his men leave to return.[5]

Roger, with Humphrey de Bohun, son of the earl of Hereford, and their army had been forced into a humiliating retreat and Maelienydd had been lost. For Roger, although his lordship of Radnor appears to have withstood the Welsh onslaught, the loss of Gwerthrynion in 1256 and Maelienydd in 1262 were major blows to his power and prestige in the March.

In the spring of 1263 Simon de Montfort returned to England. He gathered round him discontented members of the baronage and when King Henry refused to restore the Provisions of Oxford, desultory hostilities began with the reformers in open collusion with the Welsh. Attempts at mediation during the winter of 1263-4 were unsuccessful. In December, Roger was one of the loyal barons accompanying the king when Henry found the gates of Dover Castle shut against him, and a month later he attended Henry at Amiens when the king and representatives of the barons' party put their case to Louis of France for arbitration. When the barons refused to accept Louis's decision in favour of Henry the kingdom lapsed into disorder.

Roger Mortimer appears to have been singled out by the rebel barons as being one of their most dangerous opponents as well as being an apostate of their cause. In February 1264 a baronial army combined with the Welsh to attack the royalist lords in the March and in the English border counties. The rebels and Welsh harried the Mortimer lordship of Radnor and besieged Wigmore Castle itself when Roger's enemies, some no doubt with old private scores to settle, 'immediately levied war upon Roger de Mortimer in the marches of Wales; and levelled all his castles, pillaged his lands and burnt his manors and vills; sir [Prince] Edward also, on coming to his succour with a strong force, was nearly taken prisoner'.[6] Prince Edward continued to be successful in persuading a number of reformers to abandon Simon de Montfort and the barons' party, and by now he had assumed control of the elderly king's war-effort. He retaliated against the rebels by invading Brecon, a lordship of the reformer Humphrey de Bohun, granted it to Roger, and when the barons' army withdrew eastwards across the Severn as a condition of a truce, Roger

regained control of Radnor. His tenure of Brecon, however, was a short one, perhaps a temporary arrangement, as the next year, 1265, it was granted to Gilbert de Clare, earl of Gloucester, on the marriage of his heir and presumably as a reward for transferring his allegiance to the king; in any case in these troubled years lordship did not guarantee actual jurisdiction and much if not all of Brecon remained under Welsh control.

By early April 1264 Roger had left the March, and doubtless at the head of his knights and Welsh levies had joined the king's army which was gathering at Oxford; the March was the royalist reservoir of manpower—an area where men possessed greater experience of war than any other which supplied the warring parties with their forces. Roger played a prominent part in the royalist victory at Northampton, capturing a number of prisoners whom he appears to have been loath to surrender to the king when he would be likely to lose some of their ransom value.

On 14 May Simon de Montfort won a decisive victory at the battle of Lewes, and King Henry, Prince Edward, Roger Mortimer and

Henry III. (This portrait was made after his death)

61

many barons were captured. Roger and his fellow marcher lords were allowed to return to their lordships to defend them against the Welsh as part of a peace agreement, the Mise of Lewes, after Prince Edward and Henry of Almain, the king's nephew, had been surrendered as hostages. The king himself had become little more than Simon de Montfort's puppet. Simon's decision to release Roger and other lords was an overconfident and fateful one. The lords of the March constituted the one group of barons in the kingdom, associated by interest and geography, which could forge an effective military opposition to the new regime, and this they proceeded to do, with Roger Mortimer conspicuous among them.

Through the summer of 1264 Roger and his allies played for time in which to rebuild their forces. They failed to implement the Mise of Lewes by refusing to attend a parliament in June and by not surrendering the prisoners they had captured at the battle of Northampton. Simon responded with a short campaign during which Roger's estates were once again wasted and Wigmore Castle was captured. Roger and other lords agreed terms, which again they failed to keep, and by November he was ready to take the offensive. Early in that month he briefly besieged Hereford, but the city had been forewarned of the attack and withstood the assault obliging Roger to withdraw. An exasperated Simon now determined to have done with the refractory marcher lords once and for all.

After they had refused a summons to Oxford, Simon de Montfort again led an army into the border counties and the March and, with the Welsh, forced the marchers to submit at Worcester in December. One of the terms of the lords' submission was that Roger Mortimer and other leading barons were to be exiled to Ireland for a year and a day, but they found excuses and banishment was delayed, never in fact to be implemented. Meanwhile, Simon's problems were mounting and his preoccupation with other matters enabled Roger to maintain his defiance and continue plotting with possible defectors from the baronial party, but by early in 1265 he appears yet again to have made a temporary and no doubt tactical submission to Simon.

The military balance between the royalist and baronial factions was now swinging in favour of King Henry, still Simon's prisoner—a number of former supporters of Simon de Montfort had transferred their allegiance to the king, notably Gilbert de Clare, the powerful earl of Gloucester, lord of Glamorgan in the March. Roger Mortimer is credited with organising Prince Edward's escape from custody in Hereford at the end of May 1265; the prince rode to Wigmore and then on to Ludlow where he was joined by the Gilbert de Clare, Roger Mortimer and other marcher lords who united in an alliance to defeat Simon. This they accomplished on 4 August when Simon's army was cornered at Evesham. At the resulting battle Roger Mortimer commanded one of the three corps into which Prince Edward had split his army and shared in the triumph of the victory which determined the outcome of the Barons' War. Simon de Montfort's head was sent to Maud Mortimer at Wigmore—a grisly trophy from her husband who had done as much as any man to bring Simon down. As for Roger, his relationship with Prince Edward had developed into a close association of comrades-in-arms, and the prince, the power behind the throne and a shrewd judge of men and how to make the best use of their individual qualities, was now in a position to reward and employ him.

A few weeks after the battle of Evesham Roger attended a meeting of victorious magnates at Winchester when peace was proclaimed and it was ordered that the estates of Simon de Montfort's allies were to be confiscated. In the aftermath of the battle, members of the king's party had on their own account seized some of the rebel barons' lands and these had now to be surrendered to the king. Roger advocated a hard line with the rebels—one chronicler recorded that he inordinately coveted the lands of his opponents—and this brought him into conflict with the more conciliatory earl of Gloucester. Through the summer and autumn of 1266 Roger commanded a corps of the royal army during the six-month siege of Kenilworth Castle where many of those who supported de Montfort's cause had sought safety, and who had nothing to gain by surrendering if harsh terms were to be imposed. The king had meanwhile set up a committee to consider the treatment of the rebels; moderate opinion prevailed and in October the Dictum of Kenilworth laid down the procedures and conditions by which the 'disinherited' could recover their estates. Roger's name does not appear on the Dictum, possibly because of his disapproval of its provisions. He received his share of the spoils of victory, however, with as a 'Gift for good service',[7] the county of Oxford, subject to certain reservations, which had been previously held by Robert de Vere, earl of Oxford. As a result of the Dictum, de Vere was able to recover his

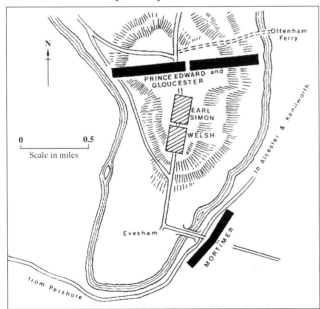

Plan of the battle of Evesham, illustrating
the pincer movement co-ordinated
by Roger Mortimer and Prince Edward

honour after paying compensation to Roger and agreeing that his eldest son, Robert, should marry Roger's daughter, Margaret.

The most interesting example of royal favour towards Roger at this time was a charter granted to him the year after the battle of Evesham concerning his estates of Cleobury and Chelmarsh in Shropshire. The two manors were to be united to form a single manor 'which, *with its members*, was henceforth to be independent of all *suits* to County or Hundred, was in fact a Hundred in itself. On the strength of this, Mortimer professed to consider not less than twenty Manors to be members of Cleobury and Chelmarsh, and consolidating them all into one Franchise, he set up his central Court at Cleobury'.[8] In 1274 there were complaints of the conduct of Roger's court which was accused of arrogating to itself royal rights, and three years later Cleobury, which in 1240 had been assessed at one knight's fee, was omitted from the list of Roger's honours in the March for which he owed knight-service.

Roger had twisted the meaning of the charter to include a much wider scope than had been intended. He had clearly turned his estates of Cleobury, Chelmarsh and other manors, formerly part of the county of Shropshire and administered as such by the king's officers, into little less than a marcher lordship with all its constitutional repercussions. Again, at Wigmore, Roger's steward began at this time to exclude royal officers and claim exemption from royal writs, taxes and the authority of the justices; Roger seems to have been at least partly successful in turning what since Saxon times had been part of an English Hundred into a private lordship.

Surprisingly, Roger appears to have got away with this sharp practice with neither Henry III nor Edward I, the latter a stickler for his rights and baronial discipline, seriously questioning his actions. The reason probably lay in the need to reward Roger handsomely for his services during the civil war and in Prince Edward's personal friendship with him. There would be little point in alienating such a prominent and staunchly loyal magnate, one who could play an absolutely vital role in Anglo-Welsh relations at such a difficult time in the March. It is, nevertheless, puzzling that Roger was permitted to retain, let alone obtain, these privileges. Prince Edward, in his maturity as king, would not, one feels, have allowed for one minute such *lèse-majesté*; but he was seemingly content to let matters rest and it was left to Roger's heir, years later, to justify the privileges which his father had so dubiously obtained.

Roger held a number of prestigious and lucrative appointments during the decade between the battle of Evesham and Edward I's Welsh war of 1276-7. He was sheriff of Herefordshire in 1266-7, and on completion of his term of office he and his household were allowed to continue living in Hereford Castle. Early in 1270 he attended the council at Westminster which would have been largely concerned with taxation to finance Prince Edward's crusade in the Holy Land. Before Edward left England later that year, Roger was appointed one of the trustees of the prince's castles and estates as well as being a 'reserve' guardian of Edward's children if the nominees for that office died. Edward did not return to England for four years, and when he did it was as king as his father had died in 1272. Roger's activities while Edward was abroad included attending parliament, holding an enquiry into complaints against a justice in Cheshire, sitting as a justice himself and dealing with a potential rebellion in the north of England. After King Henry's death, Roger and his four fellow trustees were regents of the kingdom in all but name, and their energetic and competent conduct of public affairs ensured that King Edward returned from his crusade to a well-ordered and secure kingdom.

After peace had been restored to England in 1266-7, one of the most important problems facing the king and his council had been what should be done about Wales. For years Prince Llywelyn had been able to make the running against a preoccupied and divided opposition, and his position in Wales had been little affected by the death of his ally, Simon de Montfort. King Henry appears initially to have favoured resorting to force of arms, and in the spring of 1266 Roger, who had been commissioned with other lords to attack the king's enemies, was defeated by the Welsh whilst he was trying to reconquer the lordship of Brecon. Roger, it will be recalled, had been granted the lordship by Prince Edward in 1264, during the Barons' War, but he had been soon supplanted by Gilbert de Clare for no other apparent reason than the need to reward Gilbert for deserting Simon de Montfort and joining the royalist party. This incident must have rankled with Roger and there had been another source of friction between Gilbert and himself over the treatment of the rebel barons. King Henry, plagued by political difficulties and civil disturbances in England, now realised his impotence in Wales and entered into negotiations with Prince Llywelyn; with the aid of the papal legate as honest broker, the king and prince agreed the Treaty of Montgomery in September 1267. The Welsh won what was probably the best settlement they ever obtained from the English, with the Crown recognising the conquests of Llywelyn who, as prince of Wales, did homage to the king.

The terms of the treaty were not always clear and of particular interest to Roger Mortimer was the unresolved status of Maelienydd: Llywelyn could retain the lordship if he was able to justify his claim to it and, as a compromise, Roger was allowed to build a castle there pending a resolution of the dispute. The legal right to Maelienydd never seems to have been resolved and it is doubtful whether Llywelyn ever envisaged ceding to the English a lordship which extended deep into central Wales. Just as the possession of Maelienydd between 1220 and 1240 had been the subject of a legal dispute, with the Welsh remaining its *de facto* rulers, so between 1267 and 1276 the Welsh retained control in spite of Roger Mortimer's claim.

After the Treaty of Montgomery the Welsh prince's relationship with King Henry was reasonably amicable, but with Henry's death and the return to

England of his heir as King Edward I an open breach soon developed between the English and the Welsh. Edward insisted that Llywelyn do homage to him and this the prince refused to do until grievances he had were satisfied. By the autumn of 1276 the king had determined to resolve his protracted dispute with Llywelyn, if necessary by force, and Roger was one of the magnates who, meeting with the king at Westminster in November, considered an offer by the prince to do homage under certain conditions, among them that Roger would be one of the guarantors of his safety. Llywelyn's offer was rejected, he was declared a rebel and war broke out almost at once.

The marcher lords were to the fore, eager at last to turn the tables on the Welsh. Roger was one of the three commanders of the king's forces and was appointed captain of the king's army in Shropshire, Staffordshire and Herefordshire with his base at the royal castle of Montgomery. He was responsible for the central sector of the Anglo-Welsh front and for the state and security of the roads which would be used by the advancing English armies; he had to restore fortifications and he was authorised to raise troops and enlist Welsh 'friendlies' by agreement with local Welsh lords. He also sought reinforcements from a Florentine merchant who was granted royal protection during his journey to France to fetch 12 warhorses. Quality warhorses were always scarce in medieval England, and indeed in western Europe; they were expensive and Roger's 12 warhorses would have represented a substantial capital investment. A few years later, in 1282, Edward I was to lament the dearth of great warhorses in England, and he ordered those of his subjects who had at least £30 in landed income to keep a powerful warhorse, complete with armour, ready to serve the king when needed.

Montgomery Castle, looking to the inner bailey from the ditch
alongside the outer bailey

*Montgomery Castle: the ruins of the gateway to the inner bailey
from the outer*

During the summer of 1277, men from Maelienydd, Gwerthrynion and elsewhere in the March were sent to reinforce the English army in the north. Roger's and the earl of Lincoln's forces advanced meanwhile into central Wales, annexing Welsh lands as they went, including the *cantrefi* of Ceri and Cedewain, and recovering the lordships of Builth and Gwerthrynion. Commanding part of what was arguably the best led, equipped and organised army in Britain since William the Conqueror's, Roger finally took part in the blockade of Llywelyn's mountain fortress of Gwynedd. By July, when the king himself took the field, Llywelyn's authority had been constricted to the mountainous north-west of Wales and in November he submitted conditionally to the king who had no wish to prolong an expensive campaign into the winter. The Treaty of Conway of 1277 resurrected the humiliating Treaty of Woodstock 30 years earlier and the English were once again lords of most of Wales; the treaty did permit Llywelyn to retain his title of prince of Wales, but this was now an empty honour as his territories were restricted to Gwynedd west of the Conway.

In 1279 Roger was once more rewarded for his services to the Crown with a grant of his conquests of the *cantrefi* of Ceri, which abutted the northern border of Maelienydd, and of Cedewain with Llywelyn's castle of Dolforwyn. Llywelyn had built or rebuilt this castle *c.*1273 as a counterpoise to the great royal fortress of Montgomery some four miles away, but it had been captured with little difficulty in 1277 when, 'a little after Easter, the earl of Lincoln

Looking out from the ruins of Dolforwyn Castle
towards the area just to the south of Montgomery

The remains of Llanfair Chapel, later St. Mary's Church, at Newtown.
This chapel, on the inside of a bend in the River Severn, was the focal point
of Roger Mortimer's new borough. First mentioned in 1253, the chapel had
become independent of the mother church of Llanllwchaiarn by 1291. A motte
and bailey was built on the north-eastern side of the new settlement

and Roger de Mortimer came to lay siege to the prince's castle of Dolforwyn. And they took it by the end of a fortnight for lack of water'.[9] Roger repaired the castle and established the market town of Newtown five miles away to replace Llywelyn's town just outside the castle. After the war the long-standing animosity between Llywelyn and Roger Mortimer appears to have moderated. In 1281, the year before both men died, they agreed a treaty swearing to support each other in peace and war, saving their fealty to the king. Llywelyn showed every sign at this stage of wanting the post-war rearrangement of Wales to work and needed a friend at court, while Roger would have appreciated the Welsh prince's support and influence in his dealings with the Welsh lords of his new lands.

The years between the two Welsh wars, 1277-1282, were the high summer of Roger's career. For 35 years his fortunes had ebbed and flowed but all had now come right for him; he had regained his lands and acquired new ones, he had held high offices, and as a result his status and influence in the kingdom had increased immeasurably. He might not be among King Edward's chosen administrators and lawyers, but when a military man of action was required, he was one of the king's first choices—as the renewal of his appointment as 'captain' at the beginning of the second Welsh War shows. His long experience of negotiating and fighting with the Welsh must have meant that his advice on Anglo-Welsh matters, hawkish though it might be, would carry great weight in council.

In 1279 Roger held a magnificent tournament to mark the knighthoods which had been bestowed upon his three sons, Roger, William and Geoffrey.

Jousting, as illustrated in the Decretals of Gregory IX in 1234

The celebrations took place at Kenilworth, a castle of Edmund, earl of Lancaster, which Roger was holding for the earl during his absence in France. One hundred knights and their ladies, who would have been accompanied by their abundant households and numerous merchants and tradesmen attending the event, took part in the festivities preceding Roger's ten-day 'Round Table' with all its chivalric Arthurian connotations. In practice, tournaments on this scale needed royal approval, for kings viewed such gatherings of the baronage with suspicion as opportunities for the disaffected to meet together, discuss their grievances and engineer conspiracies. Years later, Roger's grandson as virtual dictator of England banned all tournaments at a time for him of great political difficulty. Tournaments were status symbols for their patrons, and the one at Kenilworth was evidence not only of Roger's prestige in the kingdom but also of the confidence that the king had both in himself and in Roger. The remains of what is known as Mortimer's Tower, the gatehouse of the castle until it was superseded by a new building in the 16th century, still overlooks the old tiltyard.

The rebellion which broke out in Wales in March 1282 took the English by surprise but King Edward responded quickly and forcefully. He appointed three commanders to sectors of the front and, 'trusting Roger's tried fidelity, circumspection and industry',[10] gave him responsibility for the central sector as he had done in 1276-7. Roger proceeded to garrison his castles at his own expense,

Kenilworth Castle showing the remains of the early 13th-century Mortimer's Tower with the 12th-century keep in the background

Kingsland Church glass, showing the coat of arms believed to have been adopted by Maud de Braose

and with money from the exchequer raised troops for the campaign and for the defence of Montgomery Castle; by the autumn he was able to send some of his infantry, very probably Welshmen from his lordships, to join the king's army. Although Roger crushed Welsh opposition in his sector it was not eliminated, and after his death that October it was reported that no revenue could be collected from his Welsh tenants because of the unsettled state of the country.

In September or October 1282 Roger fell ill. He worried about his debts to the Crown which might have hindered execution of his will, and on 27 October King Edward tried to set his mind at rest by expressly granting Roger's petition that such debts would not impede his executors. If Roger recovered, the grant would be nullified and if he died it would be left to his heirs to settle his debts; 20 years later the Fine Rolls show that his son, Edmund, was obliged to pay them off at the rate of £20 per year. Roger had probably died on the previous day at Kingsland in Herefordshire, but he would have appreciated the king's 'special favour which had never been granted to blood-relation or other before'.[11] His widow, Maud, lived on until 1301 and it is her arms which it is thought can be seen in the east window of Kingsland Church.[12]

Roger Mortimer (III) is the first of the family of whom one can with any confidence venture a judgement of character and achievement. The one element in Roger's career which cannot be denied is his success. In the secular society of the times this called for an appetite for power, toughness, unscrupulousness — including opportunist but controlled thuggery — ability to recognize and use what opportunities came his way: Roger clearly possessed these faculties in abundance. A character defect in the eyes of at least one chronicler was avarice, in particular a rapacity for land, and this apparently stood out in a baronage hardly noted for its sluggishness in this field: it was a flaw, a family trait it would seem, which more than anything was to help bring about the downfall of his grandson in 1330.

Roger was an archetypically successful magnate of late-13th-century England as well as 'one of the great architects of the late medieval March'.[13] Loyalty; high military commands; appointments as a negotiator with the Welsh; employment as councillor, administrator and justice; one of Prince Edward's trustees; an executor of William de Beauchamp, the earl of Warwick's father, and of the widow of the earl of Cornwall; in the view of a contemporary, 'the most famous man and most powerful knight known through the ages';[14]

71

here is evidence of Roger's widely recognized qualities. They justified King Edward's friendship and favour to him, as well as the letter the king wrote to Roger's son, Roger of Chirk, in which he enjoined the latter, *inter alia*, to:

> so conduct himself against the king's Welsh enemies where his father was captain of the king's garrisons that the king, so far as lies in Roger's power, may seem to recover to some extent in the son what he has lost in the father.

The king went on to pay a tribute to his old comrade, as moving an eulogy as any servant of the Crown could wish for:

> As often as the king ponders over the death of Roger's father he is disturbed and mourns the more his valour and fidelity, and his long and praiseworthy services to the late king and to him recur frequently and spontaneously to his memory. As it is certain that no one can escape death, the king is consoled, and Roger ought to be consoled on his part, because there is good hope that his father after the trials of this life has now a better state than he had.[15]

CHAPTER V

Lord Mortimer

Edmund Mortimer (I), Roger (III)'s second son, was originally destined for the Church. In 1265, shortly after the battle of Evesham, Henry III honoured a promise made to Edmund as 'clerk' to find him an ecclesiastical office by appointing him Treasurer of York with 'a stall in the choir and a place in the chapter'.[1] On the death in 1273 or 1274 of his elder brother, Ralph, Edmund became Roger (III)'s heir, but as a canon of Hereford Cathedral and entitled to the prebend of Hunderton in Herefordshire it seems that Edmund concerned himself as a clerk in minor orders mainly with clerical matters. It was to Edmund's younger brother, Roger of Chirk, and not to Edmund, that Edward I wrote the letter exhorting Roger to serve him in military matters as his father had done.

Shortly before, or at about the time of his father's death in October 1282, Edmund abandoned the Church (his successor as Treasurer of York was appointed in December) and he joined his brother in the war against the Welsh. In August 1282, two months before his father died, he had been given custody of the castle and hundred of Oswestry during the minority of John Fitzalan's heir; in November he was granted his patrimony or inheritance and by December both he and his brother Roger were in the field when Llywelyn ap Gruffydd was campaigning in central Wales.

The reason for the Welsh prince's presence in the district around Builth has been the subject of much speculation and there is confusion as to the circumstances of his death there in December 1282. Llywelyn was said to have been the victim of treachery on the part of the English — namely the two Mortimer brothers who were alleged to have decoyed him into a trap by feigning disloyalty to the king; there was also talk of actual disaffection among certain marcher lords. Whether or not he had been duped, the Welsh prince had, no doubt, come from Gwynedd to see if he could profit from the situation following Roger Mortimer (III)'s death, and perhaps open up another front to relieve the English pressure in north Wales. On 11 December the Welsh were defeated to the west of the river Irfon, near Builth, and Llywelyn was killed.

One chronicler related that he met his death when he became separated, with only one retainer, from the mass of his army. Roger Lestrange, who had succeeded Roger (III) in his command, informed the king that 'Llywelyn ap Gruffydd is dead, his army broken, and all the flower of his men killed'.[2] Edmund Mortimer was reputed to have identified the corpse and taken its head to the king at Rhuddlan while the body was buried in the abbey of Cwmhir. By tradition it was interred beneath the altar and a modern stone slab marks the position amongst the ruins of the abbey. The accusation that the Mortimer brothers had enticed Llywelyn into the area has never been proved, but there must remain a strong suspicion that this was so.

Llywelyn's memorial
at Abbey Cwmhir

David, Llywelyn's brother, carried on the struggle against the English, but early in 1283 King Edward took the offensive, drawing the net ever tighter around the Welsh redoubt of Snowdonia and the hills of Merioneth. The king, anticipating a summer campaign, ordered reinforcements to muster in May and Edmund was summoned to report at Montgomery. But on 25 April the last centre of Welsh resistance, the castle of Bere seven miles south-west of Dolgelley, had surrendered. The king's army no longer faced an organised opposition and set about hunting down David who had taken to the hills. He was captured in June, handed over it is said to the English by his compatriots, and Edmund was one of the barons summoned to Shrewsbury for his trial and who condemned him to death. The war was over and Edward I had achieved the military subjugation of Wales, a project in which his predecessors had all failed.

In the summer of 1287, at the beginning of the revolt in south Wales of Rhys ap Maredudd of Dryslwyn, Edmund Mortimer was a commissioner of array, responsible for mobilizing the levies of Shropshire and Staffordshire. At the time the king was in France, and the regent, Edmund, earl of Cornwall, summoned Edmund Mortimer to Gloucester to join the English army which advanced through Brecon and for which Edmund supplied 3,000 men. He agreed with Sir Peter de Malu Lacu in August at Wigmore that:

> Peter shall stay with Edmund in the expedition of the war in Wales
> against Rhys, son of Mereduc, and his accomplices, the king's enemies

and rebels, with ten barded [armoured] horses appraised at price, to wit, a black one having one white foot, price 60 marks, another black horse … In case Peter lose any or all of these horses in Edmund's service, the latter shall be bound to him for the price at which they were appraised, half thereof to be paid at the feast of the Purification next after the loss of the horses and the other half at Midsummer following.[3]

Edmund later shared responsibility with John Giffard for the defence of Radnor and the region of the upper Wye. He and other marcher lords and constables of the royal castles were instructed to remain in their lordships until the Welsh revolt was suppressed, and in December Edmund and Humphrey de Bohun, earl of Hereford, were appointed joint custodians of Carmarthen and of Cardigan to where Rhys had retreated. He was captured and taken to York and executed in 1291.

In 1288, during the suppression of the revolt, Edmund had been ordered to ensure that the roads through his lands were cleared of trees on either side so as to leave an unobstructed way a bowshot in width, a bowshot for this purpose being probably about 100 yards. Edmund appears to have neglected his duty in this respect as an indignant king sharply reminded him of the order and of the possible consequences to his person and property if he failed to carry it out. He had received similar instructions in 1283 and clearly the English lines of communication in Wales were vulnerable to ambush by guerrilla forces, a mode of warfare at which the Welsh excelled.

Edmund Mortimer was a concerned spectator in the constitutional crisis of 1290-91, when the king succeeded in disciplining two of the major marcher lords (see pp.18-19). Later he found himself defending his rights in proceedings involved in writs of *quo warranto* (see p.20); judgement in one instance had to await the king's return from France and is not recorded, and in another instance was in favour of Edmund on technical grounds, although the king reserved his right to pursue the matter in another legal form.

The Welsh revolt of 1294-5 was an altogether more serious challenge to English rule than the local revolt in south Wales of 1287-8. The summer of 1294 found King Edward deeply involved in his quarrel with King Philip of France and preparations for his expedition to Gascony and, in June, Edmund Mortimer and other magnates were summoned to a council which agreed to intervene militarily in the duchy. The king ordered the feudal host to assemble at Portsmouth by 1 September, but for some reason Edmund was excused his summons — perhaps there was already unrest in his lordships, as there was elsewhere in Wales, and which developed at the end of September into open revolt through much of the country. The Welsh leaders had, however, struck too soon, for although many English troops had been withdrawn from Wales for service in Gascony, much of the expeditionary force had not sailed. The king transferred his administrative energy to Wales. Within a few weeks three English armies were campaigning in the country and by the summer of 1295 the fighting was over with Edward tightening the English grip on Wales by castle-building, administrative measures and instituting enquiries into the reasons for the revolt. Edmund had probably been in the March at, or soon after, the outbreak of hostilities and he served under the earl of Hereford and John Giffard who were responsible for the defence of the March between Brecon and Montgomery. The king did not forget his quarrel with France and sent forces to Gascony late in 1294; the next year Edmund and other lords were ordered 'to take into the king's hands all lands and goods of all alien religious of the power of the king of France'.[4]

King Edward had political confrontations with barons other than the marcher lords whom he had so successfully brought to heel in 1290-91. Resentment at the king's methods of government came to a head in 1297 when the earls of Norfolk and Hereford took the lead in resisting the king's plans to raise armies, particularly the financial arrangements, for campaigns against France in Gascony and Flanders. Edmund supported the two earls, and in March of that year probably attended the conference in Wyre Forest, part of the Mortimer liberty of Cleobury, at which Norfolk and his allies discussed their grievances. Edmund was summoned for service abroad in July and was ordered to send 200 men from his lands in the March to join the expeditionary force; but he and other magnates remained in England insisting on satisfaction of their complaints as well as the confirmation of Magna Carta. In spite of the delicate political situation the king sailed for Flanders, although with a smaller force than he had hoped for. The crisis in the kingdom developed as the regents wrestled with the problem of avoiding what for a time seemed to be a risk of civil war. Edmund and other dissidents were included in a summons to 220 knights and others to come in arms to join the king's son, Prince Edward, at Rochester, and Edmund was called to a parliament which was to meet on 30 September. Then, in the middle of that month, came news from Scotland of the battle of Stirling where William Wallace had defeated the earl of Surrey and had invaded northern England.

This disaster was the catalyst which united the baronial factions in England in a common cause in the autumn of 1297, and a parallel can be found 617 years later when the outbreak of the First World War transcended in the national consciousness the train of events in Ireland. The earls of Norfolk and Hereford and other dissidents, including Edmund Mortimer, were pardoned, steps were taken to defend the north of England and preparations begun for a great offensive against the Scots the following year. Edmund was not listed as being present at the English victory at Falkirk in July 1298, although Roger of Chirk was, but the king's army did include infantry from both Edmund's lands and those of his mother (see p.28).

Edmund was summoned on a number of occasions for service in the Scottish wars, but seems never to have held a major command, and was also called to parliaments as Lord Mortimer. In 1300, when Pope Boniface VIII tried to interfere in the king's plans for Scotland by ordering Edward to cease hostilities in what the pope was pleased to call a papal fief, Edmund was one of seven earls and many barons who early the next year signed a letter of remonstrance to Boniface. It seems, however, that the letter was never sent for fear of aggravating the situation. In 1301, Edmund was granted the lands of his mother who had recently died and he himself died in July 1304. He was buried like so many of his forebears and descendants in Wigmore Abbey, and left as his heir his son Roger.

In neither his first marriage, nor his second to Margaret de Fiennes, did Edmund show the acumen displayed by his father and his son in making hugely profitable marriages, for Margaret, although a second cousin of Queen Eleanor, seems to have brought little to augment the fortunes of the Mortimers. Margaret was to survive her husband by 30 years and aristocratic widows were important pieces on the medieval political chessboard. They were entitled to one third of their husbands' estates and any lands which they had inherited or which they held jointly with their husbands. Margaret held as her dower Knighton, Norton, Presteigne, Gwerthrynion and Radnor throughout the life of her son and her husband's heir, Roger (IV). She may well have acted in accordance with 'family policy', nevertheless dower significantly reduced Roger's resources. Dower became an acute problem for the Mortimers for a few years after Roger's death in 1330 when three Mortimer dowagers were alive — his mother, his widow and his heir's widow.

Edmund never built a career in royal service or achieved great office under the Crown. Whether he was unambitious or untrustworthy is not clear, but King Edward seems to have doubted his ability to hold down an important office, or to have mistrusted him, and Edmund's relationship with the king appears never to have been a close one. Edmund was, however, in no way disgraced; he was granted the right to hold markets and fairs, he was regularly summoned to parliaments and for military service, and in common with other members of the baronage he had other duties to perform such as being appointed to a commission 'to enquire touching the magnates and others who have narrowed and increased in height their weirs on the river Severn between the towns of Gloucester and Shrewsbury, so that vessels cannot pass through as they were wont, and to pull the same down where necessary'.[5]

Causes or symptoms of the coolness between the king and Edmund can be found in several incidents. The marcher lords were deeply offended by some of Edward's actions, particularly the events of 1290-91 and the taxation measures of 1292 (see p.20), and Edmund was far from alone among the lords of the March in incurring the king's displeasure or in suffering from royal interference in his affairs. He may have been imprudent and too forthright in protesting to the king; perhaps he presumed too much on being the son of Edward's trusted friend and lieutenant and expected the royal indulgence that his father had enjoyed. In 1290 the king confiscated Edmund's liberty of Wigmore after Edmund had executed a man from the royal lordship of Montgomery (see p.20). Five years later, when Edmund refused to serve overseas, the king ordered distraint of his lands for payment of his debts to the Crown.

In 1297 the men of Maelienydd submitted a list of grievances to the king. Edward summoned Edmund to attend a meeting before himself and the council when the Welshmen would present their complaints and Edmund would be called upon to answer them; in the meantime Edmund was ordered not to aggrieve or molest his men in any way:

> The king has received diverse complaints from the community of Welshmen of Melenith, Edmund's men and tenants, setting out that he grievously disquiets and molests them by imprisonment of their bodies and the taking and carrying way of their goods and chattels and by various ransoms, wilfully and without reasonable cause, contrary to justice and contrary to the law and custom of those parts, so that they are now so impoverished that they have little or nothing to live upon, as they assert.[6]

Edward appears to have pressured Edmund into granting two charters to the Welsh of Maelienydd — for which they had to pay £500. In the Statute of Westminster of 1275 the king had promised the peoples of the March, 'as their sovereign lord', to do justice in the March 'where the king's writ does not run' to all who complained. His intervention may also have been connected with the investigation into Welsh grievances which he had instigated after the rebellion of 1295. Yet another of Edmund's grudges would have been the loss in unrecorded circumstances of Cwmwd Deuddwr, a small lordship to the west of Gwerthrynion, which the king took from him.

Edmund Mortimer (I)'s somewhat undistinguished career contrasted strongly with that of his father, a not uncommon circumstance for the son of an energetic and successful parent, but political circumstances beyond his control militated against Edmund continuing his father's empire-building. It was his ill-fortune to be head of the house of Mortimer, along with the Corbets and the Braoses the longest-established family of the March, just when the expansion of the Mortimer empire had been halted by the royal conquest of Wales, and the lords' freedom of action limited by the interventionism of a forceful king. These magnates now found that the danger to their interests in Wales came not from the Welsh, but from royal interference in their affairs. The 14th and 15th centuries were to demonstrate that the Crown's authority in Wales was only as effective as the king was powerful, but it was during Edward I's reign, and Edmund (I)'s lifetime, that threatening clouds began to gather over the constitutional status of the March and its lords.

CHAPTER VI

Earl of March

Edmund Mortimer (I)'s heir, Roger, is the one member of the Mortimer family who receives more than a cursory mention in general histories of England. His career can be conveniently divided into three phases: until he was about 30 years old he devoted most of his energy to promoting his interests in Wales and Ireland; after 1318 he played a more prominent part in the kingdom's politics, broke with the king, and in 1323 escaped from imprisonment into exile; the last phase comprised Roger's return to England in 1326, the consolidation of his position as the most powerful man in England, his downfall and execution for treason in 1330.

Roger (IV) was probably born in 1287 and, as he was a minor at the time of his father's death in 1304, Edward I made him a ward of Peter de Gaveston, a close friend of Prince Edward, the king's son and heir. In 1306 Roger obtained the right to his lands by paying off Gaveston and these were in due course augmented by the lands inherited by his bride, Joan de Genevile, whom he had married in 1301: a moiety — not necessarily a half share — of the lordship of Ludlow together with the castle, the lordship of Ewyas Lacy, manors in Herefordshire and Shropshire and, in Ireland, the lordship of Trim with which went a moiety of Meath.[1]

In the spring of 1306 Edward I began preparations for yet another campaign in Scotland. On Whit Sunday, Prince Edward and nearly 300 other young men, including Roger Mortimer, were knighted in a splendid ceremony at Westminster staged to mobilize the youth of the country. The old king was carried to the festivities in a litter and there he swore vengeance on the recently crowned Robert Bruce who, through the murder of John Comyn in which he was implicated, had changed the Scottish political landscape. Roger served in the English army in Scotland and was one of a number of knights, among them his uncle, Roger of Chirk, and Peter de Gaveston, who left the army 'without licence before the war was ended, deserting the king and his son in those parts in contempt of the king and to the retarding of the king's business there'.[2]

The south-east gatehouse at Trim Castle, Co. Meath

King Edward, growing ever more irascible with advancing years and ill-health, disciplined the offenders, confiscating Roger's lands although he soon returned them together with a pardon. Roger was subsequently summoned for service against the Scots on several occasions in the early years of Edward II, once being ordered to raise '200 foot soldiers instead of 500 from his lordship of Mollennyght [Maelienydd] and his other lordships in Wales'.[3]

Roger was called to parliament for the first time in 1307, the year of Edward I's death, and at Edward II's coronation the following year he had the honour of being one of the four bearers of the royal robes. Roger was clearly favoured by the new king, most probably through his association with Peter de Gaveston, and at the age of 20 or so he would have felt more at home at the court of the young Edward II than in the service of the king's formidable father.

The justiciar in Ireland was ordered to hand over to Roger the lands which constituted his inheritance in December 1307, and Geoffrey de Genevile was authorised to transfer to Roger and his wife (Geoffrey's granddaughter) the estates in Ireland which he had been holding for her. In the following April Roger was granted a charter to hold a weekly market and annual fair at Ardmulchan in Meath. Roger Mortimer's thoughts at this time must have turned towards the family estates in Ireland, and in October 1308 he and Joan crossed the Irish Sea to make what is the first recorded visit to Ireland by the head of the family. The Mortimers had held lands in Ireland for over 60 years but, understandably preoccupied with their affairs in Wales and politics in England, they seem to have taken little interest in them. The Irish lands in Meath which had come to Roger in the right of his wife, when added to his inheritance in Leix (western Leinster) from his grandmother, Maud, made him one of the principal lords of Ireland, but he needed to assert his rights in a disturbed country and in face of hostility from some of the Anglo-Irish magnates.

The remoter regions of Ireland had never been brought under English control, and outside the counties and lordships the Anglo-Irish and the native Irish had always squabbled and fought among themselves. By the beginning of the 14th century the government, with its seat in Dublin and under the authority of the justiciar, administered — at least nominally — about three-quarters of Ireland, and although Edward I never visited the country, English domination was probably more complete than it had ever been. But this authority was relative; Ireland was a divided country with relatively peaceful areas, mainly in the east, and areas where warfare and lawlessness were endemic. Absentee landlords like the Mortimers, who were disliked by the resident Anglo-Irish magnates, contributed little to the community. They often preferred to transfer profits from their estates to England, and did not take their full share in the defence of Anglo-Irish lands and society against the Irish from both the untamed lands in the west and from scattered pockets of land among the lordships which had never come under effective Anglo-Irish control. With the justiciar's administration ineffective in many regions and his authority widely flouted, the sword remained the ultimate source of power of the Anglo-Irish in much of the country, and by it they settled disputes among themselves and with the Irish. For a lord of the Welsh March this was a familiar political environment and Roger Mortimer remained for the rest of his life alert to opportunities in Ireland, building up an empire there just as he was to do in Wales.

Roger and Joan arrived in Ireland to face claims to their lands from the Lacys and Verduns who disputed Joan's inheritance, and a few years later by an invasion by the Scots; it was to be another ten years before the Mortimer titles to their lands were secure and their status in Ireland assured. Ireland was not Roger's only concern during this period, but it is convenient to narrate here his progress to power in that country and turn later to his contemporary activities in England and Wales.

The Irish were encouraged by the Scottish victory over the English at Bannockburn in 1314 to attempt to recover their independence, and they welcomed an offer of support from Robert Bruce and his brother, Edward, who were eager to discomfort the English and extend Scottish influence into Ireland. In May of the following year a Scottish army under Edward Bruce's command landed in Ulster with the avowed intention of overthrowing the English and restoring the ancient Irish kingdoms. The Lacys had helped to persuade Bruce to invade Ireland, had written to the pope in his support, and, with no love lost between them and the Mortimers and hoping to profit from the situation, they had joined forces with the Scots. Bruce with his Irish allies won a number of victories, and advancing into Meath defeated Roger Mortimer early in 1316 at Kells.

For a time the position of the English in Ireland was desperate, and abandoning his Irish estates Roger fled to Dublin and made his way to England; an inquest of 1323 found that Roger's castle of Dunamase had been burned and the manor ruined — probable evidence of the havoc wrought by the Scots in 1316-17. Roger was not blamed for the Irish debacle and indeed in November 1316 he was appointed the king's lieutenant and *custos* in Ireland. Edward II and the council ordered that 'Roger de Mortuo Mari of Wyggemor shall be at Haverford at the above feast [of the Purification, 2 February] with a multitude of men for the purpose of proceeding to Ireland to repel the invasion of that country by Edward de Brus and his accomplices, Scotch rebels'.[4] Roger mustered his army at Haverfordwest and landed at Youghal in Ireland early in April 1317, while the king provided him with support by entering into an indenture with Sir Antoyne Pessaigne, knight of Genoa and a mercenary, who was to provide '5 galleys well found, each equipped with 200 men armed in plate, to be landed in Dublin for the war in Ireland'.[5] The Scots retreated northwards and, in a two-day battle in June, Roger gained his revenge on the Lacys; they fled westwards into Connaught and he confiscated their estates in the name of the king who in due course granted them to him in recognition of his services. As Roger regained territory lost to the English he energetically restored the administration, sought out Edward Bruce's supporters and confiscated their lands, granted pardons and rewarded those who had remained loyal to the king besides no doubt feathering his own nest. Bruce himself was killed in battle in 1318. According to one account his head was brought to England and:

> unexpectedly laid, with other heads, on a table before Edward II., while seated at a banquet, with ambassadors from Scotland … The Scotch ambassadors, rising from the table, hurried, horror-stricken from the apartment … the King of England received the head with great delight, and was 'right blithe' of the present, glad to be so delivered of 'a felon foe'.[6]

In the same year Roger was recalled to England, but in 1319 returned to Ireland as justiciar, the nominee of the Middle Party (more moderate magnates and churchmen who formed a group around the earl of Pembroke, as opposed to the more radical Ordainers) now in the political ascendancy in England. He held the justiciarship for nearly two years, but in January 1321, as his relations with the king worsened, he was relieved of his office. The previous autumn he had in fact appointed the earl of Kildare as his deputy and had returned to England, presumably to look after his interests there and in Wales where the political situation was rapidly deteriorating.

Roger had come to Ireland to assert his wife's rights and had found himself defending the Anglo-Irish supremacy against both the Irish and the Scots; he had been appointed to the command of the expeditionary force which had been sent to reimpose English rule and had ended up by becoming justiciar. His ability was evident and his removal from office seems to have been on account of his differences with the king over developments in south Wales and the growing influence at court of the Despencers, rather than mismanagement of affairs in Ireland. The seeds of Roger's ambition would have grown quickly as a result of his success in Ireland, and his record there foretold the formidable figure that he would cut in the crisis which would soon break in England.

Roger's commitments in Ireland did not mean that he neglected his interests in Wales which, throughout his career, he recognized as the primary source of his power and which provided him with military muscle during the crises of Edward II's reign and his subsequent political ascendancy in the early years of Edward III. An influential bloc of the peerage had similar concerns in Wales, indeed when Edward II came to the throne seven out of the ten English earls were also lords of the Welsh March. Edward I had kept the marchers on a tight rein, reacting violently to any tendency to individual or group aggrandisement, but under Edward II the political environment was more conducive to private empire-building. A weak king and lax, faction-ridden administration provided

Medieval glass in Ludlow Church showing the Mortimer arms

political conditions in which the marcher lords, resentful of all superior authority, could flourish, and while Wales no longer offered the scope or the threat it once had done, there were still opportunities for the lords of the March to build up their power as individuals and as a group.

In 1309 Roger was granted Cwmwd Deuddwr which his father had been forced to surrender to Edward I and the following year he was granted custody of Builth Castle. He was soon succeeded at Builth by Philip ap Hywel, but custody of royal castles such as Builth, and Roscommon, Randown and Athlone in Ireland, provided him with opportunities for exploiting his influence and patronage; under weak central government these bastions of power, nominally the Crown's, could be manipulated by unscrupulous custodians for their own purposes. A dispute which arose over the lordship of Powys in 1309 gave Roger a chance to try his hand at power politics in Wales. Powys was claimed by both Gruffydd de la Pole and John Charlton; while the former's claim was backed by the grandee, Thomas, earl of Lancaster and his political faction, the latter's claim had the support of the king. Roger had an interest in the matter as Powys bordered his lands and it was his uncle, Roger of Chirk, who as justiciar of Wales had been ordered to evict Gruffydd. Armed intervention on the king's orders, perhaps involving Roger's

The figures of Roger (IV) and Edmund (III) Mortimer and their arms as shown in the glass by Willement in the 19th century in Ludlow Church

forces, resulted in Charlton establishing himself as lord of Powys although the dispute was to drag on for some years. Roger was rewarded for his support with a grant of land in Powys and with the marriage of Charlton's son, another John, to his daughter, Maud.

Roger may well have been on the fringe of the developing baronial opposition to the king when he attended a tournament at Dunstable in the spring of 1309. It was here that the magnates are likely to have discussed the demands for reform which they were to make in parliament, but Roger's part in the political infighting in which the Ordainers, with Thomas of Lancaster at their head, forced through the Ordinances of 1311 is not clear. The Ordinances limited the king's freedom of action and removed Gaveston from the court. Although at this time Roger may not have overtly supported the Ordainers, he could well have sided with them over one issue. In 1308 he had acknowledged a debt of £80 to Italian bankers, the Frescobaldi. The Frescobaldi were suspected by the Ordainers of mischief-making, of wielding undue influence over the king through his debts to them and providing him with a degree of financial independence free of their supervision. Whether Roger settled his debt is not known, but for those barons who were in debt to the Frescobaldi, national and private interest were neatly served when the bankers were forced to flee the country leaving the baronage's debts to them unpaid.

In 1313 Roger visited Gascony on the king's service with his expenses of £100 being found by the sheriffs of Shropshire and Herefordshire, and by the bailiff of Builth. His mission was probably connected with the delicate constitutional position of King Edward as duke of Aquitaine vis-à-vis the French king, a bone of contention which a peace conference, the Process of Périgueux, had failed to settle two years earlier. By the time of Roger's visit to Gascony the king had won back some of the independence that he had lost to the Ordainers, and his employment of Roger on a diplomatic mission suggests that Roger's support of the Crown over the Powys succession, and possibly at the time of the Ordinances and over other matters, had brought him into King Edward's circle of trusted servants.

Roger and his uncle were among the marcher lords who in 1315-16 suppressed the revolt of Llywelyn Bren in Glamorgan. At the time the English administration was still reeling from the defeat of Bannockburn and trying to repel Scottish raids into northern England, besides being under great pressure in Ireland. There were fears that the revolt might spill over into the rest of Wales while the nightmare of a Scottish army, victorious in Ireland and crossing the Irish Sea to assist the Welsh, haunted the king and his advisers. Also in 1316, Roger assisted the earl of Pembroke in putting down a rising in Bristol where the burgesses had driven out the city's officers; it needed the deployment of siege engines around the walls to force the city to surrender. There was at this time widespread unrest throughout the kingdom, and indeed much of Europe, which had been sparked off by acute deprivation after the ruined harvest of 1315.

It was in 1318, the year that Roger Mortimer returned to England after his successful campaign in Ireland, that he began to play a more prominent part in English politics. By now in his early thirties, with his status bolstered by his achievements in Ireland, he was well placed to take part in government, a self-aggrandising role which he would pursue for the rest of his life. Edward II's humiliation at Bannockburn had strengthened the hand of Thomas, earl of Lancaster, and the reformist Ordainers. Thomas, was, however, the leader of only a section of the baronage, and the more moderate Middle Party sought a reconciliation between the king and the earl. Roger appears to have supported the moderate group which favoured a measure of reform, but which was in fact close to the Crown with its leaders believing that they could manage the wayward king. In the summer of 1318 the Treaty of Leake established a *modus vivendi* between the contending parties and the king, perhaps, getting slightly the better of the bargain. Roger played a part in the negotiations, no doubt fearing that Edward II's patronage might be at risk if reform was allowed to go too far, and his opposition to earl Thomas's more extreme demands hardened when he received from the king a grant of marriage of the three-year-old earl of Warwick to his daughter Catherine. (The marriage settled a quarrel between the Mortimers and the Beauchamp earls of Warwick over the marcher lordship of Elfael, with Roger probably renouncing his claim as part of Catherine's marriage portion.)

The Treaty of Leake brought Roger into the limelight; he was nominated one of the king's sureties, appointed one of the 17 members of the new council with effective control over the king's actions and he was also a member of a committee which was to consider ways of reforming the king's household. The following year, as previously noted, he became justiciar of Ireland.

For nearly two years the Treaty of Leake provided a fragile political peace, but in 1320-1 it was wrecked by the king's mishandling of the territorial ambitions and growing influence at court of two prominent barons — the Despencers, Hugh the elder and his son, Hugh the younger. Hugh le Despencer the younger had married a sister and co-heiress of Gilbert de Clare, earl of Gloucester, who had been killed at Bannockburn in 1314. Not content with his wife's inheritance of Glamorgan, Hugh had claimed other lands in Wales of the Clares and indeed had set his sights on becoming earl of Gloucester. Hugh's high-handed methods and his apparently irresistible influence over the king were violently resented by many barons, particularly the marcher lords, and matters came to a head when William de Braose let it be known that he was willing to sell his lordship of Gower.

William had been negotiating with a number of barons: Hugh le Despencer the younger, Roger Mortimer of Wigmore and Roger Mortimer of Chirk,

Humphrey de Bohun and John Mowbray, William's son-in-law, all hoped to obtain Gower. It appears that William de Braose granted the lordship to John Mowbray who immediately took possession of it. Hugh le Despencer's confident expectations had been thwarted by Mowbray and he now persuaded the king that William de Braose's alienation of his lordship had been illegal, on the grounds that lands held in chief of the Crown could not be transferred without a royal licence, and if a tenant did so his lands were forfeit. This raised the question of the Law and Custom of the March and the relevance of the royal prerogative, a subject close to the heart of every lord of the March and a delicate one ever since Edward I's assault on it 30 years earlier. The law of alienation in England had never been accepted by the marcher lords and few decisions by a king could have provoked a more united and fervent opposition from them than Edward II's ruling over the lordship of Gower. Not only at issue were Hugh le Despencer's conduct and influence over the king, but also the royal attack on the Law and Custom of the March and therefore on the marcher lords themselves. Edward I had successfully meddled in the marcher lords' affairs, but at a time and on ground of his own choosing; Edward II had neither the prestige nor the resources to repeat his father's success. Like the succession dispute in Powys a few years earlier, the quarrel over Gower was basically a local issue. It could probably have been settled by the king with a little political finesse or by the threat of overwhelming force, as his father would surely have done, but in their absence it was allowed to degenerate first into a dangerous political crisis and then open hostilities. The solution of the underlying problem of the Despencers' influence over King Edward was another matter, but this again lay in the king's hands.

The ensuing civil war between the king and elements of the baronage involved the Mortimers of Wigmore and of Chirk. Roger of Chirk had like his nephew prospered since the accession of Edward II (see chapter 8). Among other favours he had been appointed justiciar of Wales and granted the lordship of Blaenllyfni; he was an active supporter of the earl of Pembroke, and at the heart of the kingdom's administration he felt his authority as justiciar of Wales under threat from Hugh the younger. Roger of Wigmore for his part saw in Hugh an *arriviste* — a splendid example of the pot calling the kettle black — who, with the likely support of the king would threaten the existing composition and administration of the March; indeed Hugh had made clear his designs on a number of Roger's castles. Both Mortimers feared Hugh's ambition to take revenge on them for the death of his grandfather who had been killed in the Barons' War of 1264-5. In matters affecting the wellbeing of the Mortimer family, uncle and nephew saw eye to eye and they formed a dangerous combination at the heart of the opposition to Edward II's misgovernment and to the two Despencers. At this time, and for apparently blatant, political reasons, Roger of Wigmore and other marcher lords concerned themselves with an obscure monastic dispute in East Anglia. By dramatically protesting to the king over a minor matter which does not seem to have involved their interests in any way, they were sending a warning shot across the king's bows.

By early in 1321 Hugh le Despencer was garrisoning his castles and attacking Gower, while an alliance of marcher lords approached Earl Thomas of Lancaster, who was lord of Kidwelly adjacent to Gower, for support. Thomas clearly had a vital interest in the fortunes of Gower but declined to be drawn into the dispute leaving Humphrey de Bohun, earl of Hereford, the Mortimers and other lords determined to resist Hugh, and if necessary the king, by force. Among prominent marcher lords only the earls of Pembroke and Arundel were conspicuously loyal to King Edward. In March, Humphrey and Roger of Wigmore refused a summons to attend the king at Gloucester, and proceeded to ignore instructions to keep the peace and an order on 1 May not to attack Hugh le Despencer. Three days later they and their allies launched an assault on the Despencer lordships in south Wales and for some five days harried Hugh's lands before widening the conflict to other estates of the Despencers. In the ensuing sporadic warfare Roger won Clun Castle from Edmund Fitzalan, earl of Arundel, whose heir had married, or was soon to do so, Hugh the younger's daughter.

Thomas of Lancaster now assumed a more prominent role in the opposition to the king and the Despencers and called a conference of his vassals, northern barons and lords of the Welsh March. The two Mortimers were among the magnates who assembled at the end of June 1321 at Sherburn, near Thomas's castle of Pontefract, and drew up a list of grievances and an indictment of the Despencers.

The king's inclination had been to support the Despencers militarily but he was persuaded first to summon a parliament to meet at Westminster in July. The dissident barons were determined to put on a show of

The 'Keep' at Clun Castle built in the late 13th or early 14th century, peculiarly sited on the edge of the motte

The gateway to the priory precincts of the Order of St. John, Clerkenwell

force, and the Wigmore chronicler relates that Roger of Wigmore, as one of their commanders, marched into London with his men dressed in a livery of green with yellow sleeves (or hands); he stayed in the capital at the priory of the Knights of St. John in Clerkenwell. After some days of negotiation the king agreed to demands that the Despencers be banished, and Roger with the other rebels were formally pardoned. As soon, however, as they had dispersed Edward set about regaining the political initiative. He met Hugh the younger at Harwich to plan his revenge and, winning support from a number of barons who had never wholeheartedly supported the dissidents, he manu-factured an opportunity in mid-October to take the offensive by isolating one of the rebel barons, Bartholomew, Lord Badlesmere.

Besides being political allies, Badlesmere and Roger Mortimer were connected through the marriage in 1316 of Roger's heir, Edmund, to Badlesmere's daughter, Elizabeth; Badlesmere had paid £2,000 for the marriage and in return Elizabeth had received five of Roger's manors and other benefits. In 1321 Badlesmere was constable of the royal castle of Leeds in Kent but was absent when Queen Isabella had asked for hospitality during her travels. Badlesmere's wife was adamant that she needed her husband's permission before allowing anyone admission and the king took this insult as justification for laying siege to the castle. Humphrey of Hereford and the two Mortimers hurried to Badlesmere's assistance; they mustered their forces at Kingston-on-Thames preparatory to marching to the relief of Leeds, but before the army, which had been joined by Badlesmere himself, could leave Kingston, Thomas of Lancaster — no friend of Badlesmere — intervened by strongly suggesting that they should proceed no further. The king scented victory, refused to listen to the rebels' proposals for a solution to the quarrel, and a few days later forced the castle to surrender. The rebels were humiliated and Lady Badlesmere was consigned to the Tower where she spent the next year.

The Mortimers and other rebels had badly misjudged the situation, and when Earl Humphrey, the Mortimers and Badlesmere retired to the north to attend another meeting called by Earl Thomas for the end of November, they must have been suspicious, justifiably so, of the earl's political sympathies. There were a number of defections to the king's cause and he maintained pressure on the rebel alliance by forbidding 122 named men, including the Mortimers of Wigmore and Chirk, from attending Thomas's conference at Doncaster; there is in fact some doubt whether this took place on the scale that Thomas intended. The king had won the upper hand. He declared the Despencers' exile illegal, ordered the arrest of the Mortimers and other rebel lords, and in reply to a petition from Thomas's meeting at Doncaster he made clear that he was determined to have done with the rebel marcher lords once and for all, but that he had no personal quarrel with Thomas himself. The rebels returned to their estates in early December, knowing that the king had ordered his army to assemble at Cirencester in the middle of the month and that the royal forces in Wales were being called out against them.

Edward II spent Christmas 1321 at Cirencester and a few days later marched with his army to Worcester. Earl Humphrey had meanwhile garrisoned Gloucester and with his allies held the vital river crossings over the lower and middle Severn against the king. Unable to cross the river at Worcester, the king marched north to Bridgnorth, where he found the Mortimers and Humphrey had destroyed the bridge before his advance guard could secure it, and then moved further upstream to Shrewsbury. In the meantime Worcester had fallen to the rebels, and when Humphrey returned to Gloucester he left the Mortimers on the west bank of the Severn covering the royal army as it made its way up the east bank of the river. The Mortimers had by now assembled a sizeable army and had been reinforced by troops sent by Adam de Orleton, bishop of Hereford; Bromyard and Ledbury in Herefordshire, and no doubt other towns and the countryside, suffered from the ill-discipline of Roger of Wigmore's men.

The rebels did not for some reason destroy the bridge across the Severn at Shrewsbury and the king and his army were able to cross over to the west bank on 14 January. The rebels were now faced by a much superior force and were also threatened by another army advancing on them from north Wales; their only hope lay in the military intervention of Thomas of Lancaster and this did not materialise. On 20 January the king issued a safe conduct to Roger of

Wigmore 'and all those he brings with him or who will come to the king's will, Bartholomew Badlesmere excepted',[7] so that he could negotiate a surrender. The time limit was extended twice and at last Roger and his uncle gave themselves up at the end of January. The rebel alliance now fell apart. While Edward marched triumphantly through the lands of his enemies, from Shrewsbury to Hereford and on to Gloucester, some rebels followed the Mortimers' example but others, including Earl Humphrey, made their way northwards to join forces with Thomas of Lancaster who had at last openly defied the king and was negotiating for support from the Scots.

By the end of March 1322 both earls were dead: Humphrey killed at the battle of Borougbridge and Thomas captured the day after the battle and executed outside his castle at Pontefract. The two Mortimers were tried by a commission consisting of the treasurer, the mayor of London, two justices and a baron of the exchequer for 'notorious treasons'[8] which the king recorded against them. They had no chance of justice as the king's word, or record, was legally incontrovertible and conviction more or less automatic. Both of them were condemned to death in July, but were fortunate enough to be reprieved and began sentences of life imprisonment in the Tower in spite of a Welsh petition that they should be shown no mercy,

The removal from the political scene of the earls of Lancaster and Hereford, the two Mortimers and other rebels, had widespread implications for the March. King Edward rewarded his supporters with confiscated estates, parliamentary proceedings against the Despencers were annulled and they resumed their part in government, receiving lavish gifts from the king. The Mortimers may have escaped with their lives but their estates were seized and most appear to have been granted to their old opponent, Edmund, earl of Arundel; an inventory of the goods and chattels at Wigmore Castle and abbey at this time has survived.[9] Edward and the Despencers learned little from the crisis of 1321-2. Within three years the barons' animosity towards the Despencers, the ignominious if sensible truce with King Robert (the Bruce) of Scotland, the escape of Roger Mortimer of Wigmore from the Tower and the desertion of Edward by his queen once again placed the king in jeopardy.

Although many barons would have been relieved to see Roger of Wigmore behind bars he retained at least one influential supporter, Adam de Orleton, the bishop of Hereford whom the pope had refused to remove from his see in spite of the king's demands and his prominent role in the rebellion. Orleton was said to have had a large part in Roger's escape from the Tower in August 1323. Accounts variously describe how one of the Tower's officers was suborned, the constable and others drugged, a hole cut through the wall into Roger's cell and a rope ladder and a boat provided to take him and a fellow conspirator across the Thames to the south bank. Horses awaited them to ride to the coast where a ship was ready to sail. One can sense the ensuing panic in the government from the king's numerous writs to his officers enjoining them to do everything they could to capture Roger. Edward suspected reasonably enough that he would try to make for Ireland or France, and commanded Edmund, earl of Kent, constable of Dover Castle and warden of the Cinque Ports to:

> appoint spies in all the said ports and to cause diligent search to be made for the aforesaid Roger, and to take him alive or dead if he come thither, and to enquire, in case Roger have crossed the sea from those ports, who have taken him out of the realm.[10]

Roger in fact fled to Paris where he offered his services to Charles IV in his war in Gascony against Edward II and planned his revenge. He did not take long before acting. In November a man confessed in London to having been sent from St. Omer to organise the assassination of the chancellor, Robert Baldock, the Despencers and other enemies of Roger Mortimer.

Relations between Edward and Queen Isabella now became more and more strained and in 1325 the queen crossed to France, ostensibly to mediate at the papal nuncio's suggestion, between Kings Edward and Charles — her husband and her brother — but very probably largely to escape from Edward's control. She was soon joined by Prince Edward, her 13-year-old son and the heir apparent, whom the king allowed to go in place of himself to do homage to Charles as part of a peace agreement negotiated by the queen. Now that Isabella had her son with her she refused to return to England with the prince as long as Hugh le Despencer the younger remained at court, and in her defiance of the king she became associated with Roger Mortimer and the other rebels who had fled to France. Her political relationship with Roger soon developed into a personal liaison which gave rise to comment and scandal. At the pope's instigation an embarrassed King Charles demonstrated his disapproval of the state of affairs and Isabella, with Roger and the other exiles, moved to the Low Countries. It will never be known whether the affair between Isabella and Roger was based on genuine affection, or on opportunist exploitation to promote their political ambitions by one of the other, or indeed by both of each other; they were equally devious and ruthless where their interests were concerned. In the Low Countries Count William II of Hainault, who felt himself wronged by King Edward over trade and shipping matters, agreed to support Isabella in a military expedition to England to remove the Despencers from power, and if necessary the king from his throne. Count William named his price for assisting Isabella and Roger as the betrothal of his daughter, Philippa, to Prince Edward. Meanwhile King Edward had appealed in vain to Isabella to return, and now alert to the danger of invasion had taken military precautions as well as threatening Roger of Wigmore with death if he ever again set foot in England.

Isabella and her small force of some 700 exiles and mercenaries under the command of Roger Mortimer and John, the count of Hainault's brother, landed in Suffolk late in September 1326. They were unopposed by the English fleet which was said to have refused to obey the king's orders. On land, in spite of the king's precautions, when for instance he ordered Daniel de Burgham 'to select and lead all the horse and foot who will go with him against Roger de Mortuo Mari and the rebels who have invaded the realm, and to take him alive or dead',[11] the rebels marched towards London gathering adherents along the way. The king abandoned his capital and with the Despencers and their allies retreated westwards towards Wales. Edward's best chance of surviving the crisis was to unite forces from the lordships of the Despencers with those from the Principality in north and west Wales where, since his investment as prince of Wales 25 years earlier, he had built up a strong bond of loyalty and service. This contrasted sharply with the enmity of the Welsh towards the Mortimers of Wigmore and Chirk. Nothing came of Edward's attempts to rally support in Wales; time was not on his side as the rebel army soon reached Wales in pursuit of their quarry. The elder Despencer was captured, tried and executed when Bristol surrendered, and in November a contingent of the queen's army seized the king, the younger Despencer and a group of their supporters in Neath Abbey. Despencer was tried and executed in Hereford, which Isabella and Roger Mortimer had made their headquarters after the capture of Bristol, and they ordered that the king be held in close custody. After a meeting of parliament Edward II unwillingly resigned the crown and Roger attended the coronation of the young Edward III on 1 February 1327.

Looking down the nave at Neath Abbey

The deposition of the king and the destruction of the Despencers caused little disruption within the kingdom and, apart from some violence in London, was remarkably quick and bloodless. In addition to the Despencers, the earl of Arundel — Roger Mortimer's rival for power in the March and the one earl who had remained loyal to the king — was dispatched along with some supporters, but there were no widespread reprisals against Edward II's men; indeed the new government appears to have wisely adopted a conciliatory policy towards its erstwhile opponents.

As the most prominent surviving rebel of 1321-2 — Roger Mortimer of Chirk had died in the Tower in 1326 — Roger of Wigmore had played a pivotal role in the rebels' success. He had brought his considerable energy and ability to bear on the rebellion and his influence over Queen Isabella had given him great power, while his authority increased with the rebellion's success and the establishment of the new regime. Those of the baronage who distrusted Roger's ambition, who were acquainted with his avarice and who now feared that one unprincipled regime would be replaced by another, were wise if they kept their misgivings to themselves in the mood of widespread relief that followed the removal of the Despencers and their patron.

Roger could have followed the honourable political example of William Marshal when he became regent for Henry III a century and more earlier, but the temptations presented to him at the centre of power in England seem to have swamped his conscience and good sense. Rather than assume a formal position of authority in the new administration he preferred to pull the strings of power from behind the scenes. Earl Henry of Lancaster, brother and heir to the earl executed in 1322 and who with other magnates had come to the support of Isabella and Roger when they had landed in England, became Edward III's 'keeper' at the head of a regency council. Surprisingly, Roger was not a member of the council though he could surely have had a seat if he so wished. It is conceivable that he hoped to defuse baronial resentment and suspicion by declining office as part of the regime's conciliatory policy, but from what we know of him, adverse reaction among the baronage to his political advancement would not have unduly concerned him, and it is more likely that he wanted power without overt responsibility for the actions of the government. Roger's partisans on the council, among them Bishops Hotham of Ely and Orleton of Hereford, ensured that his views were forcibly represented while his influence over the queen gave him a unique status in the kingdom, largely at the expense of the council's control of affairs and Earl Henry's authority. Parliament formally pardoned him for breaking out of the Tower and other offences, revoked the sentence of imprisonment on the ground, *inter alia*, that he had not been tried by his peers as decreed in Magna Carta, and returned his lands to him.

Evidence of Roger's standing can be found in references to him as 'the king's kinsman' in some of the grants which he received over the next three years. During the 14th and 15th centuries the Mortimers liked to draw attention to their descent from King John, and they also attached great importance to their Welsh descent from Gwladus Ddu and back to Cadwalader and indeed Brutus. Adam of Usk's later panegyric of the Mortimers sums up their claims as grandees of the kingdom: 'Besides this noble descent from the kings of Britain, Italy, Troy, England, France and Spain, see how flourished the royal race of the earls of March'.[12]

Now that Roger was in a position to satisfy his cupidity, he displayed in this respect little of the sensitivity, or deviousness, that he had shown in veiling his authority as the most powerful man in England. Over the next three years he was able to acquire estates and offices — anything which would generate income or from which he could obtain prestige and patronage — in an almost compulsive manner, His brazen avarice became as notorious and as much resented as the Despencers' had been and this did much to undermine the regime's authority. Roger Mortimer always remembered that he was a lord of the Welsh March and that it had been in Wales and the borderlands that his family had first won power. Wales was the natural heart of his burgeoning empire and it was there that Roger concentrated his territorial ambitions. Many of the estates he acquired had been held by the Despencers and the earl of Arundel, his former rivals for power in Wales who had so conveniently been executed under his auspices.

From the host of grants and preferments which fell into Roger's hands, some indication of the power and wealth which he amassed between 1327 and 1330 can be gained from the following examples. In 1327 he acquired control of the elder Despencer's large and important lordship of Denbigh and temporary custody of the younger Despencer's lordships of Glamorgan and Morgannwg. The following year, however, and no doubt much to his chagrin, he surrendered the custody of Glamorgan and Morgannwg to Hugh's widow, Eleanor, who had 'prayed the king to cause her lands, etc, to be restored to her, and the king does not consider it consonant with reason that her lands should be deemed forfeited by Hugh's forfeiture'.[13] He obtained Oswestry, Shrawardine, Clun and other lands in Shropshire and the March which had been forfeited by the earl of Arundel. Roger also claimed that he was the heir of his uncle, the late Roger Mortimer of Chirk, and appears to have acquired Roger of Chirk's lordships of Chirk, Blaenllyfni, Narberth and part of St. Clears in what looks very much like a piece of chicanery at the expense of Roger of Chirk's son; Roger graciously allowed his cousin some minor estates, including Tedstone Wafre in Herefordshire for which he had to pay Roger a token rent. Roger was later granted Church Stretton, Queen Isabella's interest in the hundred of Chirbury with Builth and Montgomery Castles (later Montgomery Castle in fee) and the lordships of Clifford and Glasbury.

As well as land, Roger gained a number of profitable offices. He was appointed justiciar of Wales for life — a key administrative and remunerative post long held by his uncle — with power in the Crown lands 'to remove constables, bailiffs and other ministers in Wales found incompetent',[14] and he was made 'chief keeper of the peace' in Herefordshire, Gloucestershire and Worcestershire. He became justiciar of the dioceses of Llandaff and St. Davids. In July 1330 one of the last offices to come his way before his downfall was his appointment as chief commissioner of array and captain of Herefordshire,

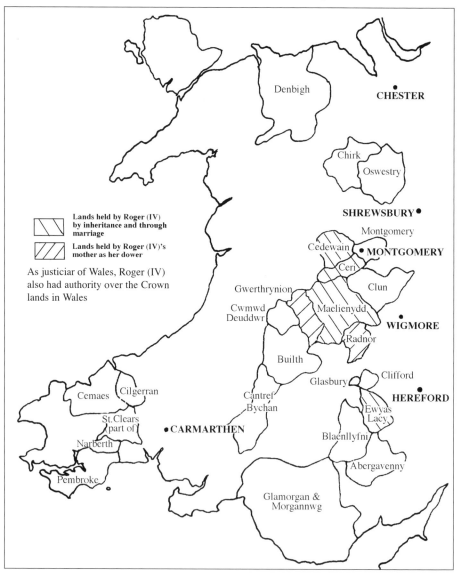

The Mortimers' hold on Wales between 1327 and 1330

Gloucestershire, Worcestershire and Shropshire. Two years earlier, in October 1328, Roger had had himself created *Comes Marchia Walliae* — earl of March — a new honour and the first earldom in the kingdom to be unrelated to a county. His choice of 'March' served to emphasize his independent status as a marcher lord, his preeminence in the region and the importance he placed on his Welsh power-base. He may also have wanted to mark his wife's descent from the counts of La Marche. In any event it was a title which staggered at least one chronicler, while another noted that Roger bore himself so haughtily that it was a wonder to watch. By 1330 his domination of Wales and the border-lands was in one way or another complete.

Roger obtained other estates and offices in England. Wardships were profit-able grants and in 1327, for instance, he was granted the custody of the lands of Thomas, earl of Warwick, during his minority, and the custody of the estates of James, heir to Nicholas de Audley; Roger's daughters, Catherine and Joan, married respectively Thomas and James. He was granted Droitwich together with the custody of Bristol and the city's castle. He procured charters to hold fairs in Oswestry, Chipping Norton and Ludlow.

In Ireland, too, Roger augmented the Mortimer interests. Trim (East Meath) had been restored to him in 1327 and this was soon followed by a grant of land in Uriel (Louth). He obtained custody of Athlone Castle. Finally in 1330, to crown his achievements in Ireland where his success as an officer of King Edward II a decade earlier had launched his political career, Roger and his wife procured palatine status in their lands in Meath and Uriel, enabling them to exercise royal jurisdiction in their lands, a right similar to their prerogative in the Welsh March.

Roger, earl of March, who as a chronicler observed had taken 'castles, towns, lands and rents, in great harm and loss unto the crown, and of the king's state also, out of measure',[15] naturally lived in grand style and in 1328 was granted the privilege of retaining an armed retinue, largely made up of fighting men drawn from his Welsh lordships who accompanied him on his travels, securing his safety and intimidating his fellow magnates and the people. In the same year he held a Round Table at Bedford and a great tournament at Hereford, the latter in the presence of the king and Isabella to celebrate the marriages of two of his daughters which the royal pair had also attended. Soon afterwards Roger entertained the king and Isabella in his castles at Wigmore and Ludlow. After the debacle of his Scottish campaign (see p.101), Roger may well have adopted a policy of 'bread and circuses' to defuse political tensions in the baronage.

Any financial difficulties that Roger experienced were eased by the many lucrative positions he held and the privileges which were granted to him. Shortly after receiving his earldom he was allowed £10 a year from the dues of Shropshire and Staffordshire; then, in 1330, all his debts to the exchequer,

ULSTER

URIEL

CONNAUGHT

Kells
(1316)

Roscommon
Castle

Randown
Castle

•Trim

MEATH

•Athlone
Castle

Dublin

•Dunamase
Castle

LEIX

LEINSTER

Youghal

Map of Ireland showing places mentioned in the text

and those of his ancestors, were cancelled and he was granted 500 marks a year from the issues of Wales in addition to his normal fees as justiciar.

Roger probably felt little need to court ecclesiastics when he could rely on the support of Bishop Orleton of Hereford, who was translated to Worcester in 1327, and Bishop Hotham of Ely, and there is scant evidence of Roger's religious benefactions. Wigmore Abbey was maintained in fitting style for reasons of prestige if nothing else, and the Wigmore chronicler states that Roger founded St. Peter's Chapel in the outer bailey of Ludlow Castle to mark his gratitude for his escape from the Tower in 1323 on the feast of St. Peter ad Vincula (1 August). He financed two chaplains to say mass in a chapel in the castle — presumably St. Peter's — for the king and the queen, his wife, their ancestors and descendants. Roger also endowed nine chaplains of Leintwardine Church with 100 marks a year to perform the same service; nine were apparently soon thought insufficient for this onerous duty and their number was increased to ten.

Roger Mortimer's career for the last three years of his life was intimately bound up with the kingdom's history, and it is likely that no major political, diplomatic or military decision was taken by the council without his accedence. His record between 1327 and 1330 was a discreditable one. He showed little interest in innovative administrative and economic policies, unlike, perhaps surprisingly, Hugh le Despencer the younger, and he has been held responsible for two actions in particular that have incurred obloquy: his part in the murder of Edward II, and in the judicial murder of Edmund, earl of Kent.

Although the deposition of Edward II had dethroned the king, he remained a danger to the new regime and, given what had gone before, to the life of Roger Mortimer. Edward was a figure around which any opposition could rally, and plots and rumours of plots to rescue Edward from Kenilworth and Berkeley castles are evidence that such opposition did exist. In the interests of security Edward was moved from Kenilworth to Berkeley early in April 1327 where he was imprisoned in reasonable comfort in the custody of Lord Berkeley and his brother-in-law Sir John Maltravers. Thomas, Lord Berkeley, Roger's son-in-law (he had married Margaret Mortimer) had suffered under Edward II's government. His father had died in prison and he, too, had been imprisoned and his castle and estates plundered by the Despencers. Roger had chosen well in appointing Berkeley as the ex-king's jailor and Maltravers, too, had reason to hate Edward.

Three months after the move to Berkeley, a plot to rescue Edward, engineered by a Thomas Dunhead, a Dominican friar, succeeded and he was free for a short time, seemingly taking refuge in Corfe Castle in Dorset before being recaptured. He was returned to Berkeley and imprisoned more closely, while the castle's garrison was kept on high alert to prevent a further rescue attempt. In early September Roger Mortimer was informed of yet another conspiracy, this time organised by Sir Griffith Lloyd who had campaigned against the Mortimers in 1321-2 and had remained loyal to Edward. In the circumstances the leadership of the country had, as pragmatic governments before and since have had, little choice but to remove the former ruler permanently from the scene.

So, it has been alleged, when Roger received a letter from the justiciar of Wales warning him of Sir Griffith Lloyd's plans to free Edward, he forwarded the letter to Maltravers and Thomas Gurney at Berkeley with a suggestion of the obvious solution to the danger. The deed was done though one would like

King Edward II's room at Berkeley Castle

to think that Roger had no hand in the barbaric method said by Geoffrey le Baker to have been used in effecting it:

> … on 22 September, having suddenly seized him lying in bed and having pressed him down and suffocated him with great pillows and a weight heavier than fifteen robust men, with a plumber's iron heated red hot, through a horn applied leading to the privy parts of the bowel, they burned out the respiratory organs past the intestines, fearing lest, a wound having been found on the royal body where wounds are usually required by any friend of justice, his tormentors would be bound to answer for an obvious offence and pay the penalty for it.[16]

Like others involved in this murky affair, the whole truth of which will probably never be known, Roger successfully covered most of his tracks, but his countrymen had little doubt as to his guilt, and at his trial he was accused of being responsible for the king's death — his accusers, however, would have been none too punctilious in assessing the facts of the case, determined as they were to put an end to him. Whether Edward was murdered, escaped, or was clandestinely permitted to go into exile will probably remain uncertain, and Isabella's role in events remains even more shrouded than Roger's; but it would be surprising if she had not been aware in general terms of his intentions towards her husband.

As for the infamous letter, Geoffrey le Baker, who wrote his chronicle some 30 years after Edward's death, describes how Adam de Orleton supposedly composed it, to include the sentence: *Edwardum occidere nolite timere bonum est*. Depending on the position of any comma this can be read as 'Do not fear to kill Edward, it is a good thing' or 'Do not kill Edward, it is good to be afraid'. This is but one instance of the mystery and subsequent disinformation which surrounds Edward's death and the part of Roger and his associates in it; Orleton was far away in Avignon and remote from the rapidly unfolding events in England at the time the letter is supposed to have been sent.

As serious for Roger's reputation was his part in the execution or judicial murder of Edmund, earl of Kent and Edward II's half-brother, for here *raisons d'état* provided no mitigating circumstances. A breach had soon developed in the regency council and coalition of 1327 between Roger and Isabella and their supporters on the one hand, and Henry of Lancaster and his party on the other. By 1330 opposition to Roger and Isabella had, as will be recounted, manifested itself in a half-hearted and abortive show of armed resistance led by the earl of Lancaster. Among Lancaster's supporters had been Edmund of Kent who had been in Isabella's party when she had landed in England in 1326 and who had served on the regency council. Although Edmund soon deserted Lancaster, Roger considered him too dangerous a potential opponent to leave at large, or indeed alive. By an unscrupulous intrigue Isabella's and Roger's *agents provocateurs* led Edmund not only to believe that the late king was alive but also to become privy to an imaginary plot to rescue him. In March 1330, when Edmund had been thoroughly compromised, Roger ordered his arrest; he was sentenced to death and executed and Roger's son, Geoffrey, received many of the earl's lands. For Roger the adverse reaction to Edmund's contrived death far outweighed the advantage he had gained in eliminating him and the chroniclers recorded the public revulsion at the execution which served only to encourage further opposition to the regime.

It was not only Roger's greed and inordinate corruption, and his relationship with Isabella, that provoked opposition. Lancaster complained that he was being excluded from government, implicitly blaming Roger and Isabella who meanwhile replaced officials who were Lancastrian sympathisers with their own supporters, and in their efforts to win support quickly disposed of the considerable sum left in Edward II's treasury at the time of his deposition. One issue which was condemned by the chroniclers was the treaty with Scotland of 1328. The Treaty of Northampton was negotiated by the English in ignominious circumstances after the king's — in fact Roger and Isabella's — ineffective campaign against the Scots in County Durham during the summer of 1327. The treaty appears to have been the personal policy of Roger and Isabella and to have been carried through in opposition to the wishes of Edward III and a large faction of the baronage.

Contemporaries alleged that treaty negotiations were pursued by Roger and Isabella for their private financial benefit and they certainly managed to lay their hands on substantial sums paid by the Scots in accordance with the treaty's terms. It can be argued that the cessation of hostilities for whatever motive, and it seems that Roger and Isabella were unable to finance a continuation of the war, was in fact in the kingdom's interest; the English had been unable to extinguish Robert Bruce's claim to the throne of an independent Scotland and the north of England had been devastated by years of Scottish raids. What stuck in the gullets of the king and the English baronage was that the treaty with its concessions to Scotland had been negotiated from weakness and for the apparent benefit of Roger Mortimer and Isabella. A further cause for complaint was that, as part of the treaty, a number of magnates had been summarily disinherited of their Scottish lands. Rumours abounded in the febrile situation and it was even alleged that Roger aimed to have himself made king with the aid of the Scots. Roger and Isabella appreciated the political dangers, especially the outrage of the disinherited lords, and by summoning a parliament they tried to unload onto it responsibility for the treaty's provisions. Many lords were, however, unwilling to be associated with the treaty, and the poor attendance at the Northampton parliament which ratified it was later somewhat disingenuously used as justification for denying that the treaty had ever been properly agreed. 'Accursed be the time when this parliament was ordained at Northampton', wrote one chronicler, 'for there through false counsel the king was fraudulently disinherited',[17] and for this Roger and Isabella were blamed, while Roger's military reputation was compromised.

Henry of Lancaster's break with Roger and Isabella came in the autumn of 1328, some months after the infamous treaty which he seemingly had not dared to oppose overtly when he attended the Northampton parliament. Lancaster and his supporters protested that the council had become no more than a cipher, the king had not enough to maintain himself and the queen should live off her dower and not impose on the people. The earl declined to attend the parliament at Salisbury during which Roger received the earldom of March. Roger appears to have ignored Lancaster's protest and turned a blind eye to his snub at Salisbury and there were attempts to reconcile the two grandees; but when Lancaster in alliance with the earls of Kent and Norfolk began to recruit support in London and elsewhere, Roger with an Anglo-Welsh army raided Lancaster's lands in Leicestershire. Lancaster's rebellion was technically against King Edward, although it was in practice a trial of strength with Roger Mortimer, and the king condemned the rebels as he was neither ready to move against Roger nor had he any wish to replace Roger's patronage with Lancaster's. The earls of Kent and Norfolk soon deserted Lancaster, and Roger's show of force, together with the confiscation of rebels' lands, convinced Lancaster and his allies of the futility of continuing their defiance. There had been little fighting and by the end of January 1329 the rebels had submitted, in due course recovering their estates while Roger and Lancaster arrived at a semblance of a reconciliation. Roger had acted decisively and effectively. He had put Lancaster firmly in his place and, at political cost, had disposed of Edmund of Kent. As for Henry of Lancaster, he can have been under few illusions as to his safety and he now realised that he needed the support of the king if he was to make another stand against Roger and Isabella.

Edward III, now 18 years old, appears by this time to have been considering how he could free himself of Roger Mortimer. He had, however, to move carefully because of Roger's spies at court such as John Wynard, one of the king's yeomen who had been associated with Roger since at least 1327. William Montagu, a member of the royal household and Edward's confidant, went abroad, allegedly on the king's private business, in the autumn of 1329. That winter while at Avignon he secretly set out to win over Pope John XXII's sympathy for Edward's plans to oust Roger from power. The pope asked for a way he could detect the difference between Edward's personal letters and those written under his name but under Roger's influence, and it was arranged that the words *Pater Sancte* in Edward's hand would authenticate any letter as his personal communication. By mid-April 1330 Montagu was back in England, and the king and Lancaster, with Montagu and his friends, hatched a plot to arrest Roger.

Roger and Isabella were aware of the growing disaffection in the kingdom and the threat presented by a group of exiles on the Continent. In May 1330 some of Roger's supporters contracted to supply men-at-arms to protect the court in exchange for grants of land, and three months later the government took steps to thwart any landing by the exiles. Roger would have been loath to be out of the kingdom in the deteriorating political situation and he obtained a papal grant to postpone a pilgrimage: 'Prorogation for two years, of the term within which he is to fulfil his vow of visiting Santiago [de Compostella]'.[18]

In October Roger's suspicions that mischief was afoot were aroused while he was staying in Nottingham Castle for a meeting of the council or parliament — it is not clear which. Alerted by his agents to the existence of an imminent plot, he accused Montagu of treachery and ordered the gates to be locked and the walls vigilantly guarded. Proud and arrogant he was probably not unduly worried. He had his armed retinue; he had built up a powerful political faction by rewarding his family and supporters with offices and perquisites, and he had taken care to cultivate elements of society, among them the merchants of Hull, and, more importantly, the citizens of London. While visiting the capital in January 1327 he had promised to preserve the liberties of the citizens who had so decisively rejected King Edward II the previous autumn, and he had later witnessed a new charter for the city. It would not be easy to dislodge Roger

Mortimer from power and a *coup d'état* offered the best method of avoiding the very real possibility of civil war.

Montagu had learned from the castle's governor, whom he had persuaded to join the conspiracy, of the existence of an underground passage into the castle and on the night of 19 October such a coup was mounted. When he and his party which included the king emerged from the underground passage into the castle bailey they advanced on Roger's quarters. Breaking into Roger's room the conspirators killed two of his knights in a brief scuffle whilst one of Montagu's men was felled by Roger himself. Isabella had heard the commotion and entered the room, but in spite of her entreaty to her son to take pity on Roger he was overpowered. He was removed from the castle without interference from the garrison and was taken under close guard to London with two of his sons, Edmund and Geoffrey, and two of his knights. One account tells how King Edward was at first inclined to execute Roger summarily, but with political good sense decided on a trial before parliament.

When parliament met at Westminster on 26 November 1330 the major business was the trial of Roger Mortimer, earl of March, for treason. This was an undefined crime which could be made to fit many circumstances and the 'trial' was in fact something of a misnomer in the modern sense as he was neither allowed to speak in his defence — a precedent had been set by the trial of the earl of Lancaster in 1322 — nor to confront his judges.

In 1330, unlike 1322, Roger was tried by the earls, barons and peers of the realm for offences 'known to be true to you and all the people of the realm',[19] and not by the king's sole record of his guilt. Among the well-documented proceedings — 'the said things are notorious' — and under the heading 'these are the treasons, felonies and misdeeds made against our lord the king by Roger de Mortimer and others of his coven', Roger was accused of appropriating royal power and the realm's government, of procuring the use of the privy seal, of acting as if he were king, and of removing and appointing ministers on his own authority. He had, with his associates, 'traitorously, feloniously and falsely murdered' Edward II. While ordering that no one should come to the parliament at Salisbury in 1328 with an armed force, he had done so himself and had threatened those attending the parliament with violence if they opposed him. He had made the king create him earl of March to the Crown's loss. He had caused the king to take up arms against the earl of Lancaster and his allies, and had exacted unduly severe ransoms contrary to Magna Carta and law.

The charges continued: he had deceived the earl of Kent into believing that his brother (half-brother, Edward II) was still alive and had then brought about his death — in response to this charge Roger was said to have privately admitted Kent's innocence. He had manipulated the king into giving him, his children and associates, castles, towns, manors and franchises at the expense of the Crown. He had appropriated fines and ransoms arising from levies for the war in Gascony, and had also taken for himself 20,000 marks paid by the Scots as part of the Treaty of Northampton. He had 'falsely and maliciously occasioned discord between the king's father and the queen' — this was the only reference to Isabella's and Roger's relationship, no doubt a tactful and political ploy to avoid prolonging the scandal. He had purloined money and jewels from the treasury leaving the king with nothing with which to maintain himself. He had procured 200 pardons for those who had killed lords and others in Ireland who were loyal to the king, contrary to law and parliament, and when the king would have preferred revenge.

The verdict was a foregone conclusion. Earls, barons and peers, as judges in parliament, unanimously declared that the articles of the indictment were indeed notorious, with the gravamen of the charges being Roger's part in Edward II's death. With the king's agreement Roger's judges sentenced him to death as a traitor and enemy of the king and his realm. This time the death sentence was not commuted as it had been eight years earlier, and on 29 November Roger Mortimer, earl of March, was drawn to Tyburn where he was hanged like a common criminal. It does not seem that he was beheaded and quartered as was customary in such cases, but his body hung in the gallows for two days and nights and was then buried in the Greyfriars Abbey in Coventry with which Isabella was connected. His wife petitioned the king that he be reinterred in Wigmore Abbey but her request was rejected, although it is just possible that in due course, with the political rehabilitation of the Mortimers, Roger may have been permitted to join his ancestors at Wigmore.

A number of the charges brought against Roger had mentioned his associates. Sir Simon de Bereford, one of Roger's placemen on the council who had been seized with Roger at Nottingham, was also tried and executed, but the records suggest that there was little other blood-letting among Roger's colleagues and many pardons were granted. Roger's family was not treated harshly and indeed his heir, Edmund, obtained surprising leniency while provision was made for his widow. As for Isabella, she forfeited her wealth and retired from public life with an ample financial allowance, while Adam de Orleton, Roger's long-standing accomplice, was pardoned and went on to a distinguished diplomatic career in the service of Edward III whose father he had done so much to injure.

The career of Roger Mortimer (IV) has few rivals in English history and at least three dramatists have recognised its theatrical potential: Christopher Marlowe, Ben Johnson and an anonymous 17th-century playwright in respectively, *Edward II*; *Mortimer, his Falle*; *King Edward III, with the Fall of Mortimer, earl of March*. In assessing Roger's public life, the dismal record of his last five years speaks for itself, but his career before 1323 was not unlike that of other magnates and gave rise to little comment from the chroniclers. True, he rebelled against Edward II — so did others; he was ambitious for personal power and was avaricious — so were others; but he also proved an energetic and capable officer of the Crown in Ireland. It was Roger's conduct after 1323 that was so reprehensible and which incurred the criticism of contemporaries and the censure of historians. He had no political vision, self-indulgence was his motivation and he showed little concern with the kingdom's wellbeing. In no way can he be compared with that other and greater rebel earl who for a time attained supreme power, Simon de Montfort.

Roger possessed in excess the unattractive ambition, avarice and unscrupulousness which were hallmarks of the Mortimers, and it must be said of most successful members of the medieval baronage. If, however, as in the case of his grandfather, Roger's ability and energy had been channelled into royal service by a strong monarch, his career might have commanded respect instead of condemnation. It was his country's misfortune and the cause of his ruin that Roger found in the undisciplined reign of one of the most ineffectual kings of England, and in the minority of another, opportunities which he could not resist for unbridled and breathtaking self-aggrandisement.

CHAPTER VII

1330-1425: Decline or Rebirth?

The execution of Roger (IV) in 1330 could have proved the end of Mortimer fortunes. Yet, when Roger (VI) died in 1398, he held a position of great prominence among the magnates of England, was pre-eminent in Ireland, and was the lord of a vast array of estates in England, Wales and the Marches, together with extensive areas of Ireland. Even so, the period from 1330 to 1425 has been categorised by Penry Evans as one of 'decline and extinction'.[1] While it is true that the premature death of Edmund (IV) without a male heir in 1425 brought the male line of the family to an end, in less than 40 years the grandson of Edmund's sister Anne took the throne as Edward IV. This could be seen as the culmination of an ambition which had been carefully nursed since the marriage of Edmund (III) to Philippa, daughter of Lionel, duke of Clarence, in 1368, in which case the period concerned could in fact be termed one of rebirth of the family fortunes.

Edmund (II)
Considering the gravity of Roger (IV)'s offences, the family was treated with leniency by Edward III when he assumed control of the kingdom in 1330. Roger's widow Joan, who can hardly have acquiesced in her husband's liaison with Queen Isabella, was specifically exempted from the general confiscation of Roger's property and estates which followed his trial. Her jewellery and other effects were ordered to be respected by crown officials, and her own lands, including Ludlow, were subsequently returned to her as the king grew surer of his position. Edward even began to restore some of the family lands to her son Edmund. As early as October 1331, Wigmore was returned to Edmund, along with Maelienydd, Cedewain, Cwmwd Deuddwr, and the castle of Denbigh. In the following month permission was granted to the Countess Joan to bring the remains of her husband from Coventry to Wigmore Abbey for burial, although recent research suggests that this was not done. It is likely

that Edmund would have been fully restored to his estates, but for his unfortunate death from a fever at Stanton Lacy on 16 December 1331. The family and its estates were at once plunged into the uncertainties of a minority.

Roger (V)

Edmund had married Elizabeth, the daughter of Bartholomew de Badlesmere, a Kentish landowner who had been an associate of his father. She had borne him two sons, Roger, born on 11 November 1328, and John, the younger, who had died in childhood. Roger (V), who succeeded his father at the age of three, faced a long period of minority before he could gain his inheritance, which was in any case complicated in the extreme. The estates had become fragmented by dower, with shares being taken by his great-grandmother, Margaret (de Fiennes); his grandmother Joan (de Genevile); and his mother. The situation was not aided by the attempts of Joan to pass her lands to her younger son Geoffrey and her other children, nor by the widowed Elizabeth's remarriage in 1335 to William de Bohun, earl of Northampton.[2]

The estates which were not held by the three dowagers were granted by the king to various nobles during Roger's minority. Denbigh was placed in the hands of William de Montacute, earl of Salisbury, while Wigmore passed to Roger's stepfather, William de Bohun. The lordship of Chirk was granted to the earl of Arundel, who consolidated his position as the leading noble in the northern Marches. Reclaiming and reassembling this inheritance was one of Roger's greatest achievements, a process which was only just completed by the time of his premature death in 1360.

The gradual restoration of Roger's estates began before he came of age. In 1341 he received Radnor, Gwerthrynion, and the lands of Presteigne, Knighton and Norton, thanks to the efforts of five knights, two of whom were relatives, who stood surety for £250 until he gained his majority. The following year William de Bohun persuaded the king to restore Wigmore to his stepson, to which the king agreed, with de Bohun doing homage on Roger's behalf. The main factor behind Roger's full restoration to his lands was, however, his distinguished military service in France.

From an early age Roger had shown an aptitude for warlike pursuits, attracting attention at a tournament at Hereford in 1344, when he was only 17 years old. It was a fortunate time for the young man to be embarking on a military career. Following some preliminary disagreements over the succession to the French throne, in 1337 Philip IV had confiscated Edward III's lands in France. Edward had replied by seizing French property in England, and re-asserting his own claim to the French throne. In 1340 he formally assumed the title of king of France at an elaborate ceremony in Ghent, an action which prompted the Anglo-French struggle which lasted until 1453, a conflict subsequently given the name of the Hundred Years War.

After an inconclusive invasion of north-eastern France in 1338-9, Edward III followed a strategy of assisting internal rebellions. Armies were sent to Gascony and Brittany, and in 1346 a third force under the command of the king landed at la Hogue in northern France. Edward's first action after landing had been to knight his son, Edward, the Black Prince, who then bestowed the same honour upon Roger, who had accompanied the expedition with a force of 200 men drawn from Wigmore and Radnor. The army then proceeded to march on Calais.

On 26 August 1346, the English force defeated the main French army at Crécy, where the English longbowmen wrought havoc among the ill-disciplined French troops. The English troops were arranged in three divisions. Two of these formed the front line, one commanded by the earls of Arundel and Northampton and the other by the Black Prince, with the third division under the king retained as a reserve in front of the baggage. Some accounts of Crécy suggest that Roger Mortimer fought in the front line, while others claim that he remained in the rear with the king.[3] In either event, he was speedily rewarded. Less than a fortnight after the battle, Roger was granted all his father's lands, with the exception of those held in dower by his mother, even though he was still a minor. The following year, his grandmother Joan was permitted to grant him the castle and lands of Trim, together with other lands in Ireland. Roger's retainers were also rewarded, being granted pardons from any offences which they had committed before they left for France.[4]

The main action in France after Crécy was the besieging and ultimate capture of Calais in 1347. Two years later Roger was able to distinguish himself in an action which saved the city from recapture by the French. A Genoese mercenary in the employ of the English who had agreed to betray the city subsequently revealed his plans, enabling a small force under the king and the Black Prince, which also included Roger, successfully to ambush the attackers and pursue them into the surrounding countryside. Here the king became separated from his troops, and was at one point surrounded by Frenchmen, only escaping when the prince and Mortimer arrived with a relieving party.

Roger's close association with the Black Prince brought him considerable prestige and influence; like his royal patron, he was one of the founder members of the Order of the Garter in 1348. In 1350 a truce was concluded with the French and during the lull in the fighting that followed, Roger turned his attention to political and administrative matters. He had first been summoned to Parliament as a baron in 1348, and from 1350 onwards seems to have spent much time at court, where he was a frequent witness to official documents. He was also occupied with affairs in the Marches, where he held various commissions, including hearing offences against the Statute of Labourers which fixed the wage rates for farm workers, and acting as a mediator between the Dominican friars of Hereford and the diocesan bishop in a dispute over property in the city.

Roger achieved major political success in 1354, when he managed to secure the reversal of the sentence which had been passed against his grand-father in 1330. This took the form of a statement which declared that the original sentence had been invalid, as it had been passed without observing the required legal procedures, meaning, in effect, that it was nullified. Whilst Roger was able automatically to assume the title and estates of the earldom of March, the reclamation of his grandfather's forfeited estates was not achieved without a struggle. For example, Arundel and Montacute had been installed for over 20 years in Chirk and Denbigh respectively, and whilst Arundel eventu-ally gave up Narberth and other estates which had formerly belonged to Roger of Chirk, he was obdurate in holding on to Chirk itself. Roger even tried to secure it in the long term by contracting a marriage between his son Edmund and Alice, Arundel's daughter, but it came to nothing, and the Mortimers never regained Chirk.

Roger was more successful with Denbigh. William de Montacute, earl of Salisbury, was sued for possession, and claimed two royal charters as his title. He failed to prove his case, and in January 1355 Denbigh was once again in Mortimer hands. Indeed, by the end of the year, Roger had regained all the lands which had been granted to his grandfather between 1327 and 1330, with the exception of those which were still held in dower.

Meanwhile, Roger's career continued in the royal service. After the 1350 truce with France, the pope had made several attempts to mediate a permanent peace between the two countries, and in 1354 Roger was among the English envoys who were present at Avignon for one of these conferences. The collapse of this particular attempt to arrange a peace paved the way for the reopening of hostilities in 1355. The plan was that the duke of Lancaster should co-operate with Charles of Navarre in Normandy, while the Black Prince launched a simultaneous attack in Aquitaine. Roger joined Lancaster's expedition, but it was held up by contrary winds in the Channel, and by the time that it reached the Isle of Wight, Navarre had come to terms with the French. The campaign was then abandoned.

A second attempt was made in the autumn, and Roger marched to Calais with the king. Unfortunately, the Scots had taken advantage of Edward III's preoc-cupations in France to launch an invasion of England, so that the army had to make a rapid return to deal with this new threat. Roger was present at Edward Baliol's surrender at Roxburgh in January 1356, and was a witness to the treaty. Preoccupations at home meant, however, that Roger was unable to be present at the Black Prince's victory at Poitiers in September 1356. Poitiers was a much closer contest that Crécy, but it included the capture of the king of France and a large number of his leading nobles. While King John II was a prisoner in

England two half-hearted attempts were made to conclude a treaty, but Edward III was only playing for time in order to prepare a final offensive which would take advantage of the desperate situation in France. England held Aquitaine and half Brittany; the Navarese controlled Normandy, and were threatening Paris; and a series of peasant uprisings called the *jacqueries* had broken out.

As the years passed the process of regathering the Mortimer estates continued. In June 1356 Roger's mother, Elizabeth (de Badlesmere), had died, to be followed by his grandmother Joan (de Genevile) in October of the same year. This brought almost all Roger's inheritance into his hands, with the exception of some lands which were still held by Elizabeth's second husband, William de Bohun, by 'courtesy of England'. From his mother, Roger gained Cefnllys and Maelienydd, Arley in Staffordshire, and a third part of the Buckinghamshire manor of Long Crendon.[5] From her Genevile inheritance he gained the lordship of Ewyas, and half the town of Ludlow, together with a range of knights' fees based on Stanton Lacy. Among other lands received were the important Worcestershire manors of Norton and Bromsgrove, which had originally belonged to the Verduns. In 1358 Roger shrewdly exchanged Long Crendon for the Verdun moiety of Ludlow held by William de Ferrers, who had inherited it from his mother Isabel in 1349.[6] In 1358 Roger's estates were further augmented when he was restored to the lands in Ireland which had formerly been part of the de Lacy inheritance, but had been confiscated by Edward II when several members of the family had sworn allegiance to Edward Bruce. These lands were now joined to the Mortimer lordship of Trim, thus considerably increasing the family holdings in Ireland. Roger made his final acquisition in 1359, when he was restored to Montgomery, over which there had been difficulties, and was awarded the lands of his maternal uncle, Giles de Badlesmere, in Kent, Sussex and Oxfordshire.[7] With these acquisitions Roger possessed an estate which placed him among the greatest magnates in the country. He had proved his loyalty to the king, and had been duly rewarded. The disgrace which his grandfather had brought upon the family had been erased.

Before the final element in the process of consolidating and expanding the Mortimer estate was complete, Edward III belatedly made his next move in France. In October 1358 the king appointed his son, Thomas of Langley, as keeper of the kingdom during his absence, and set out for Calais. Roger was appointed constable of the expedition, and rode at the head of the army with the king, accompanied by his own contingent of 500 men-at-arms and 1,000 archers. Edward had, however, delayed his departure for too long. The Dauphin was beginning to reassert his authority, and by the time the English embarked he had reached terms with Charles of Navarre.

The English lay siege to the city of Rheims, but abandoned the attempt after a month. Roger was then sent to capture St. Florentin near Auxerre, after which he was joined by the king, and the combined force began to march towards Burgundy. On 26 February 1360, at Rouvrai near Avalon, Roger was struck down with an unknown illness and died. His bones were shipped back to England to be buried at Wigmore Abbey. Shortly after Roger's death the advance to Burgundy was halted, and the English forces fell back towards Paris, which proved too formidable to attack. With Edward in retreat, the French opened negotiations at Brétigny. In May 1360 a draft treaty was agreed, whereby Edward gave up his claims to the throne of France, but retained sovereignty over Aquitaine.

Roger was described by the family annalist as 'stout and strenuous in war, provident in counsel, and praiseworthy in his morals'.[8] He had married Philippa, the daughter of William de Montacute, second earl of Salisbury. Their eldest son Edmund had been born on 1 February 1352. A second son, Roger, had died before his father, and there were two daughters, Margaret, who later married Robert de Vere, earl of Oxford, and Elizabeth, who married John de Audley. Philippa was granted dower on 3 July 1360, and in fact outlived her son by some months, dying on 5 January 1382. She was buried at Bisham Priory near Marlow.

Edmund (III)

When Edmund (III) succeeded his father, he faced a period of 11 years before he could enter into his estates. Before setting out for France, Roger had attempted to mitigate the rigours of his son's minority in the case of his own death by creating a 'use' by which he conveyed a portion of his estates, including Ludlow and Cleobury, to a group of friends and advisers headed by William of Wykeham, bishop of Winchester, to administer on the boy's behalf.[9] This grant was approved by the king for a period of eight years in 1360. Philippa, the earl's widow, received the customary third of the remaining estates as dower, including lands in Kent, Somerset, Hereford, and Worcestershire, together with the old Chirk lands of Narberth and St. Clears in west Wales.[10] She was also granted Ceri and Cedewain, with the castles of Montgomery and Dolforwyn, but these were soon after successfully claimed by the Black Prince as part of his principality.[11] These arrangements substantially reduced the number of estates which the king took into wardship, which was then granted to bishop Wykeham and Richard, earl of Arundel. In 1352 the infant Edmund had been betrothed to Arundel's daughter Alice, but the marriage never took place.

Little is known of Edmund's early life. His father's reputation gained him royal favour, and he is known to have been something of a protégé of Roger's old associate, the Black Prince. This meant that, as a mark of royal favour, Edmund was able to regain some of his lands before he came of age. In November 1367 the king decreed that Edmund could have the lands which had been granted under the 'use' to Wykeham and the others when the eight-year term ended the following February, even though he would still be only 16 years old. In May 1368 he received an even more spectacular token of royal esteem, when he was given the king's granddaughter, Philippa — only daughter of Edward III's second son, Lionel, duke of Clarence — as his wife. The marriage came with two great prizes.

Firstly, the marriage brought a considerable inheritance. Philippa's mother, Elizabeth de Burgh, had been the heiress of Ulster as well as a large portion of the de Clare estates. A few months after the marriage Clarence died, and Edward came into his wife's estates, adding the earldom of Ulster to that of March. The Mortimers now became the leading family in Ireland, and Irish affairs were to occupy an increasingly large part of their attention. But the prize that would assume greater importance the following century, was the fact that Edmund's heirs would enter the line of succession to the throne.

As Edmund approached adulthood, he began to play a part in public affairs. In 1369 he was appointed Marshal of England, with responsibility for supervising national defences, despite being only 19 years of age. Service in the royal armies was an obligation of rank, and all non-royal earls of fighting age took part in the campaigns of 1369 and 1376 together with their retinues. Although rank rather than prowess was the main factor in the selection of commanders, the English forces were reckoned to have been better served than their French counterparts. In 1371 he was summoned to Parliament for the first time as earl of March, and was involved in a number of diplomatic and military activities. In 1369 war had again broken out with France, though the campaigns were undistinguished compared to those of Crécy and Poitiers. In 1372 Edmund was a member of an unsuccessful expedition to relieve la Rochelle, and in 1375 was a member of a similarly disastrous attempt to aid John de Montfort in his claims as duke of Brittany. In 1373 Edmund had finally received the remainder of his father's estates from the crown, a year in which he served as an ambassador firstly to France, and then to Scotland, where he acted as chief guardian of the truce then in force. It was a particularly busy year for he was also nominated as the king's lieutenant in Ireland, but although he was in the country from September 1373 to March 1374, his appointment was not confirmed until 1379.

The last years of Edward III's reign saw the development of an increasingly bitter power struggle between the Black Prince and his younger brother, John of Gaunt, duke of Lancaster, who was in effective charge of the government during his father's advancing dotage. Edmund Mortimer's close association with the prince of Wales automatically placed him in opposition to Lancaster, and the situation was exacerbated by the claims of the Mortimer heirs to the succession. Gaunt was hoping that his own children would take the throne in the increasingly likely event of the Black Prince's line coming to an end; his enmity to the Mortimers is therefore not surprising.

The rivalry between the 'constitutional' opposition and the 'court' faction under Lancaster came to a head in 1376 when the financial needs of the government made it necessary to call Parliament. The 'constitutional' party was led, in addition to the prince of Wales and earl of March, by the bishops of London, Winchester and Bath, the earls of Arundel and Salisbury, and Henry, lord Scrope of Masham. These aristocrats championed the 'popular' opposition in the Lords, and Edmund, together with his friend and associate Bishop Courtenay of London, led a committee of magnates who were appointed in April 1376 to negotiate a joint approach with the Commons. This marked the beginning of the so-called 'Good Parliament', which sat from April until July.

The events of this Parliament led to some unforeseen long-term developments. When conferring with the Lords, the Commons appointed Sir Peter de la Mare, a Herefordshire member and an indentured Mortimer retainer, to be their spokesman. De la Mare is thus generally regarded as the first Speaker of the Commons, and he certainly acted as a vigorous leader of their campaigns against the administration. Although the magnates and bishops were hesitant about confronting Gaunt, the Commons had no such inhibitions. Their traditional weapon was to refuse to grant the financial demands of the government until any grievances had been redressed, and de la Mare and his colleagues launched a devastating attack upon the corruption of officials and the wastage of public money, in the face of which Lancaster backed down. The Commons also created an important precedent by developing the process of impeachment, by which Lord Latimer, the great chamberlain, and another official were tried by the Commons for a variety of offences, including the raising of money to pay off fictitious loans, and imprisoned. This weapon was to be used with great effect in the following reign, and afterwards was to fall into disuse until resurrected by parliamentary antiquarians in the 17th century in their battles with the early Stuart kings.

The situation changed dramatically on 8 June 1376, when the death of the Black Prince robbed the opposition of their most influential leader. The Commons did, however, refuse to discuss a proposal put forward by Lancaster that the succession to the crown should be brought into line with French practice, restricting it to the male lines only. This would have effectively removed the threat of a Mortimer succession. One of the Parliament's last acts before it was dissolved in July 1376 was to secure the setting up of a permanent council, which included Edmund, and was to be in constant attendance on the ailing king.

Once Parliament had been dissolved, Gaunt, in the name of the king, repudiated all agreements he had made, and ordered the imprisonment of de la Mare in Nottingham Castle without trial. Edmund was ordered to inspect the defences of Calais, but fearing that he would be murdered while out of the country, he surrendered his office of marshal. In June 1377 the aged Edward

III finally died, and his 10-year-old grandson, the son of the Black Prince, ascended the throne as Richard II. Although Gaunt remained in control of the kingdom, he felt the need for a more conciliatory approach to his former opponents, particularly as the young Roger Mortimer was in a considerably improved position in the line of succession to the throne. De la Mare was released from prison and given a tumultuous reception when he returned to London, resuming his position as speaker as soon as Parliament reassembled. Edmund was given a significant role in Richard's coronation ceremony, and included in what amounted to a council of regency. Though he was not in a position to influence events, he enjoyed a great deal of popularity in Parliament; When the Commons compelled the remodelling of the royal council, Edmund became one of its nine members. In 1378 and 1379 he was given a number of missions to Scotland, as a negotiator and as inspector of the border defences. He was also appointed to investigate a number of alleged papal encroachments upon the rights of the crown.

In October 1379 Edmund was finally appointed king's lieutenant in Ireland, a major post to which he had been nominated six years earlier. As the largest landholder in the country he was the obvious choice for the post, and as a major political rival it was in Gaunt's interest to have him out of England. Furthermore, since 1373 the Irish had been petitioning for the earl to be required to live on his Irish estates as a means of combating the disorder in the Mortimer lands of Ulster, Connaught and Meath, which was fast becoming uncontrollable. The post was accepted for a three year term on advantageous conditions: as lieutenant he was to receive a grant of 20,000 marks (£13,330) to provide troops, and in addition was to have the crown's ordinary revenue in Ireland at his disposal, yet was not to be accountable to the crown for his expenditure.

Before setting out on such a hazardous, and what proved to be fatal, enterprise, Edmund made his will. Considerable bequests were made to religious houses throughout his territories, with Wigmore as the principal beneficiary. During his lifetime, Edmund had been a major benefactor of the house where so many of his relatives were buried, and had granted lands worth 2,000 marks a year towards the cost of a major rebuilding programme. By 1380 the walls had reached full height, and the building awaited roofing. To provide suitable fittings for the refurbished abbey, Edmund bequeathed it lavish vestments and altar cloths, images, plate and relics, which included a large piece of the True Cross, the body of St. Seiriol, and bones of St. Richard of Chichester, St. Thomas à Becket, and the local saint, Thomas Cantilupe. Plate, vestments and cash were also given to a range of religious houses in Mortimer lands including Tintern, Cwmhir, Tilty (Essex), Lesnes (Kent), Walsingham and Chirbury. In addition to these provisions, family and friends were also given valuable bequests.[12]

The expedition landed at Howth near Dublin on 15 May 1380, and Edmund proceeded to enforce his authority upon eastern Ulster, where he initially gained the support of local chieftains. He was, however, unable to exert any control over the western half of the province, where the O'Neils were firmly in control. So great, indeed was their power, that Edmund was unable to use oak from his own woods to construct a bridge over the Bann near Coleraine, and had to import timber from Penallt, near Usk, for the purpose.

Having failed to make an impression on the O'Neils, the expedition moved into Connaught, where they captured Athlone Castle from the O'Connors and gained a crossing of the Shannon. They then turned towards Munster to relieve Kilkenny Castle, which was under attack from the Tobyns. Edmund, however, contracted a chill while crossing a river at Cork, and died, presumably of pneumonia, on 27 December 1381. His perishable parts were buried in the Dominican friary at Cork, and his bones were shipped back to Wigmore to be buried in the new work which he had commissioned.

Edmund was eulogised as a model of chivalry and piety, and a successful soldier, though in fairness it must be noted that neither the Wigmore chronicler nor Adam of Usk, who had been sponsored through Oxford by Edmund, could be regarded as unbiased commentators.[13] He had, however, weathered the constitutional storms of the 1370s, and had, throughout his opposition, been firmly loyal to the crown. His final expedition to Ireland had been successful in pacifying considerable areas, even if some, like western Ulster had remained firmly outside his control.

Edmund's death ushered in another period of minority. His wife had borne him four children: two sons and two daughters. His eldest child, Elizabeth, born in 1371, was to cement family ties with the Percies by marrying Henry Hotspur. His heir Roger, was born at Usk in 1374. The second daughter, Philippa, who was to have three husbands, was born at Ludlow in 1375, while the youngest, Edmund, whose exploits with Owain Glyn Dŵr will be discussed below, was also born there in the following year. Sir Thomas Mortimer, who was executed for treason in 1423, may well have been an illegitimate son. Philippa had died a year before her husband, and was buried with great pomp at Wigmore. Her epitaph described her as 'though sprung from kings, a friend of poverty'.[14]

Roger (VI)

Roger Mortimer was seven years of age at the time of his father's death, and faced a lengthy period of minority before he could gain his inheritance. As early as 1374 Edmund (III) had followed his own father's precedent and created a 'use', whereby the lordships of Ludlow and Radnor had been granted to a consortium of friends and associates, which included the bishops of London, Winchester and Hereford. The inquest which was held on Edmund (III) on 10 January 1382 noted that long before his death, with the king's licence, and having paid the appropriate fee, Edmund had so demised his lands in Shropshire and the adjacent March, with the exception of a few small parcels of land in the Wigmore area.[15] This robbed the royal escheators of a core piece of Mortimer property, though they were soon compensated by the lands which the Countess Philippa, the grandmother of Roger (VI), had held in dower, when she died a few days after her son.

At first it was ordered that from Michaelmas 1382 all revenues from the Mortimer estates in crown hands should be used to defray the expenses of the royal household, and a number of royal administrators were appointed to run the estates in addition to, and sometimes in place of the Mortimer officials. Measures were taken to protect the rights of the young earl from attempted encroachments, such as that of the priory of Walsingham, who were attempting to gain abbey status from the pope in order to end the Mortimer right of appointing their prior.[16] These arrangements were later modified by the royal council in order to prevent the impoverishment of the young earl's estates by a grasping crown. In December 1383 custody of the estates was granted to the earls of Arundel, Warwick and Northumberland, together with John, Lord Neville of Raby, until Roger came of age. They were to pay £4,000 yearly to the Exchequer, to keep all buildings in repair, and to make no grants out of the estates without royal permission. Roger's upbringing was entrusted to Thomas Holland, earl of Kent, the king's half-brother, who also paid 1,000 marks annually for six years for his ward's marriage. As a result of this agreement, no later than early 1388, Roger was married to Eleanor Holland, Kent's eldest daughter, and the king's niece. This marriage reinforced Roger's ties with the court, though he also had links with the opposition to Richard II which was developing around Arundel. Though attempting to keep neutral in these disagreements, however, Roger was a natural follower of the royal party.

It has been claimed that as early as 1385 Parliament had proclaimed Roger as Richard II's heir presumptive, though the only source which mentions this is not renowned for its accuracy.[17] As a further mark of royal favour, he was restored to all his father's lands in 1393, even though he was still only 19 years old. In March and April 1393 he immediately undertook a tour of inspection of his Welsh and marcher lands, and the following February he received the lands which his father had held by his wife's inheritance, and the estates of his grandmother, the Countess Philippa. The family chronicler also claimed that he inherited a treasury of 40,000 marks (£26,500).[18] He was well equipped to embark upon a career in public life as one of the leading nobles of the kingdom.

In 1394 Roger was duly sent on a diplomatic mission to sort out border disputes with Scotland, but his career was to centre almost exclusively upon Ireland. Shortly after his father's death, Roger had been appointed to succeed him as lieutenant in Ireland, together with its revenues and a further 2,000

Richard II departs for Ireland in 1399

marks. *De facto* rule was to be exercised by his uncle, Sir Thomas Mortimer, the chief justice, until Roger came of age, when he would be given the option of resigning his office. This experiment with a titular juvenile lieutenant was not judged a success, and by June 1383 Sir Peter de Courtenay had been appointed viceroy for a 10 year term.

Mortimer interests in Ireland coincided with those of the crown. The Irish had caused considerable devastation throughout the Mortimer lands, and Richard II became the first English monarch since 1210 to take personal responsibility for restoring order. A massive expedition was mounted in 1394, with Roger in a leading role. The fleet left Milford Haven for Waterford in September 1394, with a Mortimer contingent of 100 men-at-arms, two bannerets, eight knights, 200 mounted archers, and 400 foot soldiers.[19] The most significant achievement of the campaign was the submission to the king of Nigel O'Neil, who in reality ruled most of Ulster. Following this triumph, Richard left Ireland in April 1395, leaving Roger, who had been appointed lieutenant of Ulster, Connaught and Meath, in charge. In 1395 Roger was awarded £1,000 by Parliament as compensation for the devastation of his Irish estates, and in the following year his lieutenancy of Ulster was renewed for a further 12 months. In 1397 Roger was appointed lord lieutenant for the whole of Ireland for a term of three years, and lived in almost regal splendour while campaigning, without much success, against the rebels.

Richard II had secured success in Ireland by a policy which combined strength and conciliation towards the native and Anglo-Irish chieftains. Towards France and Scotland he had followed a policy of peace. His rule in England was far more troublesome. As a youth of 13 he had faced the rebellious peasants at Mile End in 1381, but he had subsequently endured worse problems from the aristocratic opposition of the Lords Appellant, whose murderous purge of royal officials by the use of impeachment culminated in the Merciless Parliament of 1388. Upon assuming control of his kingdom in 1389 Richard had begun a policy of reasserting the power of the crown, which had become diminished during his grandfather's dotage and his own troubled minority. Although Richard possessed many attributes which were well-suited to kingship, he was suspicious and unforgiving, and tended increasingly to ride roughshod over the traditional liberties by which the powers of the medieval crown had been limited. Although Roger had served the king with conspicuous loyalty, he too had begun to fall under royal suspicion by 1398.

The cause of this was the king's pursuit of Sir Thomas Mortimer, Roger's uncle, and a former associate of the Appellants, who in September 1397 was accused of treason and summoned to appear for trial within six months. Sir Thomas fled to Scotland, and from there to Ireland, where writs were issued to his nephew for his apprehension. Adam of Usk saw this as a plot to ensnare the nephew by revealing his reluctance to arrest his uncle. This may have been correct.[20] In October 1397 Roger received a summons to attend Parliament, which had been prorogued from Westminster to Shrewsbury. Traditionally the calling of Parliament at Shrewsbury has been regarded as an attempt by Richard to intimidate the members with archers from his power base in Cheshire. Recent scholarship has tended to dismiss this claim as Lancastrian propaganda, and has questioned the notion of a special relationship between the king and Cheshire.[21]

Parliament met on 28 January 1398, and Roger was greeted on his arrival by a demonstration of 20,000 supporters wearing hoods in the colours of his livery, who expected him to lead the opposition to the increasingly arbitrary conduct of the king. If this demonstration was spontaneous rather than orchestrated, it suggests a considerable degree of support for the Mortimers in Shropshire and north Wales. It was not calculated to reduce Richard's suspicions, although in the event Roger was scrupulous in supporting royal measures and giving no grounds for his arrest. As soon as the session was ended he returned to Ireland, where he felt increasingly secure. Roger had still failed to hand over his uncle, and his brother-in-law and enemy Sir Thomas Holland — the Hollands were staunch supporters of Richard II against the opposition in 1397 and 1398 — was sent across the Irish Sea to capture the earl. He failed, for Roger was dead by the time Holland reached Ireland.

The abdication of Richard II

Roger appears to have had a genuine empathy with his Celtic territories, and increasingly began to adopt Irish dress and habits, in flagrant defiance of the 1366 Statute of Kilkenny which had attempted to prohibit the existence of Irish customs in the English-occupied Pale. On 20 July 1398 this brought about his downfall, when he was surprised and killed near Kells by a party of O'Brien soldiers, who had failed to recognise their victim in his native dress. This action had unforeseen consequences, for although Richard II may have decided to secure the death of Roger, the killing of one who was the putative heir to the throne could not go unpunished. The king therefore set out upon his last Irish expedition in 1399. His absence provided an opportunity for Henry Bolingbroke, who had been exiled by Richard II in 1397, to return to England to claim the estates of his father, John of Gaunt. This started a chain of events which led to the deposition of Richard by Parliament in September 1399, and the proclamation of Bolingbroke as Henry IV. Like many a 20th-century dictator, Richard had been the victim of a *coup d'état* while absent abroad.

Roger's body had meanwhile been brought back for burial with his ances-tors at Wigmore Abbey, his widow shortly afterwards marrying another marcher lord, Edward Charlton, fifth Lord Charlton of Powys. Roger left four children: Edmund, his heir, who was born in 1391; Roger, who had been born two years later; Anne, who subsequently married the earl of Cambridge, and Eleanor, who married Edward Courtenay, 11th earl of Devonshire. Once again, the Mortimer estates passed to a child.

Edmund (IV)

The death of Roger (VI) had meant that in 1398 his six-year-old son Edmund was not only heir to the vast Mortimer empire, but was also regarded as heir to the throne. Bolingbroke's *coup* in 1399 dramatically changed this situation. Henry IV's first Parliament recognised Bolingbroke's son Henry as heir apparent, and the young Edmund, as a royal ward and a potential threat to the Lancastrian interest, was kept under close scrutiny. He was, however, treated with the respect which was due to him. Although the Mortimer estates were initially split up, in February 1400 they were taken into the hands of the steward and treasurer of the Great Council in order that their revenues could be used to defray the expenses of the royal household. Edmund and his brother Roger were allowed 300 marks per year for their maintenance, and in 1402 the two boys were placed in the care of Sir Hugh Waterton at Berkhampstead Castle in Hertfordshire, where they were to be brought up with the king's younger children, John and Philippa.

Despite the king's magnanimity, the young earl's position was not made easier by the involvement of his uncle, Sir Edmund Mortimer, in the Glyn Dŵr rebellion. Wales had been experiencing growing tensions during the last quarter of the 14th century. At a time of falling agricultural revenues, the great landlords had become increasingly rapacious, exacting heavy fines and subsidies from their tenants. The Welsh clergy had become increasingly outraged at the exploitation of ecclesiastical revenues by English bishops who had been appointed to Welsh sees. Racial tensions were growing between the burgesses of 'English' boroughs and their Welsh neighbours, as shown in the granting of charters such as that received by the Mortimer borough of St. Clears in 1393 guaranteeing that cases involving burgesses should only be heard by 'English burgesses and true Englishmen.'[22] There was also a significant power vacuum at the head of Welsh society. In 1397 Richard II was in a strong enough position to take action against the noble opposition who had attacked his servants in the Merciless Parliament of 1388. The earls of Gloucester and Arundel were executed, while Warwick was stripped of his estates and exiled to Guernsey for life. In 1398, somewhat inexplicably, Richard exiled the dukes of Norfolk and Hereford, who had been engaged in a bitter personal dispute. The banishing of Hereford, better known as Henry Bolingbroke, was an action which ultimately sealed the king's doom. In the immediate context, this crackdown on the magnates, coupled with the death of Roger Mortimer (VI), meant that most of the major marcher lords had been removed. Richard II's favourites who had been appointed to the vacant lands were incapable of exercising similar authority to that of the old marcher lords, and resentment soon led to outright rebellion.

In September 1400 a territorial dispute between a north Wales squire, Owain Glyn Dŵr and his neighbour Lord Grey de Ruthin erupted into a revolt which led to Owain's proclamation as prince of Wales at his manor of Glyndyfrdwy. This was the signal for spontaneous outbreaks in north Wales, which within a matter of weeks had devastated towns like Oswestry and engulfed the whole region. The capture of Conwy Castle on Good Friday 1401, while the garrison was at prayers, was an act of great bravado which captured the imaginations of many disaffected Welshmen. By the end of 1401 the revolt had spread to parts of western and central Wales, though the government still controlled large areas, and the southern lordships were as yet untouched.

In June 1402 Owain personally led a force into mid Wales. To combat this, Sir Edmund Mortimer, uncle of the young earl, assembled an army of Herefordshire men at Ludlow, and these were later joined by a contingent from Maelienydd. The Mortimer forces met Glyn Dŵr on 22 June 1402 at Bryn Glas near Pilleth, and suffered a heavy defeat, following the defection of the Maelienydd men to the rebels. Many English soldiers were killed, and tradition states that the corpses were cruelly mutilated by the Welsh women. Mortimer was captured and taken to Snowdonia by Glyn Dŵr.

Following Bryn Glas the Percies and other relations began to raise money to ransom Sir Edmund, but the king, who had begun to suspect collusion between Mortimer and Glyn Dŵr, forbade the payment of the ransom, and ordered the confiscation of Sir Edmund's plate and jewels. Perhaps partly as a direct result of this, the king suspicions appeared to be confirmed when Edmund decided to make common cause with his captor, whose daughter he married at the end of November. This may, as Adam of Usk suggested, have been a ploy to obtain a quicker release, but there may have been deeper dynastic motives.

The marriage echoed that of Ralph (II) to Gwladus Ddu, the daughter of Llywelyn ab Iorwerth in 1228, and the Mortimers were clearly attracted by Celtic lore, and the supposed early British kings. The family genealogy and chronicle now in Chicago is preceded by a Brut, or chronicle of the ancient kings of Britain, and it is significant that this document was drawn up some time after 1376, when John of Gaunt was attempting to secure the royal succession for his heirs. The Brut was clearly a means of harnessing legendary ancestors to support the rival Mortimer claims. It is significant that two of the three Round Tables, essentially tournaments and entertainments with an Arthurian theme, which were held in the 13th and 14th centuries were hosted by the Mortimers. The first, a great four day event at Kenilworth in 1279, celebrated the knighting of the three sons of Roger (III). The third, at Bedford in 1328 was held under the auspices of Roger (IV) when he was at the height of his power.[23] In addition, the birth of Sir Edmund had been attended by strange portents which would have appealed to superstitious Celtic imaginations.[24]

By December 1402 Sir Edmund had returned to Maelienydd proclaiming that he had joined Owain to restore Richard II if he were alive, or otherwise to place his 'honoured nephew', Edmund earl of March, on the throne. Owain's claims to Wales would be respected in the event of success. The men of Maelienydd were called upon to join in the campaign. Following this, the rebels were joined by the earl of Northumberland and his son, Henry Hotspur, after their own rather complex quarrel with the king. This had originally centred around the financing of further expeditions against the Scots, and developed into 'constitutional' opposition to Henry's usurpation, based on the fiction that Richard was still alive. Despite the death of Hotspur and a number of leading rebels at the bloody engagement at Shrewsbury on 21 July 1403, Glyn Dŵr continued to make headway in south Wales, and in July 1404 concluded an alliance with the king of France. The following February, Glyn Dŵr, Sir Edmund Mortimer, and the earl of Northumberland drew up a tripartite agreement whereby England and Wales was to be divided between the three leaders. Interestingly, Sir Edmund had by this time abandoned the fiction that he was acting on behalf of his nephew, and claimed the crown for himself. It is strange that under this agreement the Mortimer family lands would have passed to Glyn Dŵr, which suggests that Mortimer may have been under some coercion. This might well confirm the view of a recent writer that Edmund Mortimer

Effigy at Montgomery Church,
purported to be of Sir Edmund Mortimer

was a rather lacklustre figure, who had been forced into the role of a rebel by the king's actions after Bryn Glas. The same work makes the interesting point that there is no mention of him taking part in any further military action until his death at Harlech in 1409.[25]

The close involvement of Sir Edmund in these treasonable conspiracies had repercussions upon his nephew, who, with his brother, was still in royal custody. The situation became grave in February 1405, when Lady Despencer, the mistress of Edmund of Langley, the boys' uncle, arranged for their abduction from Windsor. It was intended that the boys would be taken to Lady Despencer's estates in south Wales, but they were recaptured at Cheltenham and placed under closer guard. In 1406 they were placed in the custody of Richard, Lord Grey of Codnor, and in 1409 they were transferred to that of the prince of Wales. In that same year Roger, the younger of the two boys died, and Sir Edmund was killed at Harlech, when the castle was retaken for the English crown as one of the last outposts of Welsh resistance. Lady Mortimer and her daughters were taken to London, and were apparently all dead by 1413.[26]

Although there is no evidence to suggest that there was any compliance by the young earl in the treason ostensibly conducted in his name, his position was difficult, and his claim to the throne was strong. There was a real threat of conspiracies to place him on the throne after the death of Henry IV in 1413. The young Henry V therefore showed great magnanimity, and some political skill, when in June 1413 he released Edmund from his captivity and restored his estates to him. The king was rewarded by the loyalty of his former charge, which was demonstrated in 1415 when his brother-in-law, the earl of Cambridge, hatched a plot to place Edmund on the throne. Although the conspirators attempted to implicate him, the earl refused to co-operate, and revealed the plot to the king. He was rewarded with a place on the commission which ordered the immediate execution of Cambridge.

Soon after this he became active in Henry V's wars in France. In 1396 Richard II had concluded a 28-year truce with the French, but had been unable to agree a permanent peace. Henry IV had been initially too preoccupied with securing his own throne, and latterly with ill-health, to consider a resumption of hostilities. On the other hand, problems caused by the madness of Charles VI, together with the civil war between the Burgundian and Armagnac factions in France had prevented the French from exploiting Henry IV's political difficulties in England. Towards the end of Henry IV's reign, however, England had intervened on a modest scale on behalf of both Burgundians and Armagnacs in an attempt to gain some advantage, largely on the prince of Wales' instigation, but it was with the accession of Henry V that a policy of war with France was adopted.

In 1414 Henry made demands of France which went far beyond the unfulfilled terms of Brétigny concerning the transfer of certain territories to

English rule which had never taken place. The rejection of these demands provided a justification for an invasion of France. When Henry V embarked for Normandy in August 1415 he was accompanied by Edmund Mortimer with one banneret, three knights, 55 men-at-arms and 160 mounted archers. Edmund was active at the siege of Harfleur, but like many others, contracted dysentery there and was allowed to return home. This meant that he missed Agincourt, though it is possible that his troops were present at the epic English victory on 25 October. For nearly a year after Harfleur Edmund was in England, acting as a justice of the peace in Essex, Suffolk, Herefordshire and Shropshire. In August 1416 he was back in the military campaign as a captain of the naval force under John, duke of Bedford which defeated the French fleet which had cut off Harfleur.

In 1417 Henry V mounted a second expedition with the serious intention of conquering Normandy. Edmund again took part with a force of 100 lances and 300 archers. In 1418 a renewed attempt involved the invasion of the Cotentin peninsula and the siege of St. Lo, where Edmund's forces were joined by those of the duke of Gloucester, and successfully reduced the town. This success led to the appointment of Edmund as the king's lieutenant in Normandy, and in November 1418 he was present with the king at the siege of Rouen. The conquest of Normandy was an important factor leading to the Treaty of Troyes in May 1420. Equally important, however, was the political situation in France, where, following the murder of Duke John the Fearless by the Armagnacs in 1419, the Burgundians under Philip the Good threw their support behind the English. At Troyes France was effectively partitioned between Henry V, who gained much of the north and west, the Burgundians, and the Valois family, who were effectively restricted to the south. Henry was to marry Catherine, the

Rouen

A drawing of the siege of Rouen in 1418

daughter of Charles VI, upon whose death Henry and his heirs would become king of both England and France.

In February 1421 Edmund returned to England with the king and queen, and carried the queen's sceptre at her coronation. Henry V then returned to France in June 1421 for his third and final expedition to France against the forces of the Dauphin, who had refused to accept the terms of Troyes. Edmund

John, duke of Bedford

was with the king at the siege of Meaux in the winter of 1421-22, where Henry, like many of his men, contracted dysentery. After several months of illness, the king died at Bois-de-Vincennes on the last day of August 1422, leaving his nine-month-old son Henry to succeed him.

Edmund left France shortly after the king's death, and returned to a confused political situation in England. Henry V's will had provided for power to be exercised during the minority by his brothers: the duke of Gloucester in England and the duke of Bedford in France. Gloucester's ambitions for the regency were opposed by many of the other magnates, who sought to make his power firmly dependent upon the sanction of Parliament. Edmund's own position was complicated. In 1421 his illegitimate kinsman Sir John Mortimer had been arrested for treason, but had escaped the following year. Edmund himself had a claim to the throne which was as strong as that of the house of Lancaster, and he had in addition quarrelled with Gloucester shortly after returning from France. This meant that he was a potential threat to Gloucester, but at the same time his importance made it essential for him to be included on the council of regency which was set up in December 1422. The solution to Gloucester's problem was to send Edmund to Ireland, where he was less of a danger. On May 1423 he was appointed king's lieutenant in Ireland as his father and grandfather had been, for a term of nine years with an allowance of 5,000 marks per year. Edmund initially took advantage of a provision allowing him to appoint a deputy, and stayed in England while Edward Dansey, bishop of Meath governed Ireland for him. The recapture, attainder and execution of Sir John Mortimer in 1424 again highlighted the potential Mortimer threat, and Edmund was ordered to go to Ireland in person. For Edmund, like his two forebears, the appointment led to premature death. He contracted the plague, and on 18 January 1425 he died at the former de Lacy stronghold of Trim. Unusually, although his bones were returned to England, they were not buried at Wigmore but in the collegiate church at Clare in Suffolk which he had founded out of the former alien Benedictine priory. The Wigmore chronicler noted that he was called 'the Good' because of his great kindness, and was 'devout in the service of God, discreet in worldly matters, and fine and generous in his gifts'.[27]

In 1415 Edmund had married Anne Stafford, the daughter of Edmund, earl of Stafford and the granddaughter of Edward III's youngest son, Thomas of Woodstock. This had been done without the king's permission, and had incurred a fine of £2,000, as well as the calling-in of a 10,000 marks recognisance for good behaviour made two years earlier. This caused considerable financial hardship and led to the mortgaging of some of the family estates.[28] The marriage was, however, childless, and as Edmund's younger brother had died in 1409, the male line of Mortimer came to an end. His widow Anne had some difficulty in obtaining her dower from Gloucester, and at some time in 1426 married John Holland, earl of Huntingdon. Although the dynasty had come to a rather inglorious end, a far greater future awaited the descendants of Richard, duke of York, the son of Edmund's aunt, Anne Mortimer and the earl of Cambridge.

CHAPTER VIII

Branches of the Mortimer Family

Like all noble families, the Mortimers produced younger sons who had to make their own way in the world. Those who were not destined for the Church sought advancement by military service, for which the wars in Wales, Scotland and France provided abundant opportunities, or attempted to augment their meagre estates by judiciously marrying heiresses. The more successful combined both processes, while others, like the Mortimers of Homme Castle in Worcestershire (themselves a branch of the Mortimers of Richard's Castle), remained insignificant owners of a single manor.

Three Mortimer lines achieved a certain degree of size and eminence in the Marches area during the 13th and 14th centuries, and their histories form the substance of the ensuing chapter. The Mortimers of Chirk rose rapidly to great prominence, but after the fall of their founder Roger in 1322 passed rapidly into obscurity. The lands of the Chelmarsh line were far less extensive, being confined to the Welsh border counties, with the exception of estates around Luton. This line failed dramatically with the death of Sir Hugh de Mortimer at the battle of Shrewsbury in 1403. The estate then passed to a cousin, John de Cressi. Robert de Mortimer, a member of a possibly distantly related Mortimer family from Essex, established a third branch in Richard's Castle and Burford. This branch built up substantial holdings of land throughout the southern part of England, before the male line failed in 1304. The inheritance was then divided between two co-heiresses, in turn augmenting the possessions of the Cornewall and Talbot families.

The Mortimers of Chirk

The short-lived lordship of Chirk was established by Roger Mortimer, the third son of Roger (III) of Wigmore and his wife Maud de Braose. It has been suggested that Roger Mortimer and his brothers were instrumental in the fatal ambush of Llywelyn ap Gruffydd in 1282, and that the grant of Chirk was the reward for war service. Having secured a victory over the English in Gwynedd,

Llywelyn had moved south to attempt to recover lost possessions in mid-Wales. While on a reconnaissance mission near Builth, Llywelyn was surprised by some English soldiers at Cilmeri, and killed. The leaderless Welsh were then put to flight (see pp.73-74). Certainly, in the same year Edward I granted to Roger the lands formerly held by Llywelyn Fychan, Lord of Powys Fadog and Bromfield, who had died in 1269. This in effect created a new marcher lordship, and gained Roger an independent position, and he commenced erecting a strong castle, almost certainly employing Edward I's mason, Master James of St. George.[1]

Roger's career after 1282 may be divided into two phases. Until the death of Edward I his time was much taken up with military activity, whereas from 1307 until his fall in 1322 his role was primarily, though not exclusively, judicial and administrative within Wales. He was heavily involved in the wars of Edward I, providing 400 foot soldiers to fight against Rhys ap Maredud's uprising in 1287, and in 1294 followed the king to Gascony where he was made governor of the castles of Bourg and Blaye. He was again in Gascony in 1297, and the following year raised 600 Welshmen to fight against the Scots. In 1299 he was summoned to fight in person, and was present at the siege of Caerlaverock in 1300, where he was appointed one of the guides and guardians of the future Edward II. He returned to Scotland in 1303, but enthusiasm for Edward's repeated campaigns there was waning. In 1306 he was one of 22 nobles who left the army without permission to attend a tournament overseas. This incurred the royal displeasure, and led to a temporary confiscation of his lands and goods, but he was one of 16 who were pardoned in January 1307 on the intercession of Queen Margaret. No action was taken against the remaining six.[2]

The accession of Mortimer's former charge as Edward II in 1307 brought a rapid restoration of his fortunes. In January 1308 he was appointed Justice of North and South Wales, and of the lands of the bishop of St. David's, and keeper of the kings lands in north, south and west Wales. These judicial posts were held until 1322, apart from an interval between 1315 and 1316 (north Wales) and 1315 to 1317 (south Wales). The powers which he exercised were extensive, at

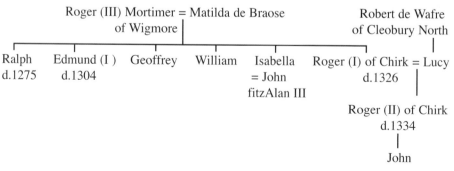

The Mortimers of Chirk

Adam's Tower — the most complete medieval feature of Chirk Castle

times requiring him to restrain a remote central administration from souring relations with friendly-disposed Welshmen. An example is the case of the threatened eviction from his lands in Carmarthenshire of David Vaughan, whose father had fortified Newcastle Emlyn against the rebels supporting Llywelyn Bren's revolt in 1316 at his own expense after its keepers had fled.[3] Much of the judicial work involved the minutiae of Welsh inheritance cases, or lengthy though comparatively trivial matters such as John de Charlton's complaint that in 1315 Philip de Middleton had stolen his horse worth £10 at Chirbury.[4]

Roger Mortimer exercised considerable power as a result of his position in Wales, and together with his nephew Roger (IV) of Wigmore utilised the opportunities which were afforded to build up a strong personal power base in the area. Links were strengthened with other rising lords on the March, such as John de Charlton, who was relieved by Mortimer when under siege in his castle of Pool (Welshpool) by his wife's uncle, Gruffydd de la Pole. In 1321, however, he joined his nephew in opposition to the Despencers, which incurred the wrath of the king. On 22 January 1322 both Mortimers were forced to surrender to Edward at Shrewsbury, and both were imprisoned in the Tower of London. Though sentenced to death, Mortimer's punishment was subsequently reduced to perpetual imprisonment. Unlike his nephew, Roger of Chirk did not escape, and died in captivity on 3 August 1326.

The disgrace of Roger brought about the effective end of the influence of the Chirk branch of the family. The Chirk lands were annexed to the Earl of Arundel, whose family, despite temporary confiscation between 1326 and 1334, began to impose their grip upon them, to the exclusion of the Mortimer heirs. Roger of Chirk had married Lucy, the daughter of Robert de Wafre of Cleobury North, by whom he had a son, also Roger. Despite the existence of this son, it was the nephew, Roger (IV) of Wigmore, who claimed upon his return in February 1327 to be the heir of Roger of Chirk, his uncle. While this act of appropriation seems to have been initially successful, the restored lands were again finally confiscated to the Crown in 1330. Roger the younger of Chirk died in 1334, to be succeeded by his infant son John. Petitions on behalf of this John to enter into his inheritance were rejected by the Crown on the grounds of his youth, and the Chirk lands were returned to Arundel in 1334. It appears that John eventually gave up his attempts, for in the Autumn of 1359 he surrendered all claims to Chirk to Arundel, and to his other lands to Roger (V) of Wigmore, second earl of March. Various references suggest that John Mortimer had settled in the Rochester area of Kent, and the line of Chirk passed into obscurity as rapidly as it had risen to prominence.

The Mortimers of Chelmarsh

Though never achieving even the brief influence and notoriety of the Chirk branch of the family, the Mortimers of Chelmarsh maintained a distinct identity, and quietly accumulated their estates both in Shropshire and beyond until the failure of the male line in 1403.

Chelmarsh formed one of a small concentration of estates on the east side of the Brown Clee which were held by Ralph Mortimer as tenant of the earl of Shrewsbury at Domesday. The *DNB* states that William, the second son of Ralph Mortimer of Wigmore was lord of Chelmarsh and Sidbury. For several generations Chelmarsh was bestowed upon younger sons of the lord of Wigmore for their lifetimes. Thus William de Mortimer held the manor by the gift of his brother Hugh (I) of Wigmore, who reassumed possession upon the death of William. A second Hugh towards the end of the 12th century held Chelmarsh and Sidbury, but was killed in a tournament at Worcester, leaving no heirs. Ralph (II) of Wigmore similarly granted Chelmarsh to his eldest son Hugh, who in turn passed it to his brother Ralph. In 1227 this Ralph succeeded to Wigmore and subsequently married Gwladus Ddu, daughter of the Welsh prince, Llywelyn ab Iorwerth. Hugh, a second son of this union was in time granted the Chelmarsh estates. He became the founder of a distinct Chelmarsh branch of the family, described by Eyton as 'though hardly of baronial rank, was of an importance very proximate'.[5]

Detailed information becomes more readily available with the emergence of Hugh (I), lord of Chelmarsh. In 1254/5 the Hundred Rolls recorded that he held five hides of geldable land, together with another four and a half virgates, a capital messuage, three mills and a 'gorth' or fish weir on the river Severn. In 1264 he was recorded at the siege of Kenilworth Castle, where he fought on the side of the king against the younger Simon de Montfort and his rebels, and

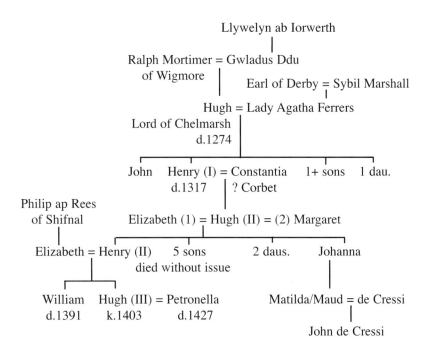

The Mortimers of Chelmarsh

lost a good horse for which he was compensated by the writing off of a debt of 40 marks.

In 1255 he made a good marriage to Lady Agatha Ferrers, daughter of the earl of Derby and Sybil Marshal, which entitled Agatha to a seventh share of a fifth part of the Honour of the Marshal earls of Pembroke. They had three, and possibly more, sons and one daughter. For the last two years of his life, which ended in 1273, Hugh served as Sheriff of Shropshire and Staffordshire, in which offices he was succeeded by his nephew Ralph, the son of Roger (III) of Wigmore. His widow lived on for over 30 years after her husband's death, and when she died in 1306 she was recorded as holding estates in Bedfordshire, Dorset and Ireland.[6]

As Hugh (I)'s eldest son John had died before his father, his younger brother, Henry (I), succeeded to his father's lands. He married one Constantia, possibly a member of the Corbet family, who brought him as her dowry Aston under Caus (Aston Rogers in Worthen) in the north-west of Shropshire. Although the manor of Aston was taken into the hands of the king in 1322, it would seem to have been restored by the time of Henry (I)'s death, as it is included among his Shropshire lands in his inquisition post mortem. Henry's Shropshire lands were further augmented by the acquisition of La Lye Hall (in Quatt) which were held jointly with his wife by enfeoffment of Mathew, rector of the church of Rossall. Away from Shropshire, Henry had received from the king a sixth part of the wealthy manor of Luton in Bedfordshire, forming the nucleus of an estate which was to be developed by his successors.[7]

In 1297 Henry was assessed as the holder of lands and rents to the value of £20 in Shropshire, and was duly summoned to serve overseas. In 1306 he did homage for his mother's inheritance, and was noted fighting in Scotland in 1309. In 1312 he represented Shropshire in a parliament held at Westminster.

Henry died in 1317, to be succeeded by his 21-year-old son Hugh (II). In common with other members of his family, Hugh would appear to have taken part in the rebellion against Edward II which ended with the the defeat of the baronial army at Boroughbridge in March 1322 and imprisonment of Roger (IV) of Wigmore and his nephew of Chirk. In 1325 he was fined £200 in ransom for his life and lands because he had joined Thomas, late earl of Lancaster in his rebellion. Hugh (II)'s first wife Elizabeth is recorded in 1331, and was the mother of six sons, all of whom except Henry (II), the eldest, died without issue, and two daughters. By 1341 Elizabeth was dead, and Hugh (II) had married his second wife, Margaret, possibly a relation of John Meriet of Bedfordshire, from whom Hugh (II) gained further lands in Luton, and estates at Magor in present-day Monmouthshire.[8]

Upon the death of Hugh (II) in 1372 the Chelmarsh line was continued by his eldest son, Henry (II), who married Elizabeth the daughter and co-heir of Philip ap Rees of Shifnal. The date of Henry (II)'s death is not known, but he was succeeded by his elder son William who was classified as an idiot. For this reason the family estates were taken into the hands of the Crown until William's death in 1391, following which the estates passed to his brother Hugh (III), the last of the male line. Unfortunately, Hugh (III) did not enjoy his estates for long, as he was killed fighting for King Henry IV at the battle of Shrewsbury in 1403. His estates were basically those of his forebear Henry (II) with augmentations. By 1403, for example, the Bedfordshire holdings had been increased to two-thirds of the manor of Luton, and contained various named properties including a horse-mill. In Shropshire were the manors of Quatt and Chelmarsh, together with a collection of hamlets in the west of the county: Bromlow, Meadow Town, and Medlicott. Magor, acquired by Hugh (II), is described in Hugh's inquisition post mortem as burnt and wasted by Owen de Glyndowdy and other traitors in his company[9] and therefore value-less. Chelmarsh, with its 'members' of Hempton and Sutton, was still held under the earl of March despite the local branch of the Mortimers having been established for five generations by 1403.

On Hugh's death, his widow Petronella, who lived until 1427, was granted dower in the manor of Quatt on condition that she did not remarry without the consent of the king. Her estate included 'one chamber where the manor formerly was, length 36 feet, width 15 feet' and 'one little toft annexed to it, length 14 feet, width ten feet'.[10]

The death of Hugh (III) without a male heir caused problems. The premature childless deaths of his five uncles meant that the inheritance passed to the issue of Johanna, the elder of his father's sisters. Johanna's daughter Matilda or Maud had married a de Cressi, and their son John de Cressi duly performed fealty for his inheritance in 1404. It is worth noting that there was a suggestion of a disputed succession, when the inquisition to the Magor estate of Sir Hugh (III) put forward Edmund Rodebergh rather than John de Cressi as the heir. The Jury commented that Rodebergh was of age 'but how he is heir is completely unknown'.[11] It is suggested that he claimed descent from a daughter of Hugh (II), but there is little evidence, and the claim does not seem to have been pursued. The line of the Mortimers of Chelmarsh had ended.

The Mortimers of Richard's Castle

The branch of the family which was established in Richard's Castle, a few miles from the centre of the Mortimer estates in Wigmore, has given rise to some controversy regarding its origins. Some 19th century genealogists such as George Morris traced its beginnings to Robert de Mortimer, son of Hugh (II) of Wigmore. This view was accepted by T.F. Tout in the *DNB*, though Penry Evans considered Robert of Richard's Castle to be a younger son of Roger (I) of Wigmore, and brother to Hugh (II).[12] The *Complete Peerage*, however, produced compelling evidence that the Sir Robert de Mortimer who founded the Richard's Castle branch of the family by his marriage to Margaret de Say was the son of Robert de Mortimer of Essex, who was probably related to the Mortimers of Attleborough in Norfolk. Recent writers such as P.M. Remfry have accepted that the Richard's Castle branch were not directly related to the 'main' Mortimer family, beyond a possible common origin in Mortemer-en-Bray.

The barony of Richard's Castle had originated with Richard Fitz Scrob, a Norman favourite of Edward the Confessor and descended to the de Say family. Upon the death of Hugh de Say in 1197, the estate was inherited by his daughter Margaret, the wife of Hugh de Ferrers. De Ferrers died some time before 1200, and Margaret appears to have been a widow for a decade before marrying Robert Mortimer in 1210. Robert (I) had seen service in the third Crusade, and had been regularly at Court in the years preceding his marriage. By marrying such an eligible widow, Mortimer acquired the extensive barony of Burford and Richard's Castle, and quickly assumed the role and responsibilities of a marcher lord. He was a loyal servant of the Crown throughout this period, fighting in Ireland and serving as a commissioner enquiring into losses experienced by the Herefordshire clergy during King John's quarrel with the pope. He remained loyal to the king during his struggle with the barons, and assisted in the restoration of normality after the accession of Henry III. Robert (I) died in July 1219, leaving a newly born son, Hugh. Shortly after, his widow

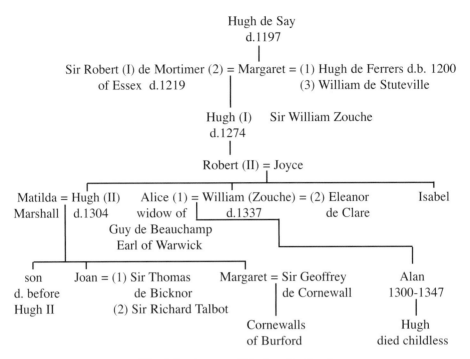

The Mortimers of Richard's Castle

made her third and final marriage to William de Stuteville from Gressenhall, Norfolk, who enjoyed possession of her estates 'by the courtesy of England' after her death in 1242 until his own in 1259. As a result, it was not until that year that Hugh (I) entered fully into his inheritance, for which he was required to pay a fine of 200 marks. The career of Hugh (I) is not particularly well documented. Remfry suggests that he may have been present at the siege of Kenilworth in 1266, where Hugh of Chelmarsh has already been noted, and it is known that in the same year he received from Henry III the grant of a weekly market at Burford.

Hugh (I) died in 1274, possessing lands in the three adjacent counties of Hereford, Shropshire and Worcester. These comprised three fairly consolidated blocks of estates, the one in the Presteigne area, the second following the Teme valley from Ludford to Homme, with an outlier at Cotheridge, and a third and smaller concentration of manors in the Droitwich area, to the north of Worcester. Although Hugh and his successors are regularly described as 'of Richard's Castle', Burford was the chief of these holdings. Richard's Castle, Stapleton, Wychbold, Cotheridge and Homme are all described in Hugh's inquisition post mortem as 'held of the king in chief by barony pertaining to Burford'.[13] There is considerable discussion of the exact significance of the status of the 'barony of Burford' at this period in *The House of Cornewall*, which, while somewhat inconclusive, underlines the importance of the manor.

(The Burford inheritance was habitually styled a barony and was held by service of five knights, yet the holders were never summoned to Parliament as barons throughout the history of the 'barony'.).[14]

Hugh (I) was succeeded by his 22-year-old son Robert, who became heavily involved in the Welsh wars. In 1277 he was called upon to perform military service against Llywelyn, together with three knights and five sergeants. In 1282 he was again summoned to join a great army which was being assembled at Rhuddlan against Llywelyn, and he evidently performed with distinction, as the following year the king exonerated him from debts amounting to the considerable sum of £287 10s. 7d. in recognition of his service. In 1283 he was summoned to attend a parliament at Shrewsbury. Robert had married an heiress, Joyce, the daughter of Sir William Zouche of Hobridge, Essex, who was the younger son of Roger de la Zouch of Ashby in Leicestershire. Joyce brought with her lands in Somerset and Northamptonshire, and when Robert died in 1286 his estates had been considerably augmented by these and other acquisitions. In addition to the nucleus in the west Midlands which he had inherited from his father, Robert possessed lands in Warwickshire, Gloucestershire, Somerset, Northamptonshire and Oxfordshire.[15] He was buried before the altar of St. Jude in Worcester Cathedral, where his widow was laid by him in March 1290.

Robert and Joyce had two sons, Hugh who inherited his father's estates, and William who took his mother's name to found the short-lived line of Zouche of Mortimer. A daughter, Isabel, was enfeoffed by her mother of lands at Huntsbere in Somerset shortly before the latter's death. Hugh was a minor at the time of his father's death, and was placed under the guardianship of William de Beauchamp, earl of Warwick. It was Warwick who made what would prove to be a possibly fatal error of securing the marriage of his ward to Matilda, a descendant of William Marshal, earl of Pembroke.

Hugh (II) came of age in 1295, and shortly afterwards began a military career. Service in Flanders in 1297 was rewarded with the writing off of £347 7s. 2d. of debts accumulated by his predecessors, and he saw subsequent service in the Scottish campaigns of Edward I. Like Roger of Chirk, Hugh (II) of Richard's Castle was among the illustrious company of English chivalry who fought at the siege of Caerlaverock in 1300. Upon his return to England, Hugh (II) confirmed a charter granting various privileges including house boot, hay boot and fire boot (the right to collect wood from commons to repair houses and fences and to use as fuel) to the burgesses of the borough of Richard's Castle in 1301. Little is known of the early history of this failed borough, the defensive earthworks of which are still visible in places. Hugh's charter may have been an attempt to retain the inhabitants, who were gradually to migrate downhill to a new settlement, the present village of Richard's Castle, although the computation of 103 burgages there in his inquisition post mortem in 1304 would suggest that the state of the town was in fact healthy, and compared not unfavourably with the 140 recorded at Wigmore in the same year.[16] His career was cut short dramatically on 30 July 1304 when he and a number of his associates died suddenly. Whether this was the result of bacterial or deliberate poisoning is not known, but the suspicion was sufficient for some of the survivors to bring an indictment against Matilda at Hereford. She was, however, pardoned by the king.

The premature death of Hugh (II) brought the male line of Richard's Castle Mortimers to an abrupt close. A son had been born some time before 1293, but had died before his father. This meant that the two daughters of the marriage, Joan, aged 12, and her eight-year-old sister Margaret now became co-heirs to a substantial collection of lands. Joan had by this time married Sir Thomas de Bicknor, who thus had an interest in the estates. Wardship was granted to Queen Margaret, who had been instrumental in obtaining the royal pardon for the girl's mother. In 1309 Joan de Bicknor came of age, and the estate was divided between the two sisters, Joan receiving the Richard's Castle moiety, and Margaret that of Burford. Margaret was given into the custody of Sir Geoffrey de Cornewall, who subsequently married her, and established the long and illustrious line of Cornewall of Burford. Joan's husband, Sir Thomas de Bicknor died without issue, and she then married Sir Richard Talbot, a younger son of Richard Lord Talbot of Eccleswall, so establishing a Richard's Castle branch of the Talbot family.

It is interesting to note the fortunes of the lesser branch of this family which had taken the name of Zouche of Mortimer. William, the younger brother of Hugh (II) of Richard's Castle married Alice, widow of Guy de Beauchamp, earl of Warwick. She was the sister of Robert de Tony of Flamstead in Hertfordshire, who was also lord of the important marcher lordships of Elfael and Glamorgan, which she brought to the marriage. Alice died in 1325, and her widower enjoyed her estates 'by courtesy of England' until his own death in 1337.[17]

William de la Zouche of Mortimer played an important role in the events surrounding the enforced abdication of Edward II. Following the landing of Roger Mortimer (IV) and Queen Isabella in September 1326, the king with Hugh Despencer the younger fled to Wales with the royal treasure, much of which they deposited in Despencer's stronghold at Caerphilly. The fugitive king and his favourite then moved to Neath Abbey, and Caerphilly was besieged by William de la Zouche of Mortimer with forces loyal to Isabella. On 30 March 1327 the castle surrendered, in return for a free pardon for the defenders, including the son of the younger Despencer brutally executed at Hereford.

In January 1329, William de la Zouche, in circumstances which are far from clear, abducted Eleanor, widow of the executed Hugh Despencer the younger

Richard's Castle from the air, showing the castle site at the crest of the ridge, and the outlines of the planned borough

from her residence at Hanley Castle in Worcestershire. It became clear that the lady had not been an unwilling participant in the affair, for the couple subsequently married and were pardoned by the king. Eleanor was a glittering prize for an ambitious man like William. In her own right, she had inherited the largest share of the vast estates of her brother Gilbert de Clare, who had died at Bannockburn in 1314 leaving no heirs. By unscrupulous means these lands had been augmented by Hugh Despencer, so that when Eleanor's estates were restored to her in 1328 she was an extremely eligible widow. By skilful marriages, William had raised himself from the position of younger son to one of influential Marcher lord. In 1332 he was on royal business overseas, and in 1333 he was given responsibility for arresting those in Wales who had taken advantage of the absence of the king and many of the major landowners in Scotland 'to cause disturbances and commit outrages'.[18] Some time afterwards he contracted an incurable disease from which he died on 28 February 1337. His widow survived him by little more than five months.

William was succeeded by his son Alan, who had been born in 1300, and died in 1347 leaving estates in Leicestershire and Sussex. These were by no means as extensive as those of his father, partly due to the successful attempt of the Beauchamps to gain the Tony lands in Wales.[19] The Despencer and Clare lands had passed to the son of Hugh Despencer upon the death of Eleanor. Alan's son Hugh succeeded at the age of seven, but although he lived almost to the age of 60, he died childless in 1399, and his estates, substantially those of his father, passed to a cousin Joyce, wife of Hugh Burnell. Thus another Mortimer line failed for want of a male heir.

CHAPTER IX

Estates and their Management

The Domesday Survey of 1086 provides a convenient starting point to a consideration of the growth and development of the Mortimer lands. Ralph (I) held considerable estates throughout England, with a concentration in Herefordshire, Shropshire, and Worcestershire. The Herefordshire estates were concentrated upon Wigmore, which rapidly replaced St. Victor-en-Caux as the chief seat of the family, while those in Shropshire were similarly centred upon Cleobury, which acquired the Mortimer name as a suffix. However, a significant difference is noticeable between these two important groups of holdings: whereas Ralph's lands in north Herefordshire were held directly from the king as tenant-in-chief, a significant number of those in Shropshire were held as under-tenant of Roger de Montgomery, earl of Shrewsbury. It was alleged much later that Ralph had been steward to the earl,[1] and this could well explain how some Mortimer land in Shropshire came to be held in this way. Other lands were spread throughout England, with significant concentrations on Humberside and in Hampshire and Berkshire. There is little indication of how these various estates may have been acquired.

The Wigmore and Cleobury lands show an interesting grouping of lesser holdings around the central manor. Evans in his 1934 University of Wales thesis suggested that this arrangement may have reflected a much earlier, possibly Celtic economy, or the piecemeal nature of conquest, whereas more recently Remfry has made a convincing case to a deliberately planned castel-lanry designed as a protective shield for the main centre.[2] Sixteen of these holdings were held as Ralph's own demesne land, while an outer ring of 13 were knight's fees which had been allotted to followers. Significantly, Remfry points out in support of his theory that these 13 vills contain 11 known castle sites, together with a further two possibles.

The subsequent history of the Mortimer possessions remains somewhat confused until the time of Ralph (II) in the second quarter of the 13th century.

Prior to that, during the troubled times of the 12th century, the family suffered the confiscation of its possessions on a number of occasions in consequence of injudicious participation in rebellions. Association with the treasonable activities of Stephen of Aumale, to whom the Mortimers were closely allied by marriage, during the reign of Henry I seems to have led to the confiscation of Mortimer lands in England, which may have been assigned to Pain FitzJohn. Hugh (I) had regained possession of his Shropshire and Herefordshire lands in the 1140s, and in 1144 the Welsh lordship of Maelienydd was brought under permanent Mortimer control, with the exception of its temporary loss in the 1260s.

The 13th century witnessed the beginning of a process whereby the Mortimer holdings were increased by judicious marriages to an extent which transformed the family from regional to national magnates. The marriage of Ralph (II) to Gwladus Ddu, the daughter of Llywelyn the Great and a grand-daughter of King John brought status, and the lands of Ceri and Cedewain as dower, though these were not permanently incorporated into the Mortimer estates until after the capture of Dolforwyn Castle by Roger (III) in 1277. In 1247 Roger (III) married Maud de Braose, the eldest daughter and co-heiress of William de Braose, whose wife was heiress of Richard Marshal, earl of Pembroke. Maud brought to the marriage a rich collection of lands, which included a third of the lordship of Brecon; Radnor; Narberth and half of St. Clears in south-west Wales; Bridgwater Castle, and a third of that borough, with other lands in Somerset and Gloucestershire; and extensive possessions in Ireland, in Kildare, Kilkenny and Carlow.[3]

The marriage of Edmund (I) to Margaret de Fiennes brought relatively little in the way of properties, and indeed she held substantial parts of the inherit-ance of Roger (IV) in dower until her death in 1334, including Wigmore itself and the Somerset lands. It was Roger (IV) who made the most spectacular acquisitions, which transformed the Mortimer holdings. His marriage to Joan de Geneville in 1301 brought into the family possession, by lease at a modest rent until the death of her mother the elder Joan in 1323, extensive lands in Shropshire and the March. These included half the town of Ludlow and the adjacent manor of Stanton Lacy, and a massive inheritance in Ireland based on the mighty de Lacy fortress of Trim. While this brought conflict with some Irish de Lacys, it laid the foundations of future Mortimer pre-eminence in Ireland.

This great accumulation of lands was further increased by grants. In 1309 Roger (IV) was granted Cwmwd Deuddwr, adjacent to the family lands in Maelienydd, while his uncle of Chirk gained Blaenllyfni, which stood in a similar relationship to the Brecon lands. Though all Roger's lands were seized in 1322 after his involvement in the rebellion against the Despencers, upon his return from exile in 1327 his estates were restored by Parliament, and his lover Queen Isabella began granting him vast estates which had been forfeited by his defeated enemies. These included the great lordship of Denbigh, formerly held by the elder Despencer, and Arundel lordships which included Oswestry, Clun and other Shropshire estates, as well as lands in other parts of the country. Shortly before his fall in 1330, Roger had also acquired Builth and Montgomery, together with Clifford and Glasbury.

Although confiscation was automatic upon Roger's fall, his son Edmund (II) was treated with leniency, and allowed to hold the traditional family lands in Cleobury, Wigmore and mid-Wales. His premature death a few months after that of his father ushered in a lengthy period when the estates were broken up, various portions being held in dower by three widows, Margaret de Fiennes, Joan de Geneville, and Edmund's own widow, Elizabeth de Badlesmere. Most of the remainder was in the hands of the king, or had been granted as a reward to those who, like William de Montacute who gained Denbigh, had assisted in the overthrow of Roger (IV).

Gradually Roger (V), who had been a child of four on his father's death in 1331, was restored to his inheritance, the most significant achievement being the result of a series of legal actions in 1354 which recovered Denbigh from the Earl of Salisbury, and various estates of Roger of Chirk, though not Chirk itself, from the earls of Arundel. The deaths of his grandmother Joan de Geneville in 1358, and of his mother in the following year brought the rest of the ancestral possessions into Roger's hands. He also purchased further lands in Somerset to add to the family holdings in that part of the country.

His son, Edmund (III) concluded a most advantageous marriage with Philippa, daughter of Lionel, duke of Clarence some

Part of the walls around the initial settlement at Denbigh
below the site of the castle

The present church at Clare Priory. Originally founded in 1248, this building initially served as the infirmary on the ground floor with accommodation above, either for students or novices and their master. After the Reformation it probably served as a barn, before becoming a school in the nineteenth century, the Augustinians returning in 1953 and establishing the church

time about 1368. This not only gave the Mortimers a direct claim to the throne, as discussed elsewhere,[4] but also the important estates of Philippa's mother, Elizabeth de Burgh. This added the lordships of Usk, Caerleon and Trellech, comprising most of present-day Monmouthshire, to the family's holdings in the southern March. In addition, Edmund gained the important Clare family lands in East Anglia and the Home Counties.[5] His position in Ireland was further enhanced by the earldom of Ulster and the lordship of Connaught. He had become the fourth largest landowner in England after the Crown, the Black Prince, and the duke of Lancaster, and also held vast estates in Ireland. These estates and their interest dominated the careers of the last two earls, although the marriage of Roger (VI) to Eleanor Holland, daughter of the king's brother, the earl of Kent, whilst tying the family more closely to the succession, added little in the way of estates. Her subsequent marriage after Roger's death to Edward Charlton, Lord Powys, did, however, involve the lordship of Usk and Caerleon passing out of Mortimer hands.

This brief account of the development of the territorial empire of the Mortimers requires some further elaboration. The male members of the family, with one or two exceptions, were not long lived. The comparative brevity of their lives was paralleled by the longevity of their wives, and both factors considerably complicated the process of succession. Although an unbroken succession of male heirs was comparatively unusual among the Marcher lords, this fortuitous state of affairs was modified by the prevalence of minorities during the 14th century. Of the six Mortimers who held the family estates between 1304 and 1425, only one, Edmund (II), succeeded as an adult to his inheritance. Roger (IV) was 17; Roger (V) was four; Edmund (III) was nine; Roger (VI) was seven; and Edmund (IV) was a few months short of the same age. In this way, for 46 years between 1300 and 1400, the Mortimer estates were subject to minority. This meant that the properties, and the revenues which they generated, with the exception of the third retained by the widow for dower, passed into the hands of the king. He would either devote the proceeds to his own usage, or would grant or lease the estates to a third party to administer them for his own benefit until the heir came of age. In this way Edmund (III) was first a royal ward, but was later put into the care of Bishop William of Wykeham and Richard, earl of Arundel. Similarly in 1398, Edward of York, earl of Albermarle and brother to Richard, was given full wardship of all possessions of Roger (VI), except those in South Wales, until Edmund (IV) came of age.

Although a remarkable degree of continuity can be observed in the administration of the Mortimer estates during times of minority, wardship represented a considerable disruption and loss of valuable revenue, and it is not surprising that during the 14th century means of avoiding it became increasingly employed. Initially this involved the creation of a joint life tenancy for husband and wife, but soon developed into a form of trust, later known as a 'use', to which the property concerned would be conveyed. The trustees would then reconvey a life interest to the donor, upon whose death the property would revert to the ownership of the trustees, who, in the case of a minority, would administer it in the interest of the heir until he or she came of age. This process deprived the crown of a considerable source of revenue. When, two centuries later, Henry VIII attempted to end the practice with Cromwell's infamous Statute of Uses, the attempt became a major grievance of the gentry rebels in 1536.

The process seems to have been adopted by Roger (IV) in the second decade of the 14th century, when in 1316 he granted to John Hothum and Philip ap Hywel the castle and manor of Wigmore and extensive estates in mid-Wales and elsewhere, with the provision for them to re-grant them to Roger and his heirs.[6] The device was later attempted by Roger (V) prior to his final departure for France. In August 1359 he conveyed a life interest in land, including Ludlow and Cleobury, in 11 counties to a group of his friends and associates led by William of Wykeham, bishop of Winchester. Shortly afterwards, a similar attempt was made with relation to the lordship of Denbigh. In this case the process of reconveyance had not taken place by the time of the earl's death, and the estates were claimed by the Prince of Wales, it not being until 1373 that the feoffees were allowed to take possession. In the case of the first group of estates, the move was successful. Edmund (III) was more successful, in 1374 conveying a similar parcel of lands to a group of friends and advisers. Following a legal action, possibly collusive, in 1379, the lands were reconveyed to the earl in January 1380 at a nominal rent for 20 years. By this means the king was deprived of control of a considerable part of the Mortimer estates when Edmund died the following year.

A problem which was less easily avoided was that of dower. The longevity of the Mortimer wives has already been mentioned in passing. A widow was entitled to a third of her husband's lands as dower, and to these would be added those which she owned either by inheritance, or by gift from her husband. This meant that these lands would be excluded from the inheritance of the heir until the death of his mother, or, if she had remarried, until the death of her husband, who could continue to hold his wife's lands by the 'courtesy of England'. In the 14th century the Mortimer estates suffered from excessive fragmentation as the result of dower.

When Edmund (I) died in 1304, he was survived for 30 years by his widow, Margaret de Fiennes, who held the Radnor lands until her death. Joan de Genevile survived Roger (IV) for 26 years, holding Ceri and Cedewain as dower, and Ewyas Lacy and a half of Ludlow in her own right. Elizabeth de Badlesmere died in 1355, some 24 years after her husband Edmund (II), holding Maelienydd and Cwmwd Deuddwr as dower, which passed by courtesy to her second husband, William de Bohun, earl of Northampton, until his death in 1360. This meant that Roger (V) was unable to incorporate large parts of inheritance into his estates until shortly before his own death. His successor, Edmund (III) was in fact outlived by his own mother, Philippa de Montacute, who survived until 1382. In this way, the Mortimer inheritance suffered considerable disruption on a number of occasions. It did, however, provide the historian with welcome sources of information, for records of the management of the estates when they were in the hands of the crown are considerably more plentiful than for the times when the family had full control of their lands.

The Tenure of the Estates

The Mortimer lordship illustrates very clearly the complexities of medieval landholding, and the changes which took place during the period between Domesday and 1425. Initially the basis of landholding under the feudal system was service. This took the form of military service for the higher echelons of society, with the lower orders performing their obligations by labour. The tenants-in-chief had an obligation to serve the crown with a specific number of troops according to their rank and the size of their holdings. They in turn granted portions of their lands to sub-tenants, who in return for their holdings would serve in their lord's retinue when it was summoned by the king. The customary period of service was 40 days, although on occasions this was exceeded voluntarily, particularly by marcher lords such as the Mortimers when campaigning against the Welsh.

The gradual sub-division of estates produced a proliferation of knights' fees — smaller estates which had been sub-let on condition of providing a knight to serve in the feudal host. Thus in 1295 Bryan de Brampton held the manor of Ashton in Herefordshire from Edmund (I) by service of 40 days guard at Wigmore Castle with a barded (armoured) horse at his own cost whenever war occurred between the king and the prince of Wales.[7] This service of castle-guard will be noted again in the context of commutation payments.

The purpose of knight-service was to provide the cavalry which was an essential basis of a medieval army. Lesser tenants were charged with providing foot soldiers and archers in return for their land. The free tenants of Radnor were each required to find a footman with a lance in time of war;[8] the manor of Winforton was held in return for providing an archer in the castle of Colwyn; while from St. Clears in Carmarthenshire, in 1281, 24 foot soldiers and one horseman were required.[9]

This system was complex and often inefficient to operate. By 1300 military developments had transformed the light horseman of the time of Domesday into a heavily armoured knight, who required a larger and more expensive horse to bear his weight and that of the horse's armour. As a partial consequence of this it became increasingly common for a quota rather than the full retinue to be summoned. This may be a recognition of the need to reach a compromise between the legal requirement and what was practically possible. There were also advantages to the king in only summoning a quota of his feudal troops. It hindered the formation of large hosts which could be used against him rather than against his enemies, and it meant that there were still reserve forces on call if needed. Each knight who was summoned was expected to be accompanied by at least

A south Wales archer as illustrated in the Littere Walliae

two mounted troopers. Thus although in 1277 Roger (III) had a quota of six knights for his lands in Herefordshire and Shropshire, and the remainder of his Braose inheritance, in total this would have meant between 20 and 30 mounted troops.[10]

Various developments contributed to the replacement of feudal levies by paid armies by the 14th century. One of these was the commutation of military service into a fine known as scutage, literally 'shield money'. While tenants-in-chief were expected to attend the king in time of war with their allotted quota of knights, it became increasingly common for lesser tenants to pay a scutage, initially of two marks (26s. 8d.) and latterly of 40 shillings for each knight's fee. This represented 40 days' service at the rate of a shilling per day, and was collected by the sheriff of the

A north Wales spearman
as illustrated in the
Littere Walliae

county. In the reign of Henry I it had become normal for ecclesiastical tenants to pay a fixed rate of scutage in lieu of knight service, and the practice had on occasions been allowed for lesser lay tenants. During the 12th century the practice was extended, and by 1159 it had become a general war tax affecting all classes of military tenants except the tenants-in-chief. During the reign of John, scutages were particularly frequent and heavy. It is interesting to note that the Mortimers' Shropshire estates appear never to have been subjected to scutage. Alone among the Shropshire baronies, that of Mortimer assumed the *de facto* status of a marcher lordship, which allowed virtual immunity from royal authority. This was confirmed by a generous royal charter of Henry III in 1266, which also exempted the lordships of Cleobury and Chelmarsh from suit at the county and hundred courts, and from the visits of royal officials. This grant was subsequently used as a pretext to extend the privilege to a further 20 manors which were not included in the actual charter.[11] A similar process of conversion at Wigmore to an independent franchise had also been completed shortly after 1266.[12] An attempt to reassert the powers of the crown was made in a series of *Quo Warranto* actions which centred upon the Mortimers' insistence that their tenants should withdraw actions from the hundred and shire courts and into those of the lordship. These attempts by the Crown failed in the case of Wigmore, and would also seem to have been unsuccessful in the cases of Cleobury and Chelmarsh, which claimed exemption by Henry III's grant. The records of the latter action, are, however, lost. Subsequently the Crown began a more oblique attack on the Mortimer immunities, by devices such as encouraging the Welsh tenants of Roger of Chirk to appeal to the king's courts against alleged ill-treatment at the hands of their lord.[13]

This does not mean that the Mortimers as marcher lords were exempt from contributing to the war effort. In practice it meant that they rather than royal officials were responsible for the collection of scutages. Like other marcher lords, the Mortimers participated enthusiastically in Edward I's Welsh wars, Roger (III) even scorning payment for his services, unlike his more mercenary colleagues from Cheshire. By the 14th century it became normal for armies to be fully professional, with a chain of command reaching from paid commanders down to humble foot soldiers. Among the latter may be noted the contingents of Welsh troops from the Mortimer estates who played a conspicuous part in the Irish wars of the late 14th and early 15th centuries.

The lower levels of rural society performed their obligations by work on the land, and here also may be seen the trend towards the replacement of labour service by money payments, even before the Black Death transformed the rural labour market. A major division, which will be noticed in other parts of this chapter, existed between the practises of the Mortimers' English and Welsh estates. The estates in those parts of Wales and the Marches which were populated predominantly by English tenants differed little in their organisation from estates in other parts of England. In the Welshries, however, many local customs continued, the conquerors having been more interested in economic exploitation than in enforcing uniformity. As late as the 14th century, the tenants of the Welshries of Denbigh were still paying *tunk*, an obscure Welsh due which had developed into a rent charge, and *consuetudines*, the original purpose of which had been long forgotten. The Wyeside manors of the lordship of Usk continued to pay *wormetak*, a form of pannage dues, at the same period.[14] Some areas were also liable to *horngeld*, a tax on cattle.

Another significance was the relative scarcity of unfree tenants in the Welshries. Bondmen had been rare in the Welsh lands, and it had proved virtually impossible to transport villeinage to them.

The division into free and unfree tenants had, at least by the 14th century, become less important in practice. Free tenants included, at the upper end of the heirarchy, those who were styled 'lords' of their townships, who could alienate their lands, and who often had sub-tenants performing labour services for them. At the lower end of the scale there was little to distinguish the condition of the free and the unfree peasants. Free tenants were bound, like their social superiors, to attend the lord's courts, the Court Leet and the Court Baron, though villeins were also bound to appear there on occasions such as the passing of a holding from father to son. Customary tenants were bound to cultivate the lord's lands, generally on a basis of a number of days per week, with extra work being required at harvest time. Most other obligations were shared by villein and free alike. Both were required to provide their best beast as heriot when renewing a tenancy; both were bound to grind their grain in the lord's mill; they were bound to render eggs at Easter and chickens at Christmas to the lord. Both kinds of tenant enjoyed (at a price) the right to graze their pigs in the lord's woods in winter, and to gather their firewood there. In theory even the unfree tenants were protected by custom against undue exploitation by their lords, and could not, for example be deprived of their holdings without good reason, such as failure to pay rent or perform labour services. In practice these checks did not always work, and the tenants of Roger of Chirk were particularly aggrieved about his arbitrary actions.[15]

The 14th century saw a marked trend in the Mortimer estates towards the commutation of labour services into money payments. This was partly due to the increasingly absentee nature of the lords themselves, which meant that the estates became primarily a source of income for the wider lordship, making money more desirable than goods and services. By 1324, all services at Wigmore had been commuted to money payments, often with indicative names such as 'reap-silver' and 'plough-silver'.[16] This process was further increased by the disastrous effects of the plagues of the mid-14th century, which drastically affected the size of the workforce. In the case of the Mortimer holdings on the March, this was often exacerbated by the devastation caused by Glyn Dŵr's rebels in the early years of the following century.

The consequent spread of wage-labour was rapid in the second half of the 14th century. In Kingsland, 206 ploughing works, extra days labour which would formerly have been compulsory for tenants, were sold at 4d. each in 1392-3; at Troy in the lordship of Usk, 116 weeding and 178 ploughing works were sold in 1409-19; and the Stanton Lacy accounts for 1388 include payments for harrowing, ditching, threshing, winnowing, mowing, sheep-shearing and a range of other agricultural tasks.[17]

The process whereby the customary tenant came to pay rent for his land and to receive wages for his labour, did not automatically make those tenants free. The end of villeinage had, indeed, been a major demand of Wat Tyler's rebels in 1381. Many landowners, including the Mortimers, resisted the trend, and in 1391 Roger (VI)'s council delivered a stinging rebuke to the bailiff of Odcombe in Somerset who had let a villein tenement to a freeman.[18] Despite rearguard actions such as this, the demise of villeinage was inevitable in the changing conditions of later medieval society.

A further dramatic change in the system of tenure which occurred at this period was the leasing of demesne lands. In 1334 the demesnes of Norton and Pembridge had been largely leased, and in 1340 the demesnes and the stock of the manor of Radnor had been let out in return for a charge of every third sheaf of corn harvested. By 1382 the whole demesne of Pilleth had been leased, while at Eardisland it had been let as small plots. In 1414 the 374 acres of demesne arable at Kingsland were leased at an annual rent of £9 7s. 3d.[19] The leasing of demesne was not confined to the Mortimer estates in the March. In the great Clare estates which passed to Edmund (III) in 1368 on the death of Lionel, duke of Clarence, the process had been well under way in 1360, and by 1400 all demesne lands had passed out of the lord's immediate possession.[20] This process dramatically ended the traditional pattern of manorial farming, and encouraged the development of a new class of independent tenant farmers who leased substantial holdings. This in turn aided the rapid decline of villeinage.

The Personnel of the Lordship

By the 14th century, when written records become more plentiful about the management of the Mortimer estates, the vast accumulation of lands in the family's possession were increasingly being run on highly organised lines, with all income and expenditure carefully accounted for. Such a process required a fairly integrated heirarchy of officials from the lord's council down to the local officers such as the reeves who collected the rents in the individual manors. It is fortunate that during the long periods when the Mortimer estates were in the hands of the Crown, there was considerable continuity in both personnel and practice with the periods when the family were in control. It is thus possible for a fairly clear picture of the organisation of the estates to be obtained.

The Mortimer lords were served by a circle of friends and advisers who served on the lord's council and witnessed documents, and acted in various legal capacities. It is fairly easy to discover the identities of these close associates by examining the various trusts created during the period. In 1359, Roger (V) created a use by granting lands to William of Wykeham, bishop of Winchester; Ralph Spigurnel; John de Bishopston; John Laundels and John Gower. A similar trust created by Edmund (III) before his departure for Ireland in 1373 consisted of William Lord Latimer of Danby; Richard Lescrop; Nicholas de Carreu; Peter de la Mare; John de Bishopston and Walter de Colmpton, clerks. Both groups consist of a combination of friends such as the bishop and the two northern magnates, Latimer and Lescrop, and professional servants such as the earl's steward, de la Mare, and the clerks Bishopston and Colmpton.

A significant number of these close associates of the Mortimer earls in the 14th century were indentured retainers who had agreed to serve in their various capacities in return for payment, generally in the form of annuities. This was the beginning of the system of so-called 'bastard feudalism' which became notorious during the Wars of the Roses in the 15th century. A number of the indentures whereby they were retained have survived, and contain information about a selection of Mortimer retainers during the period.[21]

Edmund (III) retained several knights, including Sir John de Bromwich, who had transferred from the Clare estates; Sir Ralph de Lingen, a Herefordshire tenant; and Sir Peter de la Mare. De la Mare's indentures have not survived, but he is known to have been indentured. He held the important position of steward to the earl, and his parliamentary career has already been noted.[22] There were a further six esquires, including Hugh Cheyney, who subsequently became a knight, and Richard Botirall, who held the largely honorific posts of constable, keeper and parker of Wigmore at a fee of 10d. per day. Among the professional administrators were two clerks, William Forde, and the auditor, Thomas Hildburgh, both of whom later occupied important positions in the Mortimer household. Annual salaries ranged from £66 13s. 4d for Sir John de Bromwich to £3 7s. 6d. for Hildburgh, who was at a fairly early stage in his career.

Professional administrators played a vital part in running the vast complex of Mortimer estates, which by the late 14th century extended from East Anglia to Ireland, and from Denbigh to Devon. The best documented of these is Walter Brugge, presumably a Bridgnorth man, who served the lordship for a quarter of a century prior to his death in 1396, becoming receiver-general for the whole lordship during the 1380s. His work involved oversight of the estates as a whole, particularly their financial management, as well as acting as a leading member of the lord's council. Like other officials, Brugge served the Crown when the estates were in wardship, and the earl when he was in control of his own properties. In a period when the lord was absent from his estates for prolonged periods, often in France or Ireland, it was essential to have a competent executive officer to co-ordinate the business of the lordship.

Walter Brugge was tireless in his progresses through the scattered Mortimer estates, often in the company of Thomas Hildburgh, the auditor. In 1386 they made a journey from Usk to Denbigh, via Caerleon, Wigmore, Ludlow and Montgomery. Other expeditions took Brugge to the former de Clare lands in East Anglia, and to Ireland.[23] In 1393 he made another extensive progress through Wales and the March, which took him from Ludlow to Usk, and thence to Clifford, where he spent Easter. He then proceeded to Builth and over the mountains to Carmarthen, and ultimately to the westernmost Mortimer estate at Narberth. He then made a private pilgrimage to St. David's before returning to Builth by way of Laugharne. In a 26 day journey that included 10 days on the road he had covered 300 miles.[24] As a cleric, he was rewarded with valuable preferments, which included a prebend's stall at St. David's, and the archdeaconry of Meath in Ireland.[25]

On these expeditions the work of local officials was inspected, and their accounts were meticulously examined, and items considered unauthorised or excessive were regularly struck out. In an earlier audit, for the years 1337-38 when the estates of Roger (V) were in wardship, auditors for Radnor and its members disallowed a range of items, including 16s. 8d. for cloth to make a mantle for the reeve of Gladestry, and the payment of 100s. to 60 men who had conveyed wool from Knighton to Harwich.[26]

Below the central officials such as Brugge and Hildburgh, the stewards of the individual lordships formed a middle-management layer, co-ordinating the work of the officials of the individual manors. They exercised considerable responsibility, and were generally drawn from the ranks of the lesser nobles, the class which by the mid-15th century would begin to be classified as gentlemen. Hugh Tyrel, to whom the management of Radnor was entrusted for seven years in February 1334 after the death of Margaret Mortimer (née de Fiennes), was styled 'king's yeoman'. He was a modest tenant land-holder with estates at Diddlebury and Sutton in Shropshire, and Sollers Dilwyn in Herefordshire. Towards the end of his term at Radnor he was involved in shipping wool to Flanders, and subsequently died abroad, presumably on royal business, in January 1343.[27]

Stewardship of a lordship could therefore be a step in the progression to higher services. An example is Sir John St. John, a member of an old Glamorgan family who, after serving as Sheriff of Glamorgan and steward of Gower, was appointed steward of the important Mortimer lordship of Usk in the 1390s. He subsequently progressed to Richard II's household, married a wealthy Northamptonshire widow, and represented that county in four successive parliaments. For several years he served as mayor of Bordeaux.[28] Another example of a steward who advanced to greater things was John Gour or Gower, who was steward of Radnor in 1360, and subsequently became a valued member of the lord's council.

Senior officials such as these were mostly, but not exclusively, English. Philip ap Morgan, the son of a gentry family from south-east Wales, is an exceptional example of a talented Welshman who achieved high office under the Mortimers. He rose successively through the stewardships of Usk in 1385, Clifford and Glasbury in 1388, to be appointed to the major lordship of Denbigh in 1394. In 1397 he was appointed to the council of Roger (VI), and in that year made at least three journeys to Ireland on his lord's business.[29] Another talented Welshman whose career was impressively assisted by Mortimer patronage was the chronicler, Adam of Usk, who was sponsored through Oxford University by Edmund (III).

The steward was the lord's personal representative, whose work included regular tours of the districts for which he was responsible. When the lord was absent, the steward was required to preside in his place over the various judicial bodies in his locality. These included the Great Court; the lesser courts such as the Hall-Moot (known as the foreign court in the Welshries); the forest court; the borough courts, where such existed; and the Days of March, where disputes with other lordships were mediated. These hearings incurred expenses, £12. 15s. 8d. in Radnor in 1336-7, which had to be met from the revenues of the lordship.[30] In addition to these judicial functions, the steward was responsible for the detailed supervision of the local officials under his control.

Each lordship also employed a receiver, whose role was purely financial, who was responsible for drawing the mass of accounts from the local officials into a unified whole. The Mortimers operated a particularly rigorous system, which was sometimes double-checked by teams of roving auditors. They were salaried, with their remuneration related to the size of their responsibilities. The receiver of Dolforwyn received $3^{1}/_{2}$d. per day; John de Haven, receiver for the more important lordship of Radnor was paid £9 2s. per year, with a robe worth 20s. in 1335-6; the receiver of the more important lordship of Trellech was paid £25 15s. 6d.[31] In addition to the steward and the receiver, most lordships also employed an escheator, who was required to manage the growing number of holdings which were in minority.

At grass roots level there were a range of lesser officials with particular responsibilities for administering specialised areas of the work of the manor. Most of these were also required to render accounts of their expenses, and of the revenues which they had raised. In the English manors, the bailiff and the reeve were the main officials. The bailiff or catchpole, who was responsible to the steward and the receiver, had both judicial and financial responsibilities. He was charged with maintaining law and order, assisted the steward in the courts, and delivered summonses and executed judgements. His financial responsibilities included the collection of all revenue which was not handled by the reeve, including the products of escheats, the farms of tolls and dues, and the rents of free tenants. Bailiffs were paid a wage, and could receive bonus payments if they increased the amount of revenue raised by the manor.

The reeve was basically a rent collector, with special responsibility for unfree tenants. Tenants were obliged to serve in this unpopular post for a year, during which they paid no rents and performed no customary duties, and received a wage, a food and drink allowance, and a robe. The wage of the reeve of Radnor in 1336-7 was a mere seven shillings. During his year of office the reeve had to give up his holding, and was not always sure of payment. In 1339 the non-payment of Philip de Klanrowe, reeve of Glasbury, led to an inquiry.[32]

In the Welshries different officials performed similar functions as the steward, bailiff and reeve in the English manors. The chief resident official was the *rhaglaw*, often referred to as the constable in the Mortimer Welshries, though his role was that of a steward rather than a constable of a castle. The *rhaglaw* and his predecessor the *maer* had originally been partly paid out of a rent obtained in oats, which still survived in the 14th centuries in some places as the *kylch* or *kylchmaer* which raised 12s. 8d. in Maelienydd in 1336-7. The *rhaglaw*, like the steward, was the lord's representative in the lordship, but the office was becoming more honorific than that of its English counterpart. The *rhaglaw* had authority over the *rhingyll* or bailiff, and the Welsh reeve. It is possible that the *rhingyll* dealt with the free tenants and the reeve with the bondsmen, but there is little known of their relative responsibilities. In the lord-ships of Maelienydd and Radnor the reeve was superior to the *rhingyll*, and in some manors such as Clifford and Glasbury the oat render was used to support the *rhingyll* rather than the *rhaglaw*.[33] By the 14th century the offices of reeve and *rhingyll* in the lordship of Denbigh had lost their role of rent collection, which had been farmed out.

Other local officials who rendered accounts included those who were responsible for the forests and parks. The forester of Radnor was paid 14d. weekly, or 60s. 8d. per year in 1335-6, and a forester who increased the revenue of the lordship could receive handsome bonuses. In 1336-7, Roger Perkins, the forester of Maelienydd was given a reward of 30s. 4d., half his annual salary, at the special order of Sir Ralph Spigurnell.[34] The payment of 5s. as salary to the parker at Radnor in 1336-7, suggests that, like the reeve, who was paid slightly more, the parker received other remuneration in addition to his salary.[35]

The Economic Life of the Lordships

The great collection of territories which made up the Mortimer lordships existed for the primary purpose of generating income for their lord. This was done in a variety of ways. Rents were obviously a vital source of income from the landed estates, to which must be added the multiplicity of fines and dues which tenants were required to pay. As the 14th century progressed, many parts of the estates became involved in the process of trade, particularly the export of wool, which further augmented the revenue of the lordship. The daily commercial life of towns in particular raised considerable amounts of money in the form of tolls, while the proceeds of the courts held in both rural areas and towns produced considerable sums. There were, of course expenses which had to be set against revenue, and these included salaries and wages for the various officials, the repair of buildings and equipment, as well as equipping expedi-tions to Ireland or France, and in general supporting the lavish and increasingly absentee lifestyle of the Mortimer lords.

The main elements of the Lordship — the Manor and other holdings

The manor was the basic economic unit in the rural areas. As noted previously, the number of customary tenants who held their lands in return for labour services had declined by 1300, and this decline was set to accelerate during the following century. Where customary tenants existed, they often rented land in addition to that which they held by labour services, such as the two villeins in the Mortimer manor of Stratfield Saye (Hampshire) whose rents and labour services were valued at 16s. in 1304.[36] Free tenants paid rents, but were also liable to pay a range of dues. Marriage dues were paid on the wedding of a tenant's daughter, and if she became pregnant out of wedlock, her father was liable to pay 'leyrwites', a tax on sexual incontinence.

If these payments, and those mentioned on p.149 were not enough, the tenants were also liable to other contributions to the Mortimer coffers. They were obliged to have their corn ground in the lord's mills, and as these were an area of the manor which required almost continuous repair and maintenance, such costs would have been passed on to the users in charges. Whenever the tenants were convicted in the Court Baron or another local court of an offence such as allowing their cattle on to cultivated ground, the fine would be added to the revenue of the lord.

The Mortimer lands were a vast and scattered inheritance, and an examination of the Inquisition Post Mortem of Roger (V)[37] reveals their sheer extent. Roger held property in no less than 28 English counties, all of which lay to the south of a line from Shrewsbury to the Wash. In all that area only Leicestershire, Warwickshire, Rutland and Middlesex (excluding London) contained no Mortimer possessions. It is true that away from the family heartlands in the March, manors were often scattered, with an average of less than five in most counties. However, even in counties such as Cambridge and Huntingdon, where there were comparatively few Mortimer manors, the family owned the proceeds of a number of local courts, such as those at Royston, Meldreth and Great Gransden. They also owned the advowson of a significant number of churches throughout the country, which gave them the right of presentation to the living, and its revenues during a vacancy.

The most numerous Mortimer possessions were, however, knights' fees. Originally granted as small estates for military tenants as noted earlier in this chapter,[38] over the years they had been amalgamated and sub-divided to a bewildering extent. Thus the land formerly held by William de Loversete at Idshall (Shifnal) in Shropshire amounted to one fiftieth of a knight's fee in 1398. This would have produced two shillings in annual rent. In Dorset subdivision was very common, with one eighteenth or one nineteenth of a fee being usual. This must have caused the stewards considerable inconvenience when calculating and collecting rents across the county. The number of knights' fees was considerable. Shropshire and Herefordshire, with their adjacent marches both averaged 50, many of which had become divided, but this number is not surprising in view of the early history of the area, when military support was crucial to the lord. The former Clare lands in eastern and southern England, however, contained many more knights' fees: 81 in Suffolk, and 63 in Norfolk, with similar numbers in Dorset.

Forests and Parks

Forests and parks formed a significant, if localised, feature of the Mortimer lordship. The forest of Radnor was the greatest in extent, with subsidiary woods at Northwood, Ackwood, Comergan, Badland, Hellehelde and Radnorshelde. Smaller woods existed in Maelienydd, while in England there were extensive forests at Wyre in the Cleobury lordship, and in the area around Wigmore.

Forests were a source of venison and the pleasures of the chase, which in parts of Maeliennydd had even been open to the inhabitants before 1297.[39] In 1337, the accounts of the lordship of Radnor, which was then in wardship, contain a payment of 110s. for sending the king's venison to London.[40] The forests would originally have had a primary role in supplying the castles of the lordship with meat, and an important secondary function as a source of revenue. Initially this had taken the form of dues for pannage or for collecting firewood, and particularly fines levied on those whose livestock had wandered into the forest and been impounded. By the 14th century, forests were being managed on an increasingly commercial basis, with the leasing of grazing and the sale of wood. It became increasingly common for forest land to be leased, and the passing of the traditional forest management is clearly shown in the accounts of Maelienydd in 1356-7, where dues for wood, underwood and wild honey could not be collected as the woodland had been let to the Abbey of Cwmhir.[41]

The creation of enclosed deer parks had been common in the 13th and 14th centuries, though they declined rapidly thereafter.[42] The Mortimer estates contained a significant number of parks, which were spread throughout their holdings. Despite draconian laws, parks were a prey to poaching, particularly in times of unrest, or when the lord was absent. Occasionally these incidents were sufficiently serious to demand action by the authorities. In 1315 commissions of oyer and terminer were ordered to find those who had broken into the parks of Roger of Chirk at Cleobury and Tedstone Wafre, and Roger (IV) of Wigmore at Leintwardine and Arley, Staffordshire, and hunted deer without a licence. It is not known if the perpetrators were apprehended.[43]

It is possible that such abuses led at least in part to the decline of parks. The park of Radnor contained no deer as early as 1304,[44] and was let in 1335 and 1356. The park at Pembridge was similarly let to John de Mersstone for £3 in 1356-7.[45] Certainly by 1398, when Edmund, the brother of Roger (VI) was noted as chief forester and keeper of the chase of Cranborne, and chief surveyor of the parks of Blakedon and Alreholt, also in Dorset, the position had become honorific, and very different from the post of Roger Perkins, forester of Radnor earlier in the century.[46]

Boroughs

The towns also represented a significant aspect of the economy of the Mortimer lordships, and have been described by a noted Welsh historian as 'the lordship in its trading capacity'.[47] The ground in boroughs was rented out in standard burgage plots, for which a rent of 12d. per year was normally charged. Burgage rents were not, however, the most important source of revenue produced by boroughs. Tolls of markets and fairs, and the proceeds of the borough courts could add considerably to the wealth of a lordship if the town was economically successful.

The Mortimer boroughs may be divided into those which were founded by the family, which receive some mention in connection with castle-building in the following chapter, and those which were acquired subsequently by marriage or by grant. The latter included some of the most successful Mortimer boroughs, while the former ranged from foundations like New Radnor, which were successful at least in the short term, to towns like Cefnllys and Knucklas which failed to develop significantly.

New Radnor, for which Roger (III) had first received a grant of murage in 1257 was clearly in a healthy state in 1304, when it boasted $262^{1/2}$ burgages, a market each Tuesday, and an annual fair on St. Luke's day.[48] Wigmore, which seems to have been in existence at Domesday, when it was valued at £7, contained $106^{1/4}$ plus $^{1/6}$ burgages in 1304, and also had a weekly market and annual fair. Knighton was roughly similar in size with $162^{1/3}$ burgages held by 126 burgesses, with Cleobury somewhat smaller at $102^{3/4}$. It is not known how many plots there were at Newtown, which had been founded by Roger (III) in 1279 and granted a market and fairs by Edward III in 1280, but its real expansion did not occur until the growth of flannel manufacturing in the 18th century. These towns were clearly performing a reasonably successful role as local market centres. Bala, established by Roger of Chirk around 1310, and granted a charter of privileges in 1324, was initially successful, with 42 of its 53 burgages occupied by the latter year. The planned town defences were never erected, and the town relied entirely upon local trade, declining steadily to an all-time low of 13 taxpayers in the 1540s.[49]

It is clear that other Mortimer foundations were struggling to survive even before the ravages of the Black Death. In 1332 there were only 20 burgesses at Cefnllys, occupying between them $26^{2/3}$ burgages.[50] Though it is not known how many plots had originally been laid out, it is clear that the borough was operating well below its potential. Knucklas was too small to be given a mention as a town in 1332, and although it was still styled as a borough in the 17th century, it can never have progressed much beyond its foundation.[51]

Some of the most successful Mortimer boroughs were those which they acquired through marriage or royal grants, the most striking example of which is Ludlow. The origins of the borough of Ludlow have long been a matter of controversy, but it would seem almost certain that the de Lacy family began the establishment of the town in its final form some time shortly after 1150. The growth of the wool trade, as well as the presence of a major castle, stimu-

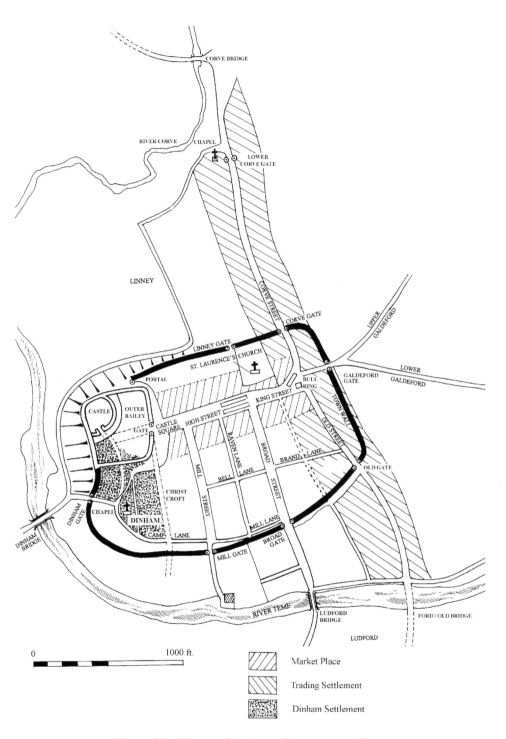

Plan of Ludlow and its immediate surroundings

lated the economic and administrative development of the borough, which by the mid-13th century was exhibiting most of the commercial and institutional features of a successful borough, although it did not receive a royal charter until 1461. Medieval Ludlow had more than 500 burgages, although it is likely that some, on the outskirts of the town, were never built upon. When the town walls, with six strong gateways, were built some time around 1260, they did not accommodate the whole of the built-up area, instead following a convenient contour line. This effectively created extensive extra-mural 'suburbs'.[52] The great size of the parish church of St. Lawrence, which occupies the most prominent position in the town, clearly reflects Ludlow's wealth and importance in the 14th and 15th centuries. The accession of the Mortimer heir to the throne as Edward IV in 1461 brought even greater prominence to the town in the following two centuries, when it developed as the administrative and judicial centre for the whole of Wales.

The Burgess Gate, one of the gateways into the walled town of Denbigh

The only other borough acquired by the Mortimers which rivalled Ludlow in size was Denbigh. This also was a de Lacy foundation, which had been established after 1282, with 47 burgage plots enclosed by walls containing two gates. Following destruction by the Welsh in 1294, the defences were considerably strengthened, particularly by the construction of a complex system of defences based on the Goblin Tower.[53] The original site of the walled town was too cramped and inconvenient for commercial life, and the town began to expand rapidly on the lowland site below the castle. In 1303 there were 183 burgages outside the walls compared with 52 within them, and by 1373 there were no less that 438 burgages in a new town outside the walls covering 57 acres. By the 17th century the walled town had become regarded as the outer ward of the castle.[54]

In the south, Usk and Trellech, which had been acquired by Edmund (III) in 1368 on the death of his father-in-law Lionel, duke of Clarence, were substantial towns, though not on the same scale as Ludlow and Denbigh. Usk had been a Clare borough, which appears to have been founded at the start of the 12th century. By 1262 there were 141 burgages. Although Usk was devastated in the wars of the late 13th century, with 180 burgages destroyed and large areas of the town left vacant, it recovered to the extent of having 269 occupied burgages in 1314.[55] Attempts at recovery were undone by further destruction by Glyn Dŵr's followers in 1402 and 1405, and by the 16th century much of the old town had converted to agriculture. Trellech, in the same lordship, was another sizeable borough which declined steadily from the end of the 14th century until 1900. Like Usk, it was burnt in 1296, but there were still 265 burgages in occupation in 1314. A year after being acquired by the Mortimers it was hit by plague, and began a steady process of decline, which was not reversed until the last century.[56] A third town in the lordship of Usk was Caerleon, formerly a Roman legionary fortress, where a medieval town was destroyed by the Welsh in 1231. Its privileges were confirmed by charters of 1324 and 1359, but relatively little is known of its history.[57] In 1324 the value of rents was 102 shillings, and there was a weekly market and annual fair.[58] Unlike Usk and Trellech, Caerleon seems to have escaped subsequent serious decline, and to have survived as a relatively prosperous market town.

The value of the lordship
It has been calculated that at the end of the 14th century, the Mortimer estates in Wales produced an annual income of around £2,750, at a time when half that sum was considered adequate to support the lifestyle of an earl.[59] This excluded the revenue from the considerable possessions which the family held in England, as well as their vast Irish estates. A valuation made in 1398 of the Welsh estates, to calculate the dower of the countess Eleanor, produced a total of £2,345, but did not include the lordships of Radnor, Gwerthrynion, and Narberth. Denbigh was the most valuable lordship at £904, followed by Usk and Caerleon at £467. Maelienydd was valued at £334; Builth, which the Mortimers held in farm from the crown was worth £200; while Wigmore was the least valued, being worth a mere £120. Previous valuations give a value of £94 for Narberth in 1366, and £314 for Radnor and Gwerthrynion in 1379.[60]

It is possible to gain information on the nature of some of this revenue from an examination of the accounts which survive from periods when the states were in crown hands during periods of minority. These include accounts from the lordships of Radnor and Maelienydd, published by Cole in the *Transactions of the Radnorshire Society*, and for Denbigh, Usk and the Somerset manors which have been analysed by Holmes. The Radnor accounts for 1335-6 show a number of interesting features. The total income for the year was £779 2s. 9¾d., with expenses of £540 17s. 7d., which left a net profit of £238 5s. 2¾d. By far the largest item of revenue were the perquisites of the various courts, which raised £264 19s. 9½d., or just under 34% of the total gross revenue of the lordship. This total conceals massive differences between the different courts, as Ceri raised £157 9s. compared with only £2 1s. from Pembridge, which is odd in view of other evidence of the prosperity of that manor.[61]

Rents produced a much smaller income, £113 7s. 10¼d., and were drawn from no less than 27 different sources, the largest of which was the *patria* or demesne of Pembridge £25 10s. 5d.), and the smallest was Stoke Bliss (13s. 4d.). Rents from the towns of Radnor, Knighton, Presteigne and Pembridge were included in the total. The accounts show that sources of revenue were already being let at farm, by which they were leased to the highest bidder who then collected and retained the rents. The 14 mills of the lordship were farmed for no less than £108 1s. 8d., the third largest source of revenue, and it is interesting to note that the mill of Gwerthrynion only produced 55 shillings, due to the scarcity of corn. The tolls of the boroughs of Radnor, Presteigne and Pembridge were all farmed, as were the various bailiwicks, confirming the point made earlier concerning the decline of the offices of reeve and bailiff in the Welshries. The Maelienydd accounts for 1356-7 show similar processes at work. The farming of tolls was widespread, and the collection of *leyrwites*, the fine for sexual incontinence was similarly farmed for 70 shillings. The process of letting demesne lands at farm, noted earlier in this chapter, is evident at Cefnllys, where they raised 26s. 8d.[62]

The accounts of the lordship of Denbigh show that a fairly constant annual revenue of about £1,000 was raised for most of the 14th century. A survey taken in 1334, when the lordship was still in Montacute hands, revealed that 53% of revenue came from rents, 16% from the farm of offices, and 12% from the profits of the courts, a rather different ordering from that seen in Radnor in the same decade. Despite the importance of the borough of Denbigh, it contributed a mere 3% to the income of the lordship.[63] Although there were some annual fluctuations, the 14th century was a period of considerable stability for the revenues of Denbigh. This came to a dramatic end in 1400, when the whole lordship was devastated by Glyn Dŵr. For a time income fell to almost nothing, and even in 1426 revenues were only between a half and two-thirds of their pre-1400 level.

The accounts for Usk, where English practices and institutions were far more common than in Denbigh, similar patterns may be seen, although the accounts are less complete. The profits of the central manor of Usk remained fairly constant for the first 30 years of the 14th century, with a tendency for rents to be increased when there was a change of tenant. By 1408-14, when accounts are again available, the devastation caused by the Glyn Dŵr uprising can be seen once more. Though the nominal value of the rents was over £56, the actual sum raised was £30 less, with rents having been reduced because of a lack of tenants.[64] At Troy the rents in 1376-7 and 1380-1 were very similar to those of 50 years earlier, but by 1409 they had fallen by nearly a third. The mill had been destroyed by the rebels, and the whole demesne had been farmed for a mere £6. Similar patterns may be seen in all the manors of the lordship, but what is significant is the fall in the overall income of the lordship which had taken place even before Glyn Dŵr had rebelled. The yield from the lordship had been £1,191 in 1330, had fallen to £967 six years later, and by 1398 was only £467.[65] This suggests that other factors were involved, and may in part reflect the outbreak of plague in 1369, which so affected the town of Trellech. It is significant that the plague is rarely, if ever, used to explain a fall in income, whereas the depredations of the Welsh were frequently blamed, both in the late 13th century and in the years after 1400.

An interesting comparison may be made between the situation in Usk and that in the Mortimers' Somerset manors. Here there was a significant loss of tenants due to the Black Death, but the decline in rents was offset by greatly increased entry fines when the holdings were re-let. This substantially increased the perquisites of the courts in certain years, but it is also clear that a decade or so after the Black Death rents had stabilised, and were to remain steady for the rest of the century.[66] Holmes concluded that there was no evidence of a long-term decline such as that which occurred at Usk.

So far the lordships have been considered as a source of income from rents, fines, fees and other traditional revenues. It has been seen that these experienced considerable fluctuations from time to time, and from place to place, but also that collectively they provided the Mortimers with an income which was more than sufficient to support their position as one of the greatest noble families in the kingdom. One further aspect of the family finances remains tantalisingly under-documented. This is the commercial activities which were undertaken by the estates, particularly sheep farming.

The estates of the earls of March and Arundel carried the greatest number of sheep in Wales and the Marches. Arundel owned 15,000 sheep in 1349, and possessed stocks of wool worth £2,042 in 1376.[67] Unfortunately no comparable statistics survive for the Mortimer flocks, but there are some useful references. Sheep farming would appear to have been adopted as an alternative either to demesne farming or to the letting out of manors at the end of the 14th century. In Stanton Lacy, the sale of 261 fleeces and the retention of a further 281 was noted in 1388-9, while in 1393-4, a further 300 were sold, and 177 retained. This suggests a flock of about 500 was kept in that manor.[68] Similarly in 1389 there were 231 sheep and 88 lambs at Clifford, and three years later the flock was increased by a further 300 which had been purchased at Knighton.[69] In 1337, 14 sacks of wool were exported from Radnor to Dordrecht in the Low Countries, by way of Shrewsbury and Harwich. The price, which was regulated by the crown, was £8 15s. per sack, slightly more than the price of Herefordshire wool in the same year.[70] Beyond these figures, however, little is known of what must have been a significant part of the overall economy of the lordship.

Conclusion

The Mortimer estates were both a source of considerable income and a potent symbol of the power and prestige of their lord. Their complexity required a sophisticated system of local administration to be integrated with a centralised executive, in which professional administrators like Walter Brugge exercised detailed supervision over all aspects of the vast operations under their control. It was an essentially absentee lordship by the 14th century, with the earls making only occasional appearances, such as the grand progress made by Roger (VI) in 1393 after entering into his inheritance. This 40 day journey through Wales and the Marches cost £162, but seems to have paid dividends in terms of gaining support. Even though most of the ensuing five years before Roger's death were spent in Ireland, his reception at the Shrewsbury parliament in 1398, where he was greeted by 30,000 supporters wearing his colours, suggests that the personal aspects of lordship were by no means insignificant at the close of the 14th century.

CHAPTER X

The Mortimer Castles and Boroughs

Professor Davies's study *Lordship and Society in the March of Wales* has drawn attention to the role played by the castle as the head of the lordship, and to the disproportionately large number of castles in Wales and the borders.[1] This can be taken further, for the concentration of sites along the borders of Wales contrasts markedly with the distribution in the Welsh hinterland.[2]

Castles played a crucial part in the initial conquest and settlement of Wales by the Anglo-Norman invaders. In the 13th century they frequently changed hands or were destroyed and rebuilt during the conflicts with the Welsh, which were essentially ended with the defeat and death of Llywelyn the last in 1282, and the conquest of Wales by Edward I — although the half dozen or so years of crisis during the rising led by Glyn Dŵr must not be ignored. Although one of the most formidable of the Mortimer castles, Chirk, was built in the immediate aftermath of Edward I's conquest, and Ludlow was transformed in the 14th century, many of the castles of the marcher lords fell into disrepair after 1300, and those of the Mortimers were no exception. Some had advanced too far in their decay to be pressed into service in the Glyn Dŵr years, though others were hastily repaired and garrisoned.

The expansion of the Mortimer territories was accompanied by the building and acquisition of castles, the latter becoming particularly important as the process of expansion advanced. Some of the castles so acquired, notably through judicious marriages, such as Radnor and Ludlow, were substantially rebuilt by their Mortimer owners. Others like Denbigh and Montgomery came to the Mortimers fully modernised, and their building history owes little to the family. It is unfortunate that with the exception of Chirk and Ludlow, and to a lesser extent Wigmore, most Mortimer building work has long been destroyed, so that some of the most spectacular castles, such as Radnor and Cefnllys, have little to show apart from their impressive earthworks. It is also unfortunate that virtually nothing in the way of building accounts has survived, other than entries for routine repairs at a number of castles during the 14th century.

The Mortimer castles — a chronology

The Domesday holdings of Ralph Mortimer in the Welsh borders centred upon the two main manors of Wigmore and Cleobury. Wigmore had previously been held by William FitzOsbern, and had been granted to Ralph Mortimer some time after an unsuccessful coup attempt against the king in which FitzOsbern's son had been implicated. It was stated in Domesday to have been built on waste land called *Merestun*, and as FitzOsbern had been killed in Flanders in 1071, the founding of the castle may be confidently dated between 1067 and 1071.[3] The site chosen for the castle was a long and narrow ridge running down from higher land to the north-west, which strategically overlooked the old Roman road from Chester to Caerleon, then still a major route.

The central manor of Wigmore was surrounded on all sides by a cluster of vills, 16 of which were held by Ralph as his own demesne or personal estate, and 13 of which were held by followers. It has been noted that the vills held by sub-tenants form a protective swathe around the north and west of Wigmore, and that these contained the sites of at least 11 subsidiary castles, generally castle mounds or mottes with or without adjacent enclosures or baileys.[4] Wigmore may well have started out as a motte and bailey castle with wooden palisades, but by the siege of 1155 at least some of the defences would have been of stone.

A similar arrangement of subsidiary manors may be observed in the vicinity of Cleobury, although it is noticeable that being situated in more settled lands some 20 miles to the east of Wigmore, there was less need for subsidiary fortifications. Little is known about Cleobury Castle, as its life was remarkably short. Hugh (II) came into conflict with Henry II shortly after he succeeded to the throne (see pp.33-34) and Cleobury Castle, which together with Wigmore and Bridgnorth had been fortified against Henry, was captured and destroyed in 1155 and was not rebuilt afterwards. It is not known whether there were any stone buildings on the site.

Pilleth was an outlier on the western flank of the Wigmore lordship, where the earthwork known as Y Foel Allt may be a castle erected by Ralph Mortimer sometime after 1086. There is, however, only one known documentary reference, which occurs as late as 1341 when it was the residence of the dowager lady of Wigmore.[5]

Mortimer expansion into mid-Wales was marked by the building of new castles and the refortifying of others captured from the Welsh. The lands of the southern part of Powys known as 'Rhwng Gwy a Hafren' ('Between Wye and Severn') were ruled in the 11th and 12th centuries by descendants of Elystan Glodrudd, a leading Welsh magnate of the 10th century who was reputed to have been the godson of the Saxon king Athelstan. This divided principality was fair game for the neighbouring Anglo-Norman families such as the Mortimers and the de Braoses, and incursions were made into this part of

Pilleth Castle, or Y Foel Allt

central Wales from an early date. In 1093/4 Ralph Mortimer defended his early gains by constructing a castle at Dineithion,[6] and it is possible that the motte and bailey castle known as the Old Mount at Cwm, south of Crossgates, was this castle.[7] At the same time he constructed a larger motte and bailey castle at Cymaron, on a bluff above the River Aran. Both these castles changed hands a number of times in the following decades, and both were destroyed between 1134 and 1136 during a major Welsh uprising led by Madog ab Idnerth, the leading Welsh lord in Maelienydd, which runs up against the eastern bank of the Wye in Rhwng Gwy a Hafren. Diniethion was possibly rebuilt by the Welsh after this, but seems to have fallen out of use by the end of the 12th century. Cymaron was rebuilt by Hugh (I) in 1144, but appears to have passed in and out of Welsh hands. When Cadwallon, the son of Madog ab Idnerth was murdered by some Mortimer followers in 1179, a bitter feud ensued between the Mortimers and Cadwallon's brothers, which finally ended with the expulsion of Cadwallon's sons from Cymaron in 1195. The Mortimers then held the castle until it was destroyed by Llywelyn ab Iorwerth and Bishop Giles de Braose of Hereford in 1215.[8]

The Mortimers also gained possession of the castles of Knighton and Norton in the eastern part of the area. These had been part of the lands of the Chandos family, who were descended from Hugh the Ass, a follower of William the Conqueror. Following an unsuccessful rebellion by Roger Chandos against Henry II in 1186, they had come into the hands of the crown, and were granted to Roger Mortimer (II) in 1207. They were not finally confirmed until

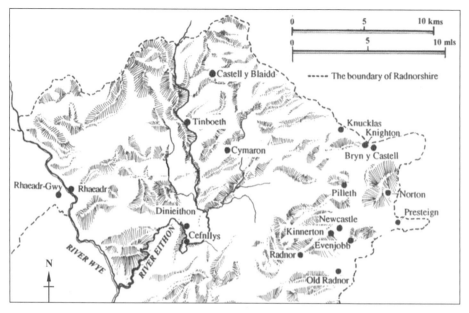

Map of the northern part of Radnorshire showing the location of Mortimer castles, together with others in the vicinity

1230, after which they remained firmly in Mortimer hands.[9] A further addition was at Rhayader, which may have been built about 1200 by the Mortimers as a replacement for the Welsh castle of Gwerthrynion, formerly a possession of the Lord Rhys. It was captured by the Welsh in 1202, but there are no further documentary references until 1307, when it was described as the site of a castle.[10]

The early 1240s was a period of difficulty for the Welsh, with Dafydd, son of Llywelyn the Great, barely being able to hold on to his titular leadership, and being forced to make disadvantageous terms with Henry III in 1241. It is not surprising that the Mortimers took advantage of this period of Welsh weakness to tighten their hold on Maelienydd and erected castles at Cefnllys in the west, and at Knucklas in the east. That at Cefnllys was begun some time prior to 1246, to replace the earlier motte at Dineithion, for following the death of Ralph (II) in that year, the crown appointed custodians of Cefnllys, Wigmore and Knucklas. It is possible that references in the Welsh chronicles to the strengthening of a castle in Maelienydd in 1242 by Ralph Mortimer may refer to improvements at Cefnllys,[11] which A.E. Brown, writing in the *Transactions of the Radnorshire Society* in 1972, identified with the northern castle on the ridge. The castle at Knucklas was apparently also built between 1242 and 1246, probably on the site of an iron age hill-fort. It consisted of a small square masonry tower, with circular angle turrets. Knucklas had a very short life, as it does not appear to have been rebuilt after its destruction by Llywelyn in 1262,[12] and was not included in the list of Mortimer castles confiscated in 1322.

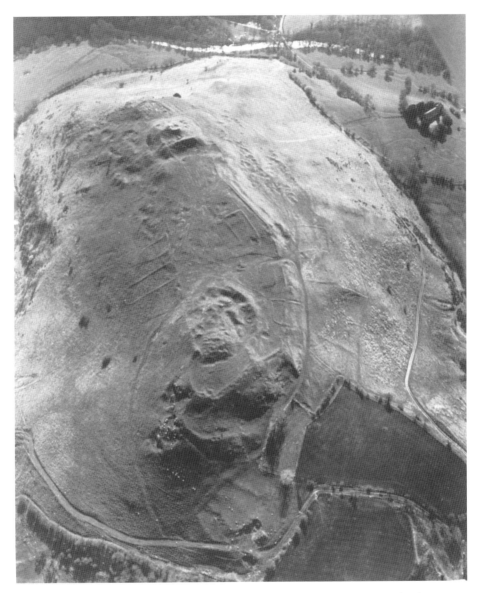

Looking south-west along the ridge on which Cefnllys was built.
The church is on the top right of the picture

The marriage of Roger (III) to Maud de Braose brought further castles into Mortimer possession, including Presteigne, which was destroyed by Llywelyn in 1262, and not subsequently rebuilt, and the major stronghold of Radnor. Ralph (II) had held the lordship and castle of Radnor in custody for the de Braoses as early as 1235, but it was not until 1252 that the de Braose inheritance was formally partitioned by the 'abbot' of Pershore between the three

Aerial view of the site of Knucklas Castle

heiresses.[13] This brought Radnor permanently into Mortimer hands, and the castle played a major role in the wars against Llywelyn ap Gruffydd.

In 1256 Llywelyn, having moved south from Gwynedd, seized Gwerthrynion contrary to the terms of the 1241 truce, thus incurring the enmity of Roger (III). The local situation then became subordinate to the conflicts between Henry III and the adherents of Simon de Montfort, which allowed the Welsh to wreak destruction in the Mortimer lands without reprisal. In April 1260, Knighton was sacked and the castle of Builth fell. Despite a truce in 1261, in the following year the Welsh of Maelienydd rose up and besieged Cefnllys. While waiting for Cefnllys to fall, Llywelyn pressed on and captured Knucklas, Presteigne, Knighton and Norton. The situation had become so desperate that Roger's forces at Cefnllys were compelled to surrender and take advantage of a safe conduct to Wigmore.

In 1263 Mortimer troops inflicted a reverse on the Welsh near Abergavenny, and, with the help of Prince Edward, expelled them from Brycheiniog, which was then granted to Roger as the de Braose heir. The situation was further complicated when England slipped into full-scale civil war, in which Roger alone among the marcher lords supported the king against de Montfort. In 1264 Llywelyn, aided by Gruffydd ap Gwenwynwen of Powys, success-fully destroyed Radnor, the last Mortimer castle in mid-Wales. The English were unable to remedy this situation until after the defeat of de Montfort at Evesham in August 1265, and in 1267 Llywelyn made peace with Henry III at Montgomery. The terms were substantially the same as those which he had agreed with the rebels two years earlier, and included the retention of Cefnllys by Roger, pending an adjudication of the rival claims of Llywelyn, which never took place. A clause in the treaty which allowed the repair of Cefnllys was apparently exploited by Roger to include the erection of a completely new fortification at the southern end of the ridge.

In 1267 the crown recaptured Builth, and began an extensive reconstruction. Builth, which later became a Mortimer possession (1327-1330; 1359-1425), was a royal castle, and was the first of Edward I's chain of fortifications designed finally to subdue the Welsh. Building work took five years, and was carried out under the supervision of Master Henry, one of Master James of St. George's assistants.[14] The structure consisted of a great tower, stone curtain walls to both inner and outer baileys, with six towers and a strong gateway to the former.[15]

At some time after 1260, a new Mortimer castle was built at Tinboeth, in the parish of Llananno, possibly as a replacement for Cymaron. This castle is also known as Dinbaud (Maud's Castle), suggesting that Maud (de Braose), the widow of Roger (III), may have been the builder. It is recorded that the castle was garrisoned by five horse and 30 foot in 1282-3, but it largely disappears from the records after 1322. It was a polygonal structure of stone, with a strong gate tower, set within impressive earthworks.[16]

The wars with Llywelyn ap Gruffydd led to the Mortimers acquiring further important castles. In the 1260s Llywelyn had obtained Ceri and Cedewain as he extended his influence southwards, and in 1273 he had built, or possibly reconstructed, a fortress and small town at Dolforwyn in order to consolidate

Tinboeth showing the one surviving piece of masonry
of the polygonal structure

The south-western walls at Dolforwyn

his gains. He had then advanced into Shropshire, as well as southwards to Brecon and Glamorgan, largely to try to stop the building of the massive de Clare castle at Caerphilly. The seriousness of these incursions was, however, eclipsed by his persistent refusal to do homage to the new king, Edward I, which led to the outbreak of full-scale war in 1277. In one facet of the campaign Roger (III) advanced from Montgomery with reinforcements under Henry de Lacy, earl of Lincoln, and laid siege to Dolforwyn. After a 10 day siege the castle surrendered, possibly due to the failure of its water supply, and it was then occupied by a Mortimer garrison while Roger proceeded to relieve Builth. As a reward for his services, the king granted Roger Mortimer the lands of Ceri and Cedewain including Dolforwyn Castle. Ten days later he was also granted a charter which allowed him to hold weekly markets and an annual fair at Llanfair in Cedewain, which soon became the 'New Town in Cedewain', eclipsing the proto-borough at Dolforwyn.[17]

The killing of Llywelyn by some Mortimer troops at Cilmeri near Builth (see pp.73-74) resulted in the granting of the lands of Llywelyn Fychan, lord of Powys Fadog in north-east Wales as a reward to Roger, the third son of Roger (III) of Wigmore, who founded the short-lived branch of the Mortimers of Chirk.[18] Here Roger set about the construction of a major new castle to serve as the *caput* of his new lordship. Rather than rebuilding the old castle near the parish church, mentioned in the Pipe Rolls in 1165 and 1212, Roger chose a new site to the west of the village, on high ground above the River Ceiriog.

Frustratingly, there are no records of the building like those which survive for Builth, but stylistically it is related so closely to the Edwardian castles of North Wales that it seems likely that Edward I's master-mason, Master James of St. George, was the designer. Traditionally the castle is said to have been finished by 1310, though there are suggestions that it was never fully completed.[19] Chirk remained in Mortimer hands for a very short period, as the family were never able to regain possession after it was confiscated in 1330 (see p.132).

Chirk was the last major fortress to be constructed by the Mortimers, as the threat from the Welsh was considerably lessened by Edward's pacification of the country. By the last quarter of the 13th century, conditions on the English side of the border had become sufficiently secure to allow the building of great houses like Stokesay and Acton Burnell, whose fortifications would have deterred few serious enemies. At some time in the early 14th century a major scheme of reconstruction was begun at Wigmore, which effectively trans-formed the castle from a fortress into a fortified palace. These works, which will be considered in more detail below, included the rebuilding of the shell keep, gatehouse and mural towers, and the construction of a new hall block and other domestic buildings in the inner bailey.

The dramatic expansion of Mortimer estates during the 14th century was accompanied by the acquisition of further important castles. The marriage of Roger (IV) to the de Lacy heiress, Joan de Genevile, brought the great fortress of Ludlow into the family's possession. Unlike Wigmore, Ludlow had been a masonry castle from its very inception, and had undergone many reconstruc-tions and extensions, particularly during the 12th century. In the years prior

The northern walls of the inner bailey at Ludlow Castle,
with the garderobe tower prominent to the left of centre,
and the three windows of the hall block to its right

Denbigh Castle: The Red Tower and remains of the 1282 curtain wall

to its acquisition by the Mortimers there had been a programme of rebuilding the domestic quarters similar to that which was taking place at Wigmore. The work at Ludlow effectively transformed the castle into an opulent palace, anticipating, at least in concept, the even more extravagant works undertaken by John of Gaunt at Kenilworth later in the century. Even if it had not been fully completed, it would have provided a fitting setting for the entertainment of Edward III and his mother as they passed through on their way into Wales in September 1329. It has traditionally been accepted that Wigmore was eclipsed by Ludlow in the 14th century, but even at Ludlow the family were hardly more than occasional visitors. An increasing amount of time was being spent at court, at war in France, on diplomatic missions, or managing the family interests in Ireland. As the family grew in importance nationally, they had less time to spend in their marcher homeland.

When Roger (IV) was in virtual control of England between 1326 and 1330, he was granted important estates by his alleged mistress, Queen Isabella. These included the great castles of Montgomery and Denbigh, with their associated walled towns. Montgomery had undergone strengthening and improvement between 1279 and 1288, and had been provided with a new hall and domestic buildings at a cost of £100. Following the fall of Roger (IV) in 1330, the castle

remained in crown hands with William FitzWarin as constable until 1355. It was restored to Roger (V) in 1359, and remained in the family's hands for a further century. The buildings had been allowed to fall into decay while in crown hands, and the Mortimer contribution to the castle buildings took the form of repairs to the curtain wall of the middle ward, and the almost complete rebuilding of the Well Tower.[20]

Denbigh was a new foundation which was commenced in 1282, when the lordship had been granted to Henry de Lacy. Master James of St. George is known to have been present at Denbigh, and the great polygonal towers, including the triple-towered gatehouse, are stylistically reminiscent of Caernarfon. Denbigh was confiscated along with the other estates of Roger (IV) in 1330, and held by William de Montacute until it was recovered by Roger (V) in 1354. Building work appears to have continued under the de Montacutes, and the contribution of the Mortimers was limited to repair works such as the re-roofing of the Red Tower in 1374.[21]

The marriage of Edmund (III) to Philippa, daughter of Lionel, duke of Clarence, in 1368 brought the lordships of Usk, Caerleon, and Trellech into the hands of the Mortimers. Trellech had ceased to be habitable as early as 1306, and Caerleon was a relatively minor castle. Usk, the most important of the three, had undergone a major reconstruction prior to its acquisition by the Mortimers. It had been expected that the military role of Usk would be taken

The motte at Trellech

over by Llangibby, some three miles away, and Usk had been remodelled, probably by Elizabeth de Burgh to provide spacious accommodation. A new hall and chapel were constructed in the inner bailey, while a solar was built projecting beyond the curtain wall. In the event, Llangibby was never completed, so that the fortifications of Usk were strengthened under the Mortimers between 1368 and 1425 by the addition of a new outer curtain wall and strong gatehouse.[22]

While these major castles still played an important role in the 14th century, some of the older Mortimer strongholds decayed rapidly. This was particularly

The walls at Usk showing the projecting solar on the right

176

true of the castles of Maelienydd, which had lost much of their *raison d'étre* after the Edwardian conquest. Cymaron was abandoned after 1282 and its garrison moved to Tinboeth, although it remained the principal marcher court for Maelienydd until 1360.[23] Tinboeth itself was listed among the Mortimer properties confiscated in 1322, but there are no further documentary references until Leland in the reign of Henry VIII noted 'the great ruines of a castle called Tynbot'.[24] Knucklas was not included in the 1322 list, and by 1406 the lordship was regarded as not having a castle.[25] Only Cefnllys and New Radnor were in a defensible condition at the time of the Glyn Dŵr revolt.

Once the accommodation of a castle was no longer in regular use, the onset of decay could be rapid, especially if the maintenance of roofs and guttering was neglected. This could lead to a situation where the rooms of a castle were uninhabitable, as at Knighton, where a room had to be hired in the town for the seneschal and members of the Mortimers' council *c*.1273.[26] This did not necessarily mean that the walls of the castle were not intact, nor that it could not be put into a state of defence if required. There is also evidence of some deliberate demolition. Excavations at Dolforwyn suggested that the lead from the roofs and glass from the windows had been taken away, perhaps to nearby Montgomery. These were valuable commodities, the removal of which would have accelerated the process of decay.[27]

Contemporary statements mentioning ruin and worthlessness should be regarded with caution. Both Montgomery and Dolforwyn were described as worthless in 1398,[28] when it is clear that both were in a defensible condition. The reference relates to the lack of revenue issuing from the castle, rather than to its capital value, and should therefore be used with caution. Even Wigmore was said to be unable to maintain itself annually in 1322, which has tended to confirm the traditional picture of abandonment in favour of Ludlow. There is, however, considerable evidence that the castle was undergoing a considerable refurbishment at this period, which will be discussed later in this chapter. Even so, in 1425 it was stated that the castle 'was ruinous and of no net value',[29] and it is probable that the real decline of Wigmore dates from this period, and not from the previous century.

Those of the lesser castles which had not been allowed to fall into decay during the 14th century appear to have been kept in some sort of repair using local materials and labour. The accounts for the lordship of Maelienydd when it was in crown hands list many such minor works at New Radnor. In 1335-6, work included repairs to the roof of the court house and byre, and repairs to the well.[30] Twenty years later, work at the castle at Radnor totalled 25s. 4d., and included repairing the steps of the hall with stones, releading the roof of the keep and thatching the barn, and providing new shackles for the prison.[31]

The spread of the Glyn Dŵr rebellion into central and southern Wales in 1401 required those castles that were defensible to be brought rapidly into commission, for that year Owain's forces burnt the abbey of Cwmhir and captured New Radnor Castle. Leland, writing in the 16th century, asserted that Glyn Dŵr had massacred the castle's garrison of 60 men, and this has been accepted by most subsequent writers. Indeed, the discovery of a large quantity of human remains when the church was rebuilt in 1845 was regarded as confirmation. Recently, however, this interpretation has been challenged by Geoffrey Hodges who has noted a number of inconsistencies in accounts of the events, and the fact that it is not mentioned by English chroniclers. Hodges suggests that the bones could be from an earlier and undocumented slaughter, but recognises that it is impossible to be categorical.[32]

In an attempt to reverse such losses, the king appointed Sir Hugh Burnell, who had inflicted an initial check on Glyn Dŵr near Welshpool in 1400, as commander of the castles of Montgomery, Dolforwyn and Cefnllys. The defection of Sir Edmund Mortimer to the rebels in late 1402, after his capture at the battle of Bryn Glas / Pilleth, forced the crown to strengthen its remaining hold on the Marches. Garrisons were reinforced and provisioned, with 12 archers and 30 spearmen being moved to Cefnllys where they were supplied with 8 quarters of wheat, 60 quarters of oats, a tun of wine, three tuns of ale, and 200 fish as provisions.[33] Royal troops were also placed in the Mortimer castles of Clifford and New Radnor, with 70 men being stationed in the latter castle in 1403, with a further increase in the following year. Between 1402 and 1405, almost £900 was spent on the defence of Radnor.[34]

Like Radnor, the great Mortimer fortress of Ludlow was garrisoned by the crown after Bryn Glas, initially under the command of Sir John Lovel, but who was soon replaced by the king's half-brother, Sir Thomas Beaufort. The situation in Shropshire was exacerbated when the Percies joined the rebellion in 1402, but it eased again after the royal victory at Shrewsbury in July 1403, when Beaufort was replaced as constable by a faithful Mortimer retainer, Sir Hugh Cheyney.[35] The history of Denbigh is somewhat different, as it had been held securely by the Percies who then rebelled. Whilst the castle remained intact, the borough was destroyed by burning.

The collapse of the rebellion ushered a period of comparative peace in Wales and the Marches, and a number of the Mortimer castles which had been defended against Glyn Dŵr now fell into further decline. Little is heard of Radnor after 1405, and the same is true of Dolforwyn. Wigmore appears to have declined steadily, and a survey of 1586 complains 'that the houses, buildings, and other edifices in the said castle being very much ruinous and decayed, will not without much charge be repaired'.[36]

Denbigh remained in occupation, and Ludlow actually increased in importance when the descendant of the Mortimers, Edward, earl of March took the throne as Edward IV in 1461. As well as granting the town privileges in compensation for its sufferings after the rout of Ludford in 1459, when the Lancastrians had sacked the town, Edward made Ludlow the seat of the Prince's Council, the forerunner of the Council in the Marches. The foundations for Ludlow's prominence in the 16th and 17th centuries had been laid.

Rather more surprising, in view of its remoteness, is the survival of Cefnllys into the 15th century. It would appear to have undergone major rebuilding under Richard, duke of York between 1431 and 1459, and the resulting works are the subject of glowing praise in a series of poems by the bard Lewis Glyn Cothi.[37] Like other Mortimer possessions, it passed into the hands of the crown in 1461, and was in ruins by the late 16th century.[38]

The Civil Wars of the 17th century were the last occasion when some of the Mortimer castles saw action. Ludlow and Denbigh were garrisoned for the Crown, the former being the last castle in Shropshire to surrender, in May 1646. Wigmore was 'slighted' by the parliamentarian Harleys of Brampton Bryan in 1643 to prevent local royalists from defending it, suggesting at least a viable structure had survived till that date. Montgomery was half-heartedly held for the king by Lord Herbert of Chirbury, and surrendered without a shot being fired in return for an undertaking that Herbert's house in the castle would be saved. Both house and castle were afterwards demolished by Parliament. Although Sir Thomas Myddleton, a leading parliamentarian, captured Montgomery, his own castle of Chirk had been seized in his absence by the local royalists and held by them for three years. After 1651 Myddleton changed sides, and following his involvement in the Cheshire uprising in 1659, Chirk Castle was 'slighted'. After the Restoration the damaged areas were rebuilt, and Chirk remains the only Mortimer castle still to be inhabited in the present day.

Ludlow and Usk are impressive ruins, and still in private ownership, though open to the public. The extensive ruins of Denbigh are cared for by CADW (Heritage in Wales) as are Dolforwyn and Montgomery, both of which have been considerably excavated to expose much detail which had formerly been deeply buried in rubble. Wigmore, which only recently (1995) came into the care of English Heritage, presents a major archaeological challenge, with many levels of building sequence to be uncovered at some time in the future. In the interim it has been decided that the ruins should be conserved and protected from further deterioration, but that the site should remain a 'romantic ruin'. Trial excavations undertaken by Marches Archaeology in 1996 and subsequent years revealed that within the curtain wall of the bailey spoil had accumulated to a depth of nearly 30 feet. The lower levels proved to belong to the 12th century, showing that the replacement of wooden fortifications had taken place at that period.[39]

Castles and town plantation

One of the most significant features of castle building in Wales and the Marches is the way in which the process was frequently accompanied by the foundation of planned towns. There were many reasons for this. Larger castles needed a community to support them with men and provisions. The lord also received economic benefits in the form of burgage rents and the tolls of markets and fairs.[40] In addition, particularly in the western part of the Marches and in Wales itself the towns, which were constructed alongside the castles, played an important role in the process of colonisation, as centres of Anglo-Norman population and culture in a predominantly Celtic land. It is small wonder that these alien towns became a focus of Welsh hatred, and were so often one of the first targets for destruction in uprisings such as that of Owain Glyn Dŵr.

The Mortimers, in common with their neighbours on the March, took an active role in the process of town plantation. Their activities may be divided into the establishment of their own settlements, and the management, and improvement where necessary, of towns which they acquired 'secondhand' by marriage, inheritance or royal grant. Most new towns were established as an adjunct of a castle, which was usually integrated into the defences of the town. Even the comparatively late foundations at Bala and Newtown were sited close to an already existing earthwork castle.

It is somewhat ironic that what was probably the first 'Mortimer' borough was not founded by the family but by their predecessor. Wigmore Castle had been founded by William FitzOsbern, and it is most likely that it was he who established the borough which was valued at £7 in the Domesday survey. This early borough was probably laid out parallel to the ridge upon which church and castle stand. While it is difficult to estimate the size of this early settlement, its extent in 1304, when it contained $106^{1/4}$ plus $^{1/6}$ burgages, suggests that it was a fairly modest settlement, about the size of a large village.[41] The same is probably true of Cleobury, the other family *caput*, though there is a complete absence of documentation to suggest a date for the founding of the borough. As already noted, the castle was destroyed in 1155 and never rebuilt, and it is likely that the town was in existence by that time. In the Inquisition of Edmund (I) in 1304, Cleobury was of a similar size to Wigmore.

The Mortimers do not appear to have become involved in establishing new towns until the middle of the 13th century. The reign of Henry III has been noted as a time when town plantation was revitalised, with a concentration of new foundations in south Wales and its eastern border.[42] This period saw the establishment of small Mortimer boroughs at Cefnllys and Knucklas, and the development of existing settlements in newly-acquired lordships at New Radnor and Knighton.

It is not clear when the borough at Cefnllys was founded, but it most likely dates from the reconstruction of the castle in 1273-4. A market charter was granted by Edmund Mortimer to the men of Maelienydd in 1297, and his Inquisition Post Mortem of 1304 mentions 25 tenants and a mill at Cefnllys.[43]

There are no documentary references to the borough after 1383, when 10 burgages had become decayed. The settlement had always been small, and was one of 20 in Wales with a population of less than 30 taxpayers in 1300.[44] Despite being virtually abandoned for generations, Cefnllys remained one of the Radnorshire parliamentary boroughs until the 1832 Reform Act. It is conjectured that the settlement lay on level ground to the west of the castle in the vicinity of St. Michael's church. Knucklas was also one of the smallest boroughs in Wales, and was very short-lived. It was most likely founded in 1240 as an adjunct of the castle, and may well have ceased effective exist-

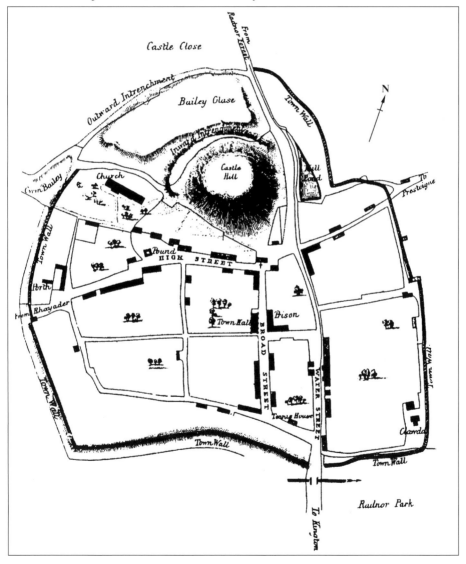

Le Keux's plan of New Radnor in 1800 showing the town walls (TRS)

ence after the capture of the castle by Llywelyn in 1262. Neither Cefnllys nor Knucklas can be regarded as successful town plantations, and were both probably too small to have been economically viable.

Both New Radnor and Knighton were, at least initially, much more successful. There was a settlement at Radnor, which had presumably been founded by the de Braoses, for which Roger (III) obtained a grant of murage in 1257. This was destroyed by Llywelyn in 1264, and the present town was established when the castle was rebuilt after peace had been restored. An area of 26 acres was enclosed by walls, with the castle integrated into the defences at the north-west angle. Murage grants were obtained in 1280, 1283, and 1290, which enabled the lord to raise a tax on goods entering the town, the proceeds of which could be used to build, upgrade, and later maintain the town defences. The defences consisted of impressive earthen embankments topped by stone walls, with four gates, one at each principal compass point. These were still in existence when Leland visited the town in the reign of Henry VIII.[45]

Radnor had been a sizeable borough in the middle ages. In 1304 there were no fewer than 262½ burgages, and the borough ranked twelfth among Welsh towns in number of taxpayers.[46] Speed's plan of 1610 reveals considerable open spaces within the walls, which may indicate the extent of decline which had taken place since the town's heyday in the 14th century. Le Keux's plan of 1800 shows the town defences very clearly, and the line may still be easily traced in the open fields to the south and west of the town.

The remains of the town walls towards the south-western corner of New Radnor, with the castle mound visible beyond the buildings

Knighton was another settlement acquired by the Mortimers, who finally gained possession in 1207. The castle was probably erected by William de Braose in 1191, some 500 yards to the west of the motte of an earlier castle, known as Bryn y Castell.[47] In 1260 and 1277 the king granted Roger (III) murage for seven years, but there is no evidence to suggest that the walls were ever constructed.[48] Soulsby even suggests that the town may have developed organically rather than as the result of plantation, citing the unusually large proportion of Welshmen in the population (60% in 1292-3). By 1304 it contained $162^1/_2$ burgages, and was, like New Radnor one of the larger towns which boasted over 100 taxpayers. The castle, a motte and bailey structure to the south-west of the town, was destroyed by the Welsh in 1262 and not rebuilt.

Rhayader, Bala and Newtown are comparatively late foundations which date from a period when town plantation had more or less ceased in south Wales, and it is possible that all three replaced existing Welsh settlements of some sort. Rhayader Castle had been built by the Lord Rhys in 1177, but there is no documentary mention of a town before 1304. The settlement was laid out to the east of the castle with two principal streets, and appears to have had earthen defences. The church lay outside the line of these ramparts, which may indicate an earlier foundation, an arrangement found in other planned towns such as Clun. Rhayader remained a local market town through the 16th century, and became a small centre for woollen manufacturing in the 18th century.

In Bala the Mortimers again utilised an existing earthwork castle which stood at the north-east angle of the later town. The borough was laid out by Roger (IV) about 1310 with a main street running from south-west to north-east, and parallel back lanes. While the charter of 1324 provided for the construction of defences linked to the former castle, there is no evidence that they were ever begun.[49] The town declined in the later middle ages, so that by the 1540s it had only 13 taxpayers. The development of a textile industry in the 18th century brought about a certain amount of revitalisation of the town.

Newtown was established by Roger (III) in 1279 as a replacement for the proto-borough which had been established by Llywelyn at Dolforwyn, which Mortimer had recently captured. As at Rhayader and Bala, the site of Newtown also possessed an existing, but undocumented,[50] motte and bailey castle, though there seems to have been no attempt to integrate this into the new settlement. Newtown received a charter in 1280 granting it an annual fair and a weekly market, and it would appear to have been regarded as a borough from at least 1330. The town became a relatively prosperous centre, and underwent considerable expansion in the 19th century with the development of the flannel industry. Newtown may be regarded as possibly the most successful of the towns which were originally established by the Mortimers.

The most substantial walled towns possessed by the Mortimers were those which they had acquired in a state of completion. Ludlow and Denbigh both boast almost complete sets of walls, each with a fine surviving gate, with Denbigh possessing a complex system of additional defences based on the outwork known as the Goblin Tower. These defences were completed before the Mortimers acquired the towns, and Ludlow had already expanded to its greatest medieval extent by 1300. The town walls, which were completed towards the end of the 13th century, enclosed a central area following a natural contour, and leaving large areas of the town as extra-mural 'suburbs'.[51] By contrast, the development of the large extra-mural settlement at Denbigh was begun early in the 14th century and was in full swing in the main period of Mortimer ownership after 1354.

Montgomery was another example of a substantial walled borough which was acquired in a state of completion by the Mortimers. The town defences were integrated with those of the castle in the customary manner, and the walls enclosed a large area. There were four town gates, together with a number of circular mural towers. There has been some disagreement as to whether the walls were constructed of stone from the start, about 1230, or whether they were originally of earth and timber construction, which was replaced in stone about 1280. In any event, they were completed by the time the borough first passed to Roger (IV) in 1330. The walls were badly damaged by Owain Glyn Dŵr's forces, and like those of New Radnor, they were not subsequently rebuilt. The borough declined in importance in the later middle ages, and today there are large open spaces within the area of the original walls. A similar situation applied in the case of Usk, where the castle occupied the north-east angle of the town, which was defended by extensive ramparts and four gates. Here also declining importance meant that large open spaces survived within the walls until the late 20th century.

The buildings

Considered chronologically, the first phase of Mortimer castle-building consisted of earthwork and timber structures, of the type loosely known as motte and bailey. Ludlow, which was stone-built from the outset, did not, of course, become a Mortimer possession until 1308. The essence of a motte and bailey castle was a castle mound or motte surmounted by a timber structure, with one or more adjacent baileys, areas surrounded with earthworks and palisades, which contained the various domestic buildings of the castle. Timber castles are generally poorly documented, but recent studies based on archaeological investigations have challenged some of the preconceptions previously held about this type of castle.[52]

It is now clear that timber castles were much more permanent than has hitherto been thought. The castle at Hen Domen near Montgomery underwent almost continuous repair and rebuilding in timber between the late 11th and the 13th centuries, and continued in use for some 50 years after the completion of the stone castle at Montgomery in the 1280s.[53] Excavations at the site of Owain Glyn Dŵr's castle at Sycharth have confirmed the continuous existence of a timber castle from the late 11th century until its destruction by Prince Henry in 1403.[54] Similarly, it is now recognised that timber and stone structures co-existed in castles for some considerable time, with timber gradually being replaced by stone. In the royal castle at Shrewsbury, the great timber motte tower collapsed as late as 1270.[55]

It is therefore likely that many of the earlier Mortimer castles remained primarily or wholly timber constructions throughout their existence. This hypothesis is strengthened by the various references to destruction and rebuilding which took place during the troubled 12th and 13th centuries. Cymaron, for example, was destroyed in the 1130s along with Dineithion, rebuilt in 1144, and finally destroyed in 1215, which suggests that the buildings may have always been of timber. Similarly the absence of references to the castle at Rhayader after its capture by the Welsh in 1202, until 1307, when it was totally decayed, suggests that it may also have been a timber structure which fell out of use and rotted away. The position with regard to Wigmore is more complicated, as most of the stonework remaining above ground appears to date from the 14th century, though it is likely that at least part of the defences had been rebuilt in stone by the time of the siege of 1155. Evidence of this and subsequent rebuilding is mostly buried in debris, and awaits large-scale archaeological excavation.

The mid-13th century provides a number of examples of castle-building in stone, with work at Cefnllys, Tinboeth, Knucklas and New Radnor dating from this period. The buildings of Cefnllys are in many ways the most complicated. The castle occupies a high ridge above the Eithon, which was originally the site of an Iron Age hill-fort. A castle was constructed at the northern end of

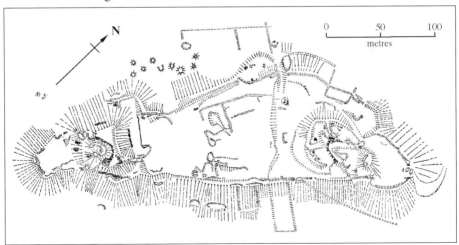

Plan of Cefnllys (TRS 1972)

this ridge at some time prior to 1246, which may possibly have involved the rebuilding of an earlier structure in stone. This northern site contains a large mound of stone, which may signify a collapsed tower rather than a motte, and two baileys which contain the foundations of buildings and a bake-oven. The site was protected on three sides by the steep slopes of the hill, but was vulnerable on the south, where the interior of the hill-fort was relatively flat.

Following the successful surprise attack by Llywelyn in 1262, a new castle was erected at the southern end of the ridge, and was separated from the rest by a strong rock-cut ditch. This provoked strong protests from Llywelyn to Henry III that the terms of the Treaty of Montgomery had been broken. The new castle consisted of a roughly square enclosure with angle towers, and a central circular or octagonal tower, which may correspond to a reference to an 'eight-sided fort' (*Kaer wythochr*) in a 15th-century poem by Lewis Glyn Cothi.[56] The arrangement of a central tower within a small bailey recalls Tretower and Skenfrith, built some 30 years earlier, and cylindrical keeps are not uncommon in south Wales in the 13th century. A polygonal keep would have been much more unusual, though there are English examples at Odiham, Hampshire, and Chilham, Kent, dating from about 1160. There may also have the more local and recent example at Hereford, thought to have had a polygonal keep erected in the latter part of the 13th century.

Cefnllys appears to have undergone rebuilding work in the 15th century under Richard, duke of York, which may have included the reconstruction of the hall. The source of this information is not completely reliable, being the series of rather sycophantic poems written in praise of the constable, Ieuan ap Philip, and his family by the bard Lewis Glyn Cothi. They do, however, emphasise that the castle had not fallen prey to the prevalent decay during the 1430s.

Tinboeth and Knucklas were far simpler structures than Cefnllys, and both appear to have occupied the sites of Iron Age hill-forts. Tinboeth was captured by Llywelyn ap Gruffydd in 1260, regained by Roger (III) Mortimer, and refortified by him in 1282, when it was garrisoned by five horse and 30 foot soldiers.[57] In 1322 it was confiscated along with Roger (IV)'s other estates, and granted to the king's brother, Edmund, earl of Kent. It was omitted from lists of Mortimer property after 1360, when it had presumably fallen into decay. Tinboeth appears to have consisted of a small polygonal bailey set within a massive, possibly Iron Age, earthwork. There are indications of a small gate-house with D-shaped towers, and a further circular tower. There do not appear to have been any other mural towers, and the castle would seem to have been a fairly simple structure. The same is true of Knucklas, which was built *c*.1242 as a small quadrangular stone building with circular angle towers and a barbican to the west. It was captured by Llywelyn in 1262, when the threat to bring up powerful siege engines was enough to make the garrison surrender. It was prob-

An aerial view of Tinboeth Castle

ably never rebuilt, as it is absent from the list of Mortimer castles confiscated in 1322, and by 1406 was regarded as a lordship without a castle.[58]

In contrast to the fairly simple castles at Tinboeth and Knucklas, New Radnor was a major fortress. Radnor was a de Braose lordship which came to Roger Mortimer (III) on his marriage, though there is some divergence of opinion on the date of the present castle. It had formerly been thought that the castle and town defences were started *de novo* by Roger Mortimer, and that references to the capture and rebuilding of a de Braose castle at Radnor refer to the site at Old Radnor. Soulsby concedes that there is some evidence that the castle of Radnor which was captured by Llywelyn ab Iorwerth in 1231 may have been the new structure, while Remfry, comparing the ditches with those of Builth and Painscastle, considers that the work may have been carried out by royal labour in 1233 on the orders of Richard, King of the Romans, the brother of Henry III.[59] The town defences would appear to have been commenced by Roger (III) after the first grant of murage in 1257, and both town and castle were subsequently destroyed by Llywelyn in 1264. This necessitated a complete rebuilding, so that the final shape of the castle and town defences is Mortimer work. It is difficult to interpret the form of the castle as no masonry work has survived, although the outlines of some stone buildings may be detected on the summit of the mound. On the drawing accompanying Speed's map of Radnorshire (1610), the building on the mound would appear to have consisted of a quadrangular structure with three square towers on the west towards the bailey, and two D-shaped towers facing the town. The massive gatehouse which is also shown on Speed's drawing served as a prison during the late medieval period when the castle had ceased to perform its primary role of defence. It is interesting to note a passing resemblance between the buildings on the motte at Radnor illustrated by Speed and those on the mound at Wigmore.

Up to this point the Mortimer castles might be regarded as substantial buildings befitting the status of important local magnates, but with little to distinguish them from those of their fellow marcher lords. At the end of the 13th century and the beginning of the 14th, as the importance of the family increased both locally and nationally, castle-building entered a new phase. This saw the construction of the massive concentric fortress at Chirk, and the conversion of Ludlow and Wigmore into stately and opulent palaces.

It is not entirely clear when the building of Chirk was started. Taylor includes it among the castles of the war of 1282-3, whereas the current National Trust history suggests a date of 1295, following the Madog uprising, in which Denbigh had been taken by the Welsh.[60] Certainly Edward I passed through Chirk in June 1295 shortly after commencing his new castle at Beaumaris, and it is not unlikely that Chirk would have been built with royal financial assistance, and the use of royal labourers and architects. Edward I encouraged and assisted the building of private castles at Denbigh, Holt and Ruthin, and his chief architect, Master James of St. George, is known to have worked for Henry de Lacy at Denbigh.[61] The close resemblance of Chirk to Beaumaris, and to a lesser extent Harlech, make it most likely that either Master James or his deputy, Walter of Hereford, was the designer.

James of St. George came to England about 1278 from the court of Savoy, where he had built the castle of St. George d'Esperance from which he took his name. In 1282 he became Master of the King's Works in Wales, and was responsible for the design of all Edward I's castles there. He also worked in Gascony and Scotland, and continued to draw the unprecedented salary of three shillings a day for his Welsh post, even when away. It has been said that 'in all the history of the king's works in medieval England, there is no other craftsman who was entrusted with such great responsibilities, no other mason who received such notable signs of his royal master's favour'.[62]

The plan of Chirk is similar to that of the inner ward of Beaumaris, comprising a rectangle with circular angle towers with a semi-circular tower midway along each wall. It is not clear whether the design was ever completed as the southern section, if it ever existed, was replaced around 1400 with a range containing the great chamber and chapel. The castle was subject to extensive damage during and after the Cheshire Uprising of 1659, following which the eastern curtain wall with its two towers was rebuilt on the old lines between 1673 and 1678. Only the north and west curtain walls survive of the original building, with Adam's Tower and the circular Distil Room Tower preserving their medieval interiors. The midway tower on the north wall was effectively

gutted in 1777-8 by John Turner of Chester to accommodate the grand staircase. The surviving medieval work does, however, give an impression of the grandeur of the original fortress, which was one of the most advanced pieces of military architecture of its day. It may well be that the *raison d'étre* for such a fortress had passed before the work was completed, or work may have stopped with the fall of Roger of Chirk in 1322. It is strange that though Chirk is the only Edwardian castle in Wales to have been continuously occupied since it was built, it was held by the Mortimers for less than 50 years.

Inside Adam's Tower, the part of Chirk Castle that was built under Roger Mortimer of Chirk in the last years of the 13th century

The character of the Mortimer work at Chirk is almost entirely military, whereas at Ludlow and Wigmore it consisted of the conversion of existing fortresses into sumptuous palaces which reflected the importance and lavish lifestyle of the family in the 14th century. At Ludlow the inner bailey of the de Lacy castle was transformed by the construction of a suite of buildings which consisted of a large first-floor hall set between two three-storied blocks of chambers — the solar on the west and the great chamber on the east. The great chamber was equipped with a massive garderobe tower of four storeys which provided two sets of lodgings with integral latrine on each floor, which discharged through a series of chutes at the base of the tower. The presence of such an easy, if unsavoury, point of entry for intruders suggests that military considerations were no longer the chief priority.

It is generally accepted that this work of conversion was commenced by the de Geneviles in the later 13th century, phased over several decades, and completed by the Mortimers. Michael Thompson in the most recent publication on Ludlow Castle suggests a date of 1250-1280 for the great hall, based on the evidence of window tracery and mouldings.[63] In the same work, R.K. Morriss argues a date in the 1280s or 1290s for the solar, quoting in evidence the prevalence of 'Y' tracery in the windows, and the use of sunk-chamfer mouldings on the window jambs. Morriss also draws attention to the use of the shouldered lintel, which, like the sunk chamfer, is found in Caernarfon Castle in the 1280s. He also suggests that the completion of the solar block may have been accelerated by the need to finish the work before the arrival of Roger (IV) in 1308, or that it was completed rapidly by the new owner prior to putting his own building programme into effect.[64]

Although there is no documentary evidence to confirm that the great chamber and garderobe tower formed part of Roger Mortimer's scheme of work, there

Looking across the Great Hall at Ludlow, with the solar block to the left and Great Chamber block to the right, with the garderobe tower beyond

are plenty of stylistic grounds for placing the buildings squarely in this period. It is significant that modern scholarship represented by Thompson agrees with St. John Hope's assessment that the work dates from *circa* 1320. The ogee arch is a feature which appears throughout this range, and is completely absent from the earlier structures immediately to its west. Although these buildings have suffered badly from later alterations and depredations, the remains of fireplaces in the great chamber and the room above it give some impression of the sumptuous nature of the accommodation which was provided.

A further building which can be definitely linked to Roger (IV) is the freestanding chapel dedicated to St. Peter ad Vincula. This was erected in thanksgiving for Roger's escape from the Tower of London in 1323, which had fortuitously occurred on the day set aside by the church to commemorate the liberation of St. Peter. This chapel has suffered more from later alteration than many other buildings in the castle, having been converted into a court house for the Council in the Marches during the presidency of Sir Henry Sidney (1560-1586). What survives is basically the nave of the chapel, which contains a blocked window with 'Y' tracery similar to that found in the domestic buildings discussed above.

More recently a somewhat different interpretation of the whole range has been put forward by the late Eric Mercer, who considered that both the east (great chamber) and the west (solar) blocks may have been built by the Geneviles, and subsequently raised in height by the Mortimers. Mercer also raised the possibility that the great hall may be a Genevile remodelling of an existing and possibly ground floor hall, and hypothesises a demolished two-storey porch with a chamber above at the entrance to the present hall.[65] While these conclusions may be controversial, few could quarrel with their author's verdict that 'the effect was one of calculated magnificence; and the building was the most imposing residence in the county, indeed throughout the Marches, and unsurpassed at the time anywhere: a fitting monument to the Mortimers, then at the height of their power and pretensions'.[66]

The work at Wigmore was also intended to transform an existing fortress into a palatial residence befitting the ancestral home of the family. Examination of the building evidence is more difficult than that in the case of Ludlow, due to the extent of the collapse which has taken place since the engraving of the site made by the Buck brothers in the second decade of the 18th century. There is, however, general agreement with the conclusion reached by the Royal Commission on Historical Monuments in 1943 that most of the visible masonry dates from the 14th century, and more specifically from the time of Roger Mortimer (IV).[67]

The remaining stone structures on the summit of the motte consist of a curtain wall, of which about 100 feet survives on the north side, with a number of turrets, two of which were rectangular, one D-shaped, and one octagonal.

The Buck brothers engraving of Wigmore

These towers, some of which may be clearly seen on the Buck engraving, have largely collapsed, though a number were still standing in 1874. That on the south-east side of the motte still stands to first floor level, though its ground floor is buried in debris. It has been suggested by Remfry that this array of towers was intended for aesthetic rather than military effect.[68] The structure bears some resemblance to the buildings on the mound at New Radnor illustrated by Speed.

Remains in the bailey consist of the curtain wall, mural towers and gatehouse, with the foundations of a number of sizeable buildings within the enclosed area. The massive gatehouse remains impressive despite being buried almost up to the base of its arch in rubble. To the west of the gatehouse are two substantial towers which provided residential accommodation, one of which, the south tower, probably accommodated the castle prison in its basement. Within the bailey on the north side, rubble mounds mark the site of a substantial range of buildings which have been tentatively identified as a hall and service area, which may have utilised the semi-octagonal north-west tower as a solar. Further foundations are indicated by rubble mounds to the west of the gatehouse, and it has been suggested that these may have been large hall ranges of timber on stone foundations, linked to lodgings in the south and south-west towers.[69]

This extensive rebuilding would have created a sumptuous palace, which probably equalled Ludlow in splendour. An artist's reconstruction, partly based on the Buck engraving gives an impression of the appearance of the castle during the 14th century, when it was at its most magnificent. If this work is to be dated to the 14th century, the traditional assertion that Wigmore became neglected by the Mortimers after the acquisition of Ludlow in 1308 must be called into question. This assumption has been accepted by scholars of the

Reconstruction drawing of Wigmore Castle
showing how it might have looked during the 14th century

eminence of Penry Evans, and more recently Rees Davies, but it does not tally with other evidence.[70] If the castle was fitted up with accommodation of large numbers of people in lodgings as commodious as those at Ludlow, it does not suggest a downgrading of the status of Wigmore. A further telling, if circumstantial piece of evidence argues in the same direction. Wigmore was both the ancestral home of the family and the site of the abbey where its leading members were buried. Wigmore Abbey itself had undergone considerable rebuilding in the 1370s at the cost of Edmund (III), and at his death in 1381 it received lavish bequests of relics, plate and vestments. All the 14th century earls were brought back to Wigmore for burial, with the exception of Roger IV, whose widow had nevertheless sought and obtained permission to do so. This attachment to Wigmore is not easily reconciled to the concept of a downgraded castle. Perhaps Edmund (IV)'s choice of his own foundation at Clare in Suffolk for his burial place in 1425 indicates a waning of family *pietas*, and it may well be that the undoubted decline which had taken place by the 1530s dates from the succession of the dukes of York to the Mortimer inheritance.[71]

The reconstructions carried out at Ludlow and Wigmore were the last major acts of castle building carried out by the Mortimers. Though these chief

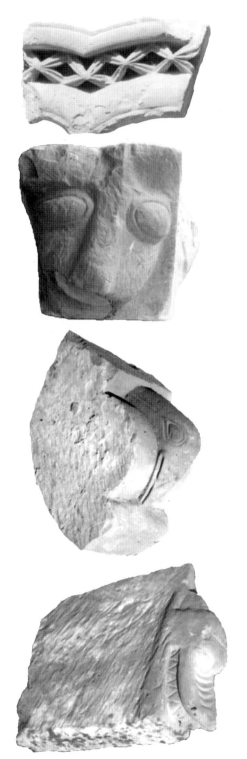

Surviving pieces of carved stone from Wigmore Abbey, including some re-erected as a pillar to a recent porch to the Grange. Under the Mortimers the abbey became extremely wealthy, but the monks were also involved in a number of scandals

Reconstruction drawing of Wigmore Abbey

seats were capable of entertaining royalty, on occasions such as the visit of the dowager queen Isabella and her son Edward III to Ludlow in September 1329, the enhanced role of the Mortimers meant that they became increasingly absentee lords who spent little time in the Marches. After 1350, work on the growing number of Mortimer castles became more a matter of repair and maintenance such as the complete rebuilding of the massive Well Tower at Montgomery, probably by Edmund (III).[72] The addition of outer defences at Usk towards the end of the 14th century, which has already been noted represents a late instance of purely military building. The reconstruction at Cefnllys during the constableship of Ieuan ap Philip, if it indeed took place, is a late example of the process of improvement of domestic accommodation, which is unusual in view of the remoteness of the site. By this time only Ludlow could really be regarded as playing anything more than a minor role in Mortimer affairs.

Use and equipment
The haphazard nature of the survival of documentary evidence concerning the Mortimer castles, and the family in general, makes it difficult to consider in depth the uses to which the castles were put, and the levels of staffing and equipment which were involved. There are, however, various areas about which it is possible to make some comment.

Information does exist concerning garrisons in time of conflict with the Welsh. The size of various Mortimer garrisons is known from the Pipe Roll of 1282, which lists 27 foot soldiers at Wigmore; eight horse and 30 foot each at Dolforwyn and Cefnllys; eight horse and 20 foot at Knucklas; five horse and 30 foot at Tinboeth; and four horse and 20 foot at New Radnor.[73] The significance of these figures may be limited, for they represent part of a chain of fortifications in mid-Wales which were held by small detachments of men while the main armies were engaging the enemy in the field elsewhere. It is known that far larger garrisons were employed during the Glyn Dŵr uprising. At Radnor the usual garrison was trebled to 70 men in June 1403, and further increased in the following January.[74]

These were, of course, exceptional times, and for most of the period between the last major Welsh uprisings in 1294 and 1295 and the outbreak of the Glyn Dŵr rebellion in 1400, the military life of most castles would have been minimal. Constables were still appointed, but the post rapidly became honorific and subordinate to the manorial officials. In peacetime the constables were subject to the receiver in all matters, even repairs, while in time of war it was the steward and not the constable who was responsible for defending, victualling and garrisoning the castle.[75] Among the lesser officials in the castle was the armourer, who was responsible for burnishing and maintaining the weaponry, and who made requisitions for new equipment through the receiver.[76] For much of the later period, when records become more plentiful, the judicial function became the most important role of the castle. Keeping a gaol was a valued marcher privilege, and prisoners were the responsibility of the janitor, an official who was rewarded with a daily stipend (2d. at Wigmore; $3^{1}/_{2}$d. at Radnor) and an annual robe.[77] Courts were held at Mortimer castles long after their other functions had ceased: at Cymaron in the 1360s, long after it was abandoned as a castle, and at Cefnllys in the 1430s. It was the presence of the Council in the Marches and its forerunners at Ludlow from the late 15th century which ensured that the castle continued to flourish until the end of the 17th century.

It is possible to discover a great deal about the equipment and furnishing of two castles, Wigmore and Dolforwyn, from inventories which were taken in 1322 when the goods of Roger (IV) were confiscated. The inventory of Wigmore contains a fascinating mixture of the mundane and the exotic. The weaponry included three springalds, (giant crossbows similar to Roman *ballistae*, which discharged stones or large iron crossbow bolts) with their winding mechanism, and three without; 14 crossbows of horn; two Saracen bows and three Saracen arrows, perhaps souvenirs of the Crusades; an Irish battle-axe; three helmets; eight shields, helmets for jousting; six tents and pavilions; and eight shields. The furniture and effects included a chess board of painted and gilded nutmeg wood with chessmen; 10 chests; six table boards; a board for tables and drafts and two damaged and broken cauldrons. There were ample provisions which included 12 bacons worth 2s.; a bacon and 14 hams worth 12d.; 200 stock fish (dried fish) worth 6s. a hundred; and three casks and a pipe of wine. In the courtyard outside the castle were stacks of wheat; 46 oxen worth 9s. each; 10 cows worth 6s. each; a boar and piglets; and five peacocks.

If this section of the inventory reflects a rather spartan lifestyle, it is probably because the family had been living in state at the abbey, which suggests that the rebuilding of the domestic ranges at the castle had not been completed, or even commenced when the inventory was taken. The items listed at the abbey included many which reveal considerable opulence and display, such as the green bed-cover with owls woven on it, with four hangings of the same pattern; a large curtain for the hall woven with popinjays and griffons; a long golden bench cover with yellow and red thread. Lady Joan's establishment contained a mattress with a muslin cover, and no less than 15 pairs of linen sheets. Both the earl and his wife boasted wardrobes of fine clothes, and Joan herself possessed luxury items such as a psalter; four books of romances; an ivory image of the Blessed Virgin; an ivory chess-set; and an ivory whip.[78]

The Dolforwyn inventory, made on 25 January 1322 by William de la Beche reveals an assortment of military equipment in the round and square towers, and a variety of everyday items of household use, often in bad condition, in the other buildings of the castle. The round tower contained a selection of weapons and armour including:

The abbot's lodgings at Wigmore Abbey to the left,
with the undercroft behind the external staircase

2 shirts of mail of the value of 13s.; 3 corsets of iron of the value of 15s.; 2 coifs of iron and one ventaile of the value of 6s.; 4 coats of metal to the value of 4 marks; 4 helms of the value of 12s.; 1 crossbow of 2 feet; 16 crossbows of 1 foot; 4 crossbows disjointed; 8 belts; 406 quarrels [crossbow bolts], and they are valued at 40s.

The square tower contained:

2 springles; 4 score bolts; 1 vice for a crossbow of vice (sic); 1 piece of cable, which contains 20 fathoms; 2 ladders, each of 20 steps; 2 ladders, each of 14 steps; 1 ladder of 12 steps; and they are not valued.

Part of the abbot's lodgings at Wigmore Abbey

The domestic rooms of the castle contained a similar assortment of furniture, mostly rather spartan and in poor condition, and of little or no value, such as the tub for bathing in the lady's chamber. Although Dolforwyn appeared to have been quite well stocked with bacon, corn, malt and even eight gallons of pea meal, most of the barrels in the cellar and the buttery were empty, save for 10 inches depth of wine in a cask in the cellar.[79]

There is a strong suggestion that Dolforwyn in 1322 was on the point of entering the cycle of decay which afflicted so many of the lesser Mortimer castles during the 14th century. Decay was not universal in the more remote parts of the Mortimer empire, and the fourth of Lewis Glyn Cothi's Cefnllys poems, written in the middle of the 15th century, and addressed to Angharad, the wife of Ieuan ap Philip, the castle's constable, provides a fascinating glimpse of castle life. The poet has been feeling the cold as winter advances, so Angharad has given him an embroidered coverlet against the cold. It was woven by a Lombard, and consisted of a dark grey sheet of cloth, with clumps of marigolds filling the white spaces, and, at the top, a yew tree had been woven into the design 'like a window at Westminster'. He concludes by wishing long life to Angharad, who had given him Greek wines at Cefnllys. There were still some luxuries, even at Cefnllys in winter.[80]

CHAPTER XI

Epilogue: Edward IV

On Edmund Mortimer's death in 1425 his immense inheritance passed to his nephew, the son of his sister Anne. She had married Richard, earl of Cambridge, and their son, Richard, had been born in 1411, four years before the execution of his father following the exposure of the plot to assassinate Henry V. Through his father Richard was a great-grandson of Edward III and, through his mother, Edward's great-great-great grandson, and it was from this descent that in due course he would base his claim to the throne (see family tree on the following page). Many years were to pass, however, before Richard and his supporters envisaged that he might become king, and indeed he appears to have been a loyal subject and servant of the Crown for the first 40 or so years of his life in spite of his superior claim to the throne.

Henry V's death in 1422 brought his son, under a year old, to the throne. Henry VI's infancy, and later his adult incapacity as a king, were a recipe for political disaster and for more than 30 years the ruling Lancastrian élite were able to intrigue and jockey for power around him at the expense of the kingdom's good administration. A chronicler described the state of the kingdom as it slid into civil war in the 1450s:

> In this same time the realm of England was out of all good governance as it had been many days before, for the king was simple and led by covetous counsel and owed more than he was worth ... Because of these misgovernances and many others the hearts of the people were turned away from those who governed the land, and their blessing was turned into cursing.[1]

Henry V's conquests were whittled away by a resurgent France in the face of inept English diplomacy and management of the war. The battle of Verneuil in 1424 was the last great English victory (won on this occasion in conjunction with Burgundian allies) of the Hundred Years War; thereafter disaster followed

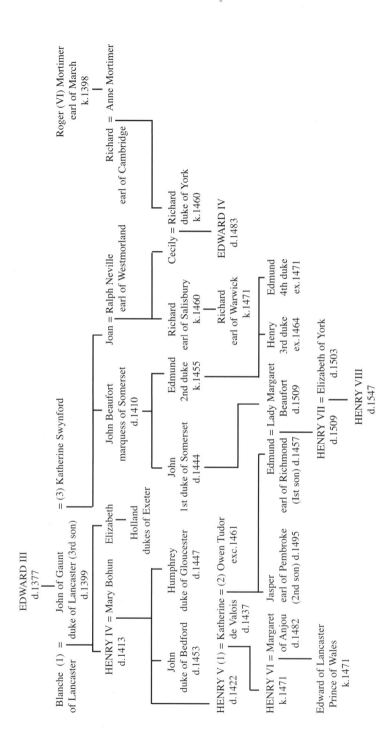

The families of York, Mortimer and Neville

disaster until, in 1453, the last English army was defeated at the battle of Castillon. All that then remained of the English possessions in France was the enclave of Calais and the Channel Islands. Henry V's empire was not viable in the long run; but this was not appreciated at the time and the gradual loss of France incited deep anger and frustration, amongst not only the baronage but also the common people who had grown accustomed to English military superiority in the field. Resentment among soldiers returning from France fed the growing disillusionment with the Lancastrian regime whose misgovernment was allowing the country to drift slowly into near anarchy. This, then, was the background to Richard's early adult life.

As duke of York, after his paternal uncle had been killed at Agincourt in 1415, and as earl of March, earl of Ulster and Lord Mortimer after the death of his maternal uncle in 1425, he became probably the wealthiest subject of the king and in 1432 he was granted livery of his estates. Some years earlier he had married Cecily, daughter of Ralph Neville, earl of Westmorland, the head of a powerful and extended family connected with many of the great baronial houses.

In 1430 Richard of York accompanied the king to France, with 12 lances (men-at-arms and their retinues) and 36 archers, and the following year was present at Henry's coronation in Notre Dame. In 1436 he was appointed lieutenant-general and governor of the kingdom of France and the duchy of Normandy for one year. This was the first of a number of appointments abroad, perhaps made to keep him relatively clear of domestic politics. He gained military experience fighting alongside John Talbot, earl of Shrewsbury, one of the foremost English military commanders of the time, but returned to England the following year in spite of being asked by the council to continue in office; it seems that he had found the financial arrangements unsatisfactory. Richard was reappointed in 1440, but owing it would appear to political disputes did not cross to France for nearly a year. He won credit for his conduct of the war against France, but in 1445 he returned to England protesting that he had not been paid large sums that the government owed him. He also had another complaint: the government had decided during his lieutenancy not to send him reinforcements, but to entrust another and larger army to John Beaufort, previously earl and now duke of Somerset, who was empowered with independent authority in France. Richard's appointment was not renewed and he was subjected to accusations of financial mismanagement during his period of office. The origins of the personal and political antagonism between the houses of York and Somerset that was to erupt into violence in the 1450s probably dates from this period. Two years later Richard was appointed to the first of two terms as the king's lieutenant in Ireland, a post amounting to banishment from the mainstream of English politics and from the war with France.

It may well be that it was his experiences in France of the government's maladministration and its incompetent prosecution of the war that first turned

Richard's thoughts to the possibility of winning a degree of political power for himself. With his royal blood he was a figure around whom an increasingly discontented element of the baronage could unite in opposition to the regime, but for some years he was to protest his loyalty to King Henry and he was probably sincere in insisting that his quarrel was with the king's counsellors and not the king himself.

Richard did not actually leave for his ten-year appointment in Ireland until 1449 and a political crisis soon brought him back to England. In June 1450 Jack Cade, a former soldier who had served in France, led a rising in Kent and, marching on London, the rebels had demanded redress of their grievances. The disturbances were distinctly pro-Yorkist in character and significantly Cade 'at the beginning took upon him the name of a gentleman and called himself Mortimer for to have the favour of the people'.[2] One of the rebels' demands was that the king should 'take about his noble person his true blood of his royal realm, that is to say, the high and mighty prince the Duke of York, exiled from our sovereign lord's person by the noising of the false traitor the Duke of Suffolk and his affinity'.[3]

In August Richard landed in Wales and gathering 4,000 armed retainers marched on London, hoping to profit from Cade's uprising. He carefully kept his distance from the disturbances, which were soon suppressed, and in an interview with the king assured him of his loyalty, but asked for political reforms and complained of moves that had been made to arrest him. The king promised to appoint a new council with Richard a member and this led to angry disputes in parliament between him and his arch enemy, Edmund, the second duke of Somerset, with the chief protagonists of both parties appearing with bodyguards of armed men.

Richard, by now heir presumptive to the throne, was slowly gaining support in the Commons and the country but in January 1452, when he again marched on London, encamping at Dartford, and tried to foment disturbances in the capital and Kent, he received little or no backing. Faced with a strong royal army, Richard was forced into face-saving but in fact humiliating negotiations. Once more he pledged his loyalty to King Henry and escaped punishment after formally pledging never to act against the king, or muster armed force, without royal licence or in his own self-defence. Rumours that Richard's son, Edward, was approaching with a large force to support his father may well have influenced the king to be lenient, and in any case Henry continued to hope for a rapprochement between the baronial factions, and indeed that summer visited Richard's castle in Ludlow.

In the summer of 1453 and under pressure of events, Henry lost his reason and, in spite of the delaying tactics of the duke of Somerset and his party, Richard was appointed Protector in March 1454. His prospects had, however, been jeopardised the previous autumn when the queen, Margaret of Anjou whom Henry had married in 1445, gave birth to a son; it was Richard who had escorted her to England to be married, but they had soon became sworn enemies with Margaret no doubt sensing the threat that Richard presented to her husband.

Richard's expectation of the throne as Henry's heir was dashed and by the end of 1454, with King Henry recovering from his illness, Richard and his supporters were politically sidelined. Having, however, tasted power, and now not even invited to attend council, Richard was not prepared to give it up without a struggle, and in May he and his allies resolved to resort to force of arms if their terms for political reform were not met. After nearly three hours of fruitless negotiations Richard's Yorkist army clashed with that of the king at St. Albans on 22 May 1455 — the first battle of that intermittent struggle for political power which was to last for some 30 years and come to be known as the Wars of the Roses. Victorious in what was not much more than a skirmish, Richard and his associates, still protesting their loyalty to King Henry, proceeded to take over the government. In November, Henry again became ill and Richard once more Protector, but when the king recovered early the next year Richard was dismissed from office although the king retained him as a councillor. The Lancastrian faction resumed control of the country's administration which was increasingly dominated by the formidable and unforgiving Queen Margaret. There ensued a three-year political stand-off, with feuds among the baronage and antipathy between Margaret and Richard only papered over with a semblance of reconciliation, while the king endeavoured to mediate between the parties and retain control of the deteriorating political situation. Both Lancastrian and Yorkist lords were now making serious preparations for war, recruiting experienced soldiers who had returned from the French wars for their retinues which were expanding into private armies. In Wales the Yorkist cause was promoted by Welsh bards recalling that Richard, duke of York, Lord Mortimer, was descended from Llywelyn the Great, through Ralph (II) de Mortimer's marriage to Llywelyn's daughter, Gwladus Ddu, in 1230.

By the summer of 1459, Richard had become convinced that Queen Margaret, now the driving force behind the Lancastrians, was intent on a military confrontation and mobilised his allies. Hostilities broke out on 23 September at Blore Heath, near Market Drayton, with Richard's ally, the earl of Salisbury, defeating a Lancastrian force when 'both hosts met and encountered and fought a deadly battle'.[4] The king now acted with uncharacteristic energy, and with an army marched to Ludlow where the Yorkist forces had converged under the command of Richard and the earls of Warwick and Salisbury. Richard and the earls protested their loyalty to the king and that they were only acting in self-defence. Outside the town, at Ludford Bridge on 12 October, the Yorkist army dissolved when many troops deserted to the royal army while others melted away without a blow being struck, leaving Richard's military reputation severely damaged.

The rebels dispersed, with Richard escaping first to Wales and then Ireland, and others making for the Yorkist safe haven of Calais. The government tried to restore its authority, taking repressive measures against suspected Yorkist sympathisers, and in November Richard and his prominent supporters were attainted in parliament 'of high treason, as false traitors and enemies'.[5] In Ireland, where he had been the king's lieutenant from 1454 until his attainder and was still widely regarded as such, Richard was popular and relatively safe. He kept in touch with his English supporters, and in March 1460 drew up plans with the earl of Warwick who visited him from Calais and who now seems to have assumed the role of the Yorkists' foremost soldier.

Towards the end of June the earls of Warwick and Salisbury took the initiative. With Richard's eldest son, Edward, earl of March since his father had probably resigned his honour in 1445, they crossed the Channel and landed with a small army at Sandwich. Virtually unopposed, they marched north and on 10 July fought the battle of Northampton, routing the Lancastrians and capturing the king, whom they took to London, assuring him of their fealty; Queen Margaret, meanwhile, fled northwards with her son. Richard landed near Chester in September:

> When the Duke of York returned from Ireland to the realm of England, landing at Red Bank near the town of Chester, there were varied and contrary rumours amongst the people about his return. Some said that his arrival was peaceful, and that he intended nothing else than to restore harmony among the quarrelling peers of the realm, and bring peace by his authority everywhere throughout the realm, and reform it. But others, amongst whom were the older and wiser in mind, suspected that he was going to be litigious and act litigiously against the king for the rights of the royal crown and claim that crown by the title of hereditary right.[6]

Richard entered parliament in London on 10 October; 'with the pomps of a great following, [he] arrived in no small exultation of spirit; for he came with horns and trumpets and men at arms, and very many other servants'.[7] He made no bones about claiming the throne by inheritance, stressing his Mortimer ancestry and the way his family had been sidelined by Henry of Bolingbroke, when his coup of 1399 had brought him to the throne as Henry IV and inaugurated the Lancastrian dynasty. He had, however, misjudged the sentiment in parliament, and after negotiations he had to be content with a compromise proposed by the lord chancellor to which King Henry agreed: Henry would remain king for life but be succeeded by Richard and his heirs. Richard was apparently reconciled with the king, now virtually a prisoner, but Queen Margaret would have none of it: she would not agree to the disinheriting of her son, and taking refuge in Wales she began to muster an army of her supporters in the Lancastrian lands of the north of England.

Sandal Castle. An engraving of 1753 of a drawing made in the reign of Elizabeth I; the castle was demolished in 1648. The chapel built by Edward IV on Wakefield Bridge in memory of his father still stands

Richard could not ignore the threat and early in December he and the earl of Salisbury marched north to suppress the rebellion, but were besieged in Richard's castle at Sandal, near Wakefield, over Christmas. Richard sent for assistance from his son, Edward, and was advised in the meantime to await his arrival in the safety of the castle. On 30 December, however, in circumstances which are not clear and protesting that he would not be caged like a bird, Richard sallied forth from Sandal Castle with his outnumbered army. In the battle of Wakefield which followed, the Yorkists were comprehensively defeated. Richard was killed, Salisbury captured and executed, and Richard's younger son, Edmund, earl of Rutland, killed in cold blood whilst escaping from the battlefield.

Richard duke of York's career can be seen on the one hand as a record of opportunist self-seeking and, on the other, as the behaviour of an honourable patriot with political responsibilities, driven by misgovernment of the country to challenge his king. His record surely shows that the latter interpretation is the fairer one, even if personal animosities and ambition progressively played a part in his actions in the last ten years of his life. His judgement and ability in military matters, other than in France in the early 1440s, are unimpressive, but his rank, great wealth and resources of manpower were crucial to the Yorkist war effort.

One of the features of the Wars of the Roses was the growing ferocity with which they were fought, ferocity to which England was unaccustomed. Civil wars are savage; in foreign wars the participants can be seen as fighting honourably for their country, in civil wars one side or the other are *ipso facto* traitors.[8] The country was unaccustomed to the summary executions of the nobility which became the practice of both sides. The French statesman, Comines, related in his memoirs how King Edward IV (Richard of York's son, Edward) told him that, 'in all the battles he had won, once victory was in sight he mounted horse and proclaimed that the commoners should be spared and the lords killed, for of the latter none or very few escaped death'.[9]

After Richard's death, the leadership of the Yorkists devolved on his eldest surviving son, Edward, earl of March. He had been born in 1442, but in spite of his youth he had gained considerable military experience by the time of his father's death, and with the benefit of hindsight we can see that the Yorkist cause had fallen into good hands. In years to come, Edward's record as a notable king is amplified by chroniclers' comments on his personality and abilities as a ruler. He developed into a capable soldier, but one who preferred diplomacy to force; he managed the kingdom's finances with conspicuous success; he had a fine physique, intelligence and the common touch, and became popular with the people who would sincerely mourn his death. All this was in the future, however. On New Year's Day 1461 the leader of the Yorkists was a relatively untried 18-year-old, his party had just suffered a disastrous

Two former signs of the Mortimer's Cross Inn.
That on the left shows a Lancastrian and Yorkist supporter with their respective red and white roses with the Monument at Kingsland, which commemorates the battle, in the background. That on the right shows the Yorkist emblem of the Sun in Splendour held by the White Lion of the March, representing Edward who is gripping the banner as part of a parhelion between red and white roses

A parhelion, as witnessed at Mortimer's Cross and which gave rise to one of Edward IV's emblems. The phenomenon is caused by ice crystals, usually at high altitude but in freezing weather also near ground level, refracting light. The parhelia or mock suns appear where a solar halo intersects a horizontal axis drawn through the sun

defeat and had been left with only one army in the field, that in the London area commanded by the earl of Warwick. The Yorkists faced two threats — one from Queen Margaret's victorious force which was soon marching towards the capital, and the other from a second Lancastrian army which was gathering in south-west Wales.

Edward spent Christmas 1460 at Shrewsbury and would have heard of his father's and brother's deaths in the first few days of January. He may have been on a recruiting drive in support of his father, but it is more likely that he was urgently recruiting a force in order to block the advance of the Lancastrian army, made up of Welsh, French and Irish troops which had assembled in Pembrokeshire under the earls of Pembroke and Ormonde. By the third week of January this army was marching north-eastwards towards England. The earls probably planned to harry the heartlands of the Yorkists — the Mortimer lordships in Wales and the Anglo-Welsh borderlands, and in particular Ludlow and Wigmore — before joining Margaret's army in a pincer movement on London. Edward's army, however, barred their way at Mortimer's Cross, near Leominster in Herefordshire and just outside the southern boundary of the lordship of Wigmore, and there on 3 February 1461, 'On the vigil of the Purification of the Blessed Virgin Mary a battle took place near Wigmore at Mortimers Cross, when the Earl of March advanced with 51,000 men against

the Earl of Pembroke with 8,000'. (The strengths of the two armies more probably consisted of between 2,000 and 3,000 men).[10]

The Yorkist victory at Mortimer's Cross was complete and was followed
by the ritual blood-letting: sweet revenge for the butchery at Wakefield.
Lancastrian lords who had been captured were summarily executed, among
them Owen Tudor, the grandfather of Henry Tudor (later King Henry VII) who
went to the scaffold in Hereford.

Queen Margaret was in the meantime advancing on London from the north,
and on 17 February encountered the earl of Warwick's Yorkist army standing
in her way. The Yorkists were defeated in the Second Battle of St. Albans, but
Warwick managed to extricate many of his men from the battle and, presumably
having heard of Edward's victory at Mortimer's Cross, retreated westwards.

The way to London lay open to the queen, now reunited with the king who
had been liberated from Warwick's custody on the battlefield. Margaret hoped
that Londoners would open the city's gates to her, but the Lancastrian army's
pillage of the countryside on its march south and its sack of St. Albans after
the battle, emboldened the citizens to refuse her entry. Margaret hesitated to
launch an attack: 'And this was the downfall of King Henry and his queen; for
if they had entered the city of London, they would have had all at their will'.[11]
With growing opposition from the large number of Yorkist sympathisers in the
capital she decided to retreat north.

On hearing of the defeat at St. Albans, Edward marched on London,
intending to secure the capital and join the remnants of Warwick's army.
The two Yorkist forces met in the Cotswolds and the gates of London were
opened to Edward and Warwick on 27 February. Five days later Edward was
proclaimed king at Westminster, in what was not a coronation but acceptance
by the capital's citizens of his new status, when 'all the people shouted that
Edward was and should be king'.[12]

A new dynasty now occupied the throne, one that largely owed its legitimacy
to its Mortimer ancestry, but Edward did not stay long in London. There was
unfinished business to attend to in the north where Henry's and the queen's
undefeated army was gathered in Yorkshire. By 22 March Edward and his army
was at Nottingham and a week later routed the Lancastrians at Towton in one of
the most bitterly fought battles in English history. Henry VI, Queen Margaret and
her son, Prince Edward, found safety in Scotland, while Edward earl of March
stayed in the north for several weeks attempting to eradicate Lancastrianism — a
task which would, in fact, take him several years and even then he would be far
from done with the indomitable Queen Margaret. He returned to London for his
coronation, and on 28 June 1461, Edward, earl of March, earl of Ulster, Lord
Mortimer, was crowned King Edward IV of England.

Notes and References

Difficulties which are sometimes experienced in tracing the descent of lordships are exemplified by the evidence for that of Narberth and part of St. Clears which were held by Roger (III), in the right of his wife, Maud, at his death in 1282 (*Cal. of Inquisitions Post Mortem*, II, no. 446). Lordship, part of Maud's dower, appears to have been conveyed to Roger of Chirk after 1282 and before 31 March 1299, when there is mention of 'Roger de Mortuo Mari's castle of Narberth and his town of St. Clear ... while he was in Gascony on the king's service'. (*Cal. Pat. Rolls 1292-1301*, 465). In view of the date it would seem that the Roger in question must have been Roger of Chirk. B.L. Harleian MS 1240 f.21 no. 16 and B.L. Additional MS 6041 f.23v no. 16 are summaries of an undated charter of Maud referring to such a conveyance to her son, Roger. A summary of a similar undated charter (B.L. Egerton Roll 8723 m.3v), in which Maud conveys the same lands to her son, *Edmund*, is perplexing. It may be a mistranscription by a careless scribe or may have been superseded by the one to Roger. (B.L. information provided by Professor Rees Davies).

Chapter I Norman Origins & English Opportunities

1. C. Lloyd, C.T. Clay and D.C. Douglas (eds.), *The Origins of some Anglo-Norman Families* (1951), vii.
2. The usual English version 'Mortimer' is used in this account except for Roger de 'Mortemer', *fl.* 11th century in Normandy. 'De Mortuo Mari', as the Mortimers were known for many years, was a whimsical play of words on a proper name, a practice adopted by others of the nobility.
3. The early Mortimers and their wives have proved fertile ground for family pedigrees. The respected genealogist J.B. Planché reviewed the evidence for Roger's ancestry nearly 150 years ago in the *Journal of the British Archaeological Association*, XXIV (1868), 21-35. His summary of the position with regard to Roger de Mortemer is as valid now as it was then: 'Until, therefore, we are fortunate enough to exhume some charter or other irreproachable instrument which may enlighten us on the subject, we have no fact to start from of an earlier date than the existence of the Roger de Mortimer commanding the troops of William Duke of Normandy in 1054, at the Battle of Mortimer'.
4. Odain, Roger's first wife (Paul Remfry, *The Mortimers of Wigmore. Part I* (1995), 2, and not Hawise (*Complete Peerage*, IX, 267), his second wife and mother of Ralph.
5. *The Ecclesiastical History of Orderic Vitalis*, Marjorie Chibnall (trans. and ed.), IV (1973), 87-9.
6. *Anglo-Saxon Chronicle*. Version in English Historical Documents, II, 168.
7. Orderic Vitalis, IV, 83.
8. The Wigmore chronicler in W. Dugdale, *Monasticon Anglicanum*, ed. J. Caley, H. Ellis and B. Bandinel, VI (1830), 348-55. There are some blatant errors in this chronicle and it must be treated with caution; presented in this edition in a somewhat muddled form, much of it is no doubt based on family oral tradition and it is likely to be more reliable when dealing with later events.
9. 'Florence of Worcester', *Chronicon ex Chronicis*, ed. B. Thorpe, II (1849), 24-6.
10. Orderic Vitalis, IV, 285.
11. *Brut y Tywysogon* or *The Chronicle of the Princes*, Peniarth M.S. 20 Version, T. Jones (trans. and ed.), (1952), 19.
12. Paul Remfry in *The Mortimers of Wigmore* (1995), 10-12, which is a valuable contribution to the history of the early Mortimers.

Chapter II Wales & the Marcher Lordships

1. *Brut y Tywysogyon or The Chronicle of the Princes*, Peniarth M.S. 20 Version, T. Jones (trans. and ed.), (1952), 34.

2. *The Itinerary and Description of Wales* by Giraldus Cambrensis, W. Llewelyn Williams (introd.), (1908), 193.
3. R.W. Eyton, *The Antiquities of Shropshire*, (1854-60), I, 235 and VII, 257. The king was 'surprised and greatly moved' at Fitzalan's bluster and ordered the implementation of the writ to levy £200.
4. *Calendar of Patent Rolls* 1461-7, 425-6.
5. *Brut*, Peniarth M.S. 20, 42.
6. *The Chronicle of Walter of Guisborough*, H. Rothwell (ed.), Camden Series LXXXIX (1957), 216.
7. *Vita Edwardi Secundi*, N. Denholm-Young (ed.), (1957), 117.
8. Such judicial difficulties were not confined to the March. In 1536 Bishop Rowland Lee, President of the Council in Wales, asked Thomas Cromwell to decide in which shire the town of Bewdley stood. Lee's efforts to administer justice were being hindered by people from the town who were indicted in Worcestershire saying that the town was in Shropshire, while those indicted in Shropshire said that the town was in Worcestershire.
9. Giraldus, xiii.
10. Giraldus, 190.
11. H.M. Colvin, *The History of the King's Works*, (1963), I , 398-9.
12. *Brut y Tywysogon* or *The Chronicle of the Princes*, Red Book of Hergest Version, T. Jones (trans. and ed.), (1955), 39.
13. *Brut*, Red Book, 247.
14. Giraldus, 205.
15. Wolsey rejected Buckingham's request, no doubt for good reason as the same year he instigated the arrest and execution of the duke for disloyalty to the king.

Chapter III Lords of the March

1. One family pedigree suggests that with Roger Mortemer being born before 990 and his grandson, Hugh, living until *c*.1180, three successive generations spanned at least 190 years. Theories have been advanced that there is a missing generation between Ralph and Hugh, or that the given dates are incorrect. The evidence for Roger succeeding Hugh as lord of Wigmore *c*.1149 [his position in a list of witnesses of a charter, *Complete Peerage*, IX (1936), 269] has been questioned in view of doubts about the charter's authenticity.
2. *The Ecclesiastical History of Orderic Vitalis*, M. Chibnall trans.and ed., VI (1978), 223.
3. *Anglo-Saxon Chronicle*. Version in English Historical Documents, II, 210.
4. William of Newburgh, 'Historia Rerum Anglicarum, Chronicles and Memorials of the Reigns of Stephen, Henry II, and Richard I, R. Howlett (ed.), (Rolls Series 1884-90), I, 105.
5. William of Newburgh, I, 105; 'Chronica Roberti de Torigneio, Chronicles and Memorials etc., IV, 184-5; *Giraldus Cambrensis, Opera*, J.S. Brewer etc. (ed.), VIII (Rolls Series 1891), 215; J.C. Dickinson and P.J. Ricketts, 'The Anglo-Norman Chronicle of Wigmore Abbey', *Transactions of the Woolhope Naturalists' Field Club*, XXXIX, 421.
6. *Brut y Tywysogyon* or *The Chronicle of the Princes*, Red Book of Hergest Version, T. Jones (trans. and ed.) (1955), 179.
7. William of Newburgh, I, 181.
8. 'The Anglo-Norman Chronicle of Wigmore Abbey', 431.
9. R.W. Eyton, *The Antiquties of Shropshire*, IV (1857), 203-4.
10. *Calendar of the Charter Rolls*, I, 155.
11. P.C. Bartrum, *Welsh Genealogies AD300-1400*, III (1974), 446, states that Gwladus was the daughter of Tangwystl, Llywelyn's mistress. Gwladus was the widow of Reginald de Braose.
12. Matthew Paris, *Chronica Majora*, H.R. Luard (ed.), IV, 319-20.

Chapter IV 'Long and Praiseworthy Services'

1. Extract from Edward I's letter, see reference 15.
2. *Brut y Tywysogon* or *The Chronicle of the Princes*, T. Jones (trans. and ed.), Peniarth M.S. 20 Version (1952), 110.
3. *Brut*, 112.
4. *Foedera, Conventiones, etc,* A. Clarke, J. Caley and F. Holbrooke (eds.), I, 398.
5. *Brut*, 112.
6. 'The Chronicles of the Mayors and Sheriffs of London', H.T. Riley (ed), *English Historical Documents*, III, 173. It is not clear whether Wigmore Castle was actually captured.
7. *Calendar of the Charter Rolls*, II, 57, 90.
8. R.W. Eyton, *The Antiquities of Shropshire*, IV (1857), 221.
9. *Brut,* 118.
10. *Welsh Rolls*, 212.
11. *Calendar of the Patent Rolls, 1281-92*, 38.
12. G. Marshall, 'Notes on Kingsland Church, Herefordshire', *Transactions of the Woolhope Naturalists' Field Club*, XXVII, 25.
13. R.R. Davies, *Lordship and Society in the Marches of Wales 1282-1400* (1978), 25.
14. The chronicler Thomas Wykes: *Annales Monastici*, IV, 290.
15. *Welsh Rolls*, 257.

Chapter V Lord Mortimer

1. *Calendar of the Patent Rolls, 1258-66*, 436,451.
2. *Calendar of Ancient Correspondence concerning Wales*, 83-4.
3. *Calendar of the Close Rolls, 1279-88*, 486.
4. *Calendar of the Fine Rolls*, I, 366.
5. *Calendar of the Patent Rolls, 1281-92*, 257.
6. *Calendar of the Close Rolls, 1296-1302*, 107.

Chapter VI Earl of March

1. Much of Roger's inheritance in England and Wales was held as dower by his mother. The family held the lordships of Wigmore, Maelienydd, Knighton, Norton, Pilleth, Presteigne, Knucklas, Gwerthrynion Ceri and Cydewain; in Herefordshire the manors of Thornbury, Marcle, Kingsland, Eardisland, Pembridge and Orleton; the manor of Cleobury in Shropshire; in Worcestershire the manors of Bewdley, Bromsgrove, Norton and one eighth of Inkberrow; the manor of Awre in Gloucestershire; in Somerset the manors of Milverton and two thirds of Odcome; in Hampshire the manors of Stratfield, Worthy Mortimer and Stratfield Saye; the manor of Crendon in Buckinghamshire; one third of the borough of Bridgwater in Somerset, lands in Ackhill in Shropshire, and in Eckington and Shrawley in Worcestershire. (*Calendar of Inquisitions Post Mortem*, IV, no. 235, and G.A. Holmes, *The Estates of the Higher Nobility in Fourteenth-Century England* (1957), 10-11. The heirs of Walter de Lacy who died in 1241 were his grand daughters Margery, who married John de Verdun, and Maud who married Geoffrey de Genevile. The Lacy lands were therefore divided into two parts. In 1283 Geoffrey and Maud gave the Lacy estates in England and Wales to their son, Peter, who died in 1292. Peter married Joan, daughter of Hugh, count of La Marche and it was their daughter, Joan, who Roger Mortimer (IV) married in 1301. Geoffrey de Genevile (d.1314) trans-ferred the Genevile lands in Ireland to the Mortimers in 1307. Although Peter de Genevile's widow, Joan, retained an interest in the English and Welsh Genevile properties until her death in 1323, Roger (IV) and his wife appear to have acquired rights over them during her lifetime, and an absolute right to a moiety of Ludlow which Geoffrey de Genevile granted to Roger in obscure circumstances.

2. *Calendar of the Fine Rolls*, I, 543.
3. *Parliamentary Writs and Writs of Military summons, Edward I and Edward II*, ed. F. Palgrave, Record Commission, II, I, 35.
4. *Calendar of the Close Rolls, 1313-18*, 450-1.
5. *Calendar of Documents Relating to Scotland*, III, No. 159.
6. J.T. Gilbert, *History of the Viceroys of Ireland* (1865), 146-8.
7. *Calendar of the Patent Rolls, 1321-24*, 51.
8. T.F. Plucknett, 'The Origin of Impeachment', *Transactions of the Royal Historical Society*, 4th series, XXIV, 57.
9. See pages 196-7.
10. *Calendar of the Close Rolls, 1323-27*, 132.
11. *Calendar of the Patent Rolls, 1324-27*, 325.
12. *Cronicon Adae de Usk 1377-1421*, trans. and ed. E.M. Thompson, (2nd ed. 1904), 166-7.
13. *Calendar of the Close Rolls, 1327-30*, 275.
14. *Calendar of the Close Rolls, 1327-30*, 317.
15. *The Brut*, ed. F.W.D. Brie, Pt I (The Early English Text Society 1906), 254.
16. *Chronicon Galfridi le Baker de Swynebroke*, E.M. Thompson ed., (1889), 31-4. See T.F. Tout's analysis of the evidence relating to Edward's death in 'The Captivity and Death of Edward of Carnarvon', in his *The Collected Papers*, III (1934), 145-190. The evidence is re-examined in G.P. Cuttino and T.W. Lyman, 'Where is Edward II?', *Speculum*, LIII (1978), 522-43, which contains a speculative version of events in which Edward escaped to Ireland and then to the Continent. Also Ian Mortimer, 'The Death of Edward II in Berkeley Castle', English Historical Review, 120 (December 2005), 1175-1214, for a persuasive argument in favour of Edward's survival.
17. A. Tuck, *Crown and Nobility 1272-1461* (1985), 97-8.
18. *Calendar of Papal Letters*, II, 349.
19. *Rotuli Parliamentorum*, II, 52-3.

Chapter VII 1330-1425: Decline or Rebirth?

1. Penry Evans, 'The Family of Mortimer', University of Wales PhD thesis (1934), 273.
2. D. Harding, in *Ludlow Castle: its History and Buildings*, (2000), 48-9.
3. The *Complete Peerage* states that he was in the first division, while the *DNB* claims that he remained in the rear.
4. Evans, (1934), 276.
5. *Calendar of Inquisitions Post Mortem*, Edward III, Volume 10, 291.
6. *Calendar of Inquisitions Post Mortem*, Edward III, Volume 9, 379. Ludlow had been divided between Maud de Genevile and Margery de Verdun after the death of their grandfather Walter de Lacy in 1244.
7. *Calendar of the Patent Rolls*.
8. Dugdale, *Monasticon*, vi, 352.
9. For a discussion of 'uses' see p.143.
10. *Calendar of the Close Rolls, 1360-64*, 46-7.
11. Evans, (1934), 292.
12. Nichols, *Royal Wills*, 104-116.
13. Dugdale, *Monasticon*, vi, 353; Adam of Usk, *Chronicon 1377-1421*, ed. Thompson, (1904), 168.
14. Adam of Usk, (1904), 168.
15. *Calendar of Inquisitions Post Mortem*, Richard II, Volume 15, 534.
16. Evans, (1934), 317.
17. *DNB*, quoting *Cont. Eulogium Historiarum*, iii, 361.
18. Dugdale, *Monasticon*, vi, 354.

19. Dugdale, *Baronage*, I, 50.
20. Adam of Usk, (1904), 159.
21. T. Thornton, Cheshire: the inner citadel of Richard II's kingdom, in G. Dodd (ed.), *The Reign of Richard II*, (2000), 85-91.
22. *Calendar of the Charter Rolls, 1341-1417*, 335.
23. M.E. Griffin, Cadwalader, Arthur, and Brutus in the Wigmore Manuscript, *Speculum*, xvi, (1941), 109-20.
24. At his birth the horses in the stables at Ludlow stood shin-deep in blood, and scabbards filled with blood. (Dugdale, *Monasticon*, vi, 354.) For dramatic effect these legends were transferred by Shakespeare to Glendower in *Henry IV, Part I*.
25. G. Hodges, *Owain Glyn Dŵr and the War of Independence in the Welsh Borders* (1995), 87.
26. They appear to have been buried at the expense of one pound at the church of St. Swithin, Cannon Street.
27. Dugdale, *Monasticon*, vi, 355.
28. Harding (2000), 55.

Chapter VIII Branches of the Mortimer Family

1. The traditional Welsh version of the grant is that the lands of Powys Fadog and Bromfield were granted to Mortimer and the earl of Surrey as guardians for the young heirs. These were drowned in the Dee in 1281 on their guardians' orders, and the lands divided between Mortimer and Surrey. (Lloyd, *History of Powys Fadog*.) In fact the boys were alive in 1283, and it was the land of their uncle which Mortimer received. (*Complete Peerage*.)
2. M. Prestwich, *Edward I*, (1997), 509-10.
3. *Calendar of the Close Rolls*, Edward II, Volume I, p.68.
4. *Calendar of the Close Rolls*, Edward II, Volume 2, p.315.
5. Eyton, *op.cit.*, Volume 3, p.38.
6. *Calendar of Inquisitions Post Mortem*, Edward I, Volume 4, 373.
7. *Calendar of Inquisitions Post Mortem*, Edward II, Volume 6, 114.
8. *Calendar of Inquisitions Post Mortem*, Henry IV, Volume 18, 751. Margaret is mentioned in the Close Rolls in 1357, where the escheator for Shropshire was ordered to deliver the manor of Quatt to Hugh de Mortuo Mari and Margaret his wife, who had granted it for life to Richard de Welles, who was by then deceased.
9. *Ibid.*, 865.
10. *Ibid.*, 751.
11. Evans, (1934), genealogical table.
12. *Calendar of Inquisitions Post Mortem*, Edward I, Volume 2, 132.
13. Foljambe, C.G.S., and Reade, C., *The House of Cornewall*, 149ff. While the holders of Burford styled themselves 'Barons of Burford', they were not entitled to sit in Parliament.
14. *Calendar of Inquisitions Post Mortem*, Edward I, Volume 2, 640.
15. *Calendar of Inquisitions Post Mortem*, Edward I, Volume 4, 221; F. Noble, Medieval Boroughs of West Herefordshire,*Woolhope Club Transactions*, Vol.38, part I, (1964), 64-65.
16. *CIPM*, Edward III, Volume 8, 112.
17. *Calendar of the Patent Rolls, Edward III, 1330-1334, 495*.
18. *Ibid.*, 662; R.R. Davies, *Lordship and Society in the March of Wales, 1282-1400*, (1978), 52.

Chapter IX Estates and their Management

1. *Calendar of Inquisitions Post Mortem*, Edward I, Volume 2, Vol. 4, 235.
2. P. Evans, (1934), 424; P.M. Remfry, *The Mortimers of Wigmore, Part 1, Wigmore Castle, 1066-1181*, (1995), 4.

3. *Calendar of Inquisitions Post Mortem*, Edward I, Volume 2, 446.
4. See above, page 113.
5. *Calendar of Inquisitions Post Mortem*, Richard II, Volume 15, 534.
6. *Calendar of the Patent Rolls,*, Edward II, Vol. 2, 491.
7. Evans, 1934, 30.
8. *Calendar of Inquisitions Post Mortem*, Edward I, Volume 4, 235.
9. *Calendar of Inquisitions Post Mortem*, Edward I, Volume 2, 446.
10. J.E. Morris, *The Welsh Wars of Edward I*, (1996), 61-2.
11. R.R. Davies, *Lordship and Society in the March of Wales*, (1978), 24-5.
12. Davies, (1978), 25.
13. Evans, (1934), 374.
14. Evans, (1934), 457.
15. *Calendar of Miscellaneous Inquisitions*, Volume 2, 1203. 18 December 1330 complaining of conversion of wasteland to forest and warren with loss of hunting rights, and the imposition of heriot and lerewytes on free tenants. The exactions had been started by Roger of Chirk and continued after his death by the earl of March.
16. Evans, (1934), 444. PRO Min.Acc 1236/18.
17. Evans, (1934), 446. PRO Min. ACC 1304/17
18. G.A. Holmes, *The Estates of the Higher Nobility in Fourteenth Century England*, (1957), 117; the document is transcribed 128-9.
19. Evans, (1934), 451. PRO Min.Acc. 1236/5
20. Holmes, (1957), 92.
21. Holmes, (1957), 60-63; an example of an indenture is printed 130-2.
22. Above, pages 114, 115.
23. R.R. Davies, *The Revolt of Owain Glyn Dŵr*, (1995), 42-3.
24. BL Egerton Roll 8732 in Davies, (1978), 214-5.
25. Davies, (1995), 43.
26. PRO, SC6/1209/7; translated by E.J.L. Cole, An Incomplete Account of 10/11 Edward III, *Transactions of the Radnorshire Society* Vol. 38, (1968), 29-43.
27. E.J.L. Cole, An Account of the Keeper of Radnor Castle, 9-10 Edward III, *Transactions of the Radnorshire Society*, Vol. 33, (1963), 42.
28. Davies, (1995), 47.
29. Davies, (1978), 206.
30. Cole, (1963), 40.
31. Evans, (1934), 408 (Dolforwyn and Trellech); Cole, (1963), 40.
32. Cole, (1968), 40. Unfortunately Mr. Cole died before publishing a promised article on this episode.
33. Evans, (1934), 416.
34. PRO, SC6/1209/11. E.J. Cole, (1963), 32.
35. PRO, SC6/1209/7. E.J. Cole, (1968), 38; 41.
36. *Calendar of Inquisitions Post Mortem*, Edward I, Volume 4, 235.
37. *Calendar of Inquisitions Post Mortem*, Richard II, Volume 17, 1184.
38. Above, page 141.
39. Evans, (1934), 458.
40. PRO, SC6/1209/7; Cole, (1968), 41.
41. PRO, SC6/1209/11; Cole, 'Maelienydd, 30-31 Edward III' in *Transactions of the Radnorshire Society*, (1964), 33.
42. T. Rowley, *The Shropshire Landscape*, (1972), 119-21.
43. *Calendar of the Patent Rolls,* 1313-17, 323.
44. *Calendar of Inquisitions Post Mortem*, Edward I, Volume 4, 235.
45. PRO, SC6/1209/11; Cole, (1964), 32.

46. *Calendar of Inquisitions Post Mortem*, Richard II, Volume I7, 1194.
47. W. Rees, *South Wales and the March*, (1924), 29; quoted in Evans, (1934), 432.
48. *Calendar of Inquisitions Post Mortem*, Edward I, Volume 4, 235.
49. I. Soulsby, *The Towns of Medieval Wales*, (1983), 74 -6.
50. *Calendar of Inquisitions Post Mortem*, Edward IV, Volume 7, 387.
51. J. Lloyd, 'Surveys of the Manors of Radnorshire; the town and borough of Knucklas',
    Archaeologia Cambrensis, 5th ser., xvii (1900), 17.
52. The latest theories on the dating of the Ludlow town defences may be found in C.J. Train,
    The Walls and Gates of Ludlow: their Origins and Early Days, (1999).
53. L.A.S. Butler, *Denbigh Castle, Town Walls and Friary*, (1976), 26.
54. Soulsby, (1983), 121.
55. Soulsby, (1983), 261.
56. Soulsby, (1983), 258-9.
57. Soulsby, (1983), 87-8.
58. *Calendar of Inquisitions Post Mortem*, Edward I, Volume 3, 244.
59. R.R. Davies, *The Age of Conquest*, (1987), 402-3.
60. PRO, SC11/23; Davies, (1978), 196.
61. All statistics taken from Cole, (1963), 37-8.
62. Cole, (1964), 34.
63. Holmes, (1957), 97.
64. Holmes, (1957), 103-4.
65. Davies, (1978), 196.
66. Holmes, (1957), 108-9.
67. Davies, (1978), 118.
68. Evans,(1934), 453.
69. Davies, (1978), 118.
70. Cole, (1968), 41-3.

Chapter X The Mortimer Castles and Boroughs

1. R.R. Davies, *Lordship and Society in the March of Wales*, (1978), 70-1.
2. A.H.A. Hogg and D.J.C. King, 'Early Castles in Wales and the Marches', *Archaeologia
   Cambrensis*, Vol. 112, (1963),78.
3. F. and C. Thoms (eds.), *Domesday Book: Herefordshire*, (1983), 1, 19 and 9, 1.
4. P.M. Remfry, *The Mortimers of Wigmore: Part I Wigmore Castle 1066 to 1181*, (1995), 4-5.
5. P.M. Remfry, *The Castles of Radnorshire*, (1996), 117. Unfortunately Remfry does not give
   the provenance for this reference, and it is not noted by Hogg and King.
6. Dugdale, *Monasticon*, vi, 349.
7. Hogg and King, (1963), 94; 110.
8. Remfry, (1996), 92.
9. Remfry, (1996), 112-113.
10. Remfry, (1996), 123; *Montgomeryshire Collections*, Vol. 30, (1898), 311.
11. A.E. Brown, 'The Castle, Borough and Park at Cefnllys', *Transactions of the Radnorshire
    Society*, (1972),12.
12. Hogg and King, 'Masonry Castles in Wales and the Marches', *Archaeologia Cambrensis*,
    (1967), 108.
13. *Calendar of the Patent Rolls*, 1247-58, 156. The prior of Pershore is erroneously styled
    'abbot'.
14. A.J. Taylor, *The King's Works in Wales, 1277-1340*, (1975), 293-99.
15. J.C. King, 'The Castles of Breconshire', *Brycheiniog*, Vol. 7, (1961), 85-6.
16. E.J. Cole, 'The Castles of Maelienydd', *Transactions of the Radnorshire Society*, (1946),
    6; Hogg and King, (1967),125.

17. R. Williams, 'Early Documents relating to Dolforwyn Castle, Newtown , etc.', *Montgomeryshire Collections*, 28, (1894), 147-50.
18. See Chapter VIII for the history of this branch of the family.
19. The National Trust guidebook (2001), 47 accepts the 1310 date. The low height of the walls and tower is sometimes cited in support of the argument that the castle was never completed, but this could be the result of Civil War adaptations.
20. J.D.K. Lloyd and J.K. Knight, *Montgomery Castle*, (1973), 10-11.
21. L.A.S. Butler, *Denbigh Castle, Town Walls, and Friary*, (1976), 13.
22. J. Newman, *The Buildings of Wales: Gwent/Monmouthshire*, (2000), 589.
23. Remfry, (1996), 93-4.
24. Hogg and King, (1967),125; Remfry, (1996), 102-3.
25. *Calendar of the Patent Rolls, 1405-8*, 145.
26. Evans, (1934), 399.
27. L.A.S. Butler, 'Dolforwyn Castle, Montgomery, Powys', *Archaeologia Cambrensis*, Vol. 144, (1995) 200.
28. *Calendar of Inquisitions Post Mortem*, Richard II, Volume 15, 534.
29. PRO, IPM, Richard II, file 20.
30. Cole, (1963), 39.
31. PRO, SC6/1209/11; Cole, (1964), 33.
32. G. Hodges, *Owain Glyn Dŵr and the War of Independence in the Welsh Borders* (1995), 53-4.
33. Cole, (1946), 17-18; CPR 1401-5, 296, quoted in Brown, (1972), 14.
34. Remfry, (1996), 65-6.
35. D. Harding, 'The Mortimer Lordship', *Ludlow Castle: Its History and Buildings*, (2000), 54.
36. BL, Lansdowne MS, ii, 82, quoted in C.J. Robinson, *A History of the Castles of Herefordshire and their Lords*, (1869), 141.
37. E.D. Jones, 'The Cefnllys poems of Lewis Glyn Cothi', *Transactions of the Radnorshire Society*, (1936), 15-21.
38. Brown, (1973), 15.
39. Information kindly provided by Richard Stone of Marches Archaeology.
40. Chapter IX, pp.157-161.
41. *CIPM*, 4, 235.
42. I. Soulsby, *The Towns of Medieval Wales*, (1983), 12.
43. *Calendar of Inquisitions Post Mortem*, Edward I, Volume 4, 235.
44. Soulsby, (1983), 22-3.
45. J. Leland, *Itinerary*, ed. L.T. Smith, (1964), 3, 10.
46. Soulsby, (1983) 21; 23. It has been assumed that the placing of New Radnor in a lower category in the table on page 23 is an error.
47. Soulsby, (1983) 155.
48. *Calendar of the Patent Rolls*, Henry III (1258-68), 67.
49. Soulsby, (1983), 74-5.
50. Soulsby, (1983), 209.
51. For a scholarly discussion of the dating of Ludlow's walls, see C.J. Train, *The Walls and Gates of Ludlow; their Origins and Early Days*, (1999).
52. R. Higham and P. Barker, *Timber Castles*, (1992).
53. R. Higham, 'Timber Castles — a re-assessment', *Fortress,* Vol. 1, (1989), 58-9.
54. D. Hague and C. Warhurst, 'Excavations at Sycharth Castle, Denbighshire, 1962-63', *Archaeologia Cambrensis*, (1966),112-113.
55. Higham, (1989),52.
56. Cefnllys poem II, line 4; Jones, (1936), 19.
57. J.E. Morris, *The Welsh Wars of Edward I*, (1996), 172.

58. *Calendar of the Patent Rolls, 1405-8*, 145. Reference kindly supplied by Ron Shoesmith.

59. Soulsby, (1983), 206; P.M. Remfry, *Radnor Castle*, (199), 19.

60. R.A. Brown, H.M. Colvin and A.J. Taylor, *A History of the King's Works*, (1974), 335; National Trust, *Chirk Castle*, (2001), 42.

61. Butler, (1976), 11.

62. Taylor, (1974), 205.

63. M. Thompson, 'The Great Hall and Chamber Block', *Ludlow Castle; its History and Buildings*, (2000), 170.

64. R.K. Morriss, 'The Solar Block', *Ludlow Castle; its History and Buildings*, (2000), 166.

65. E. Mercer, *English Architecture to 1900, The Shropshire Experience*, (forthcoming).

66. *Ibid.*

67. RCHM, *An Inventory of the Historical Monuments in Herefordshire*, Volume III, (1934), 205-8; N. Readhead, 'Wigmore Castle - A Resistivity Survey of the Outer Bailey', *Transactions of the Woolhope Natutalists' Field Club*, 46 part iii, (1990), 423; Remfry, (1995), 27.

68. Remfry, (1995), 27.

69. R. Shoesmith, *Castles and Moated Sites of Herefordshire*, (1996), 238.

70. Evans, (1934), 432; Davies, (1978), 54.

71. The kind assistance of Tony Fleming of English Heritage in regard to the foregoing paragraph is gratefully acknowledged.

72. Lloyd and Knight, (1973), 11.

73. Pipe Roll, 12 Edward I; Morris, (1976), 172.

74. Remfry, (1996), 66.

75. Evans, (1934), 400.

76. PRO, Misc. Accounts 1209/4-10 (Radnor); 1263/3, 4-5, 7-8, (Wigmore); Evans, (1934), 405.

77. *Ibid.*

78. L.B. Larking, 'Inventory of the Effects of Roger Mortimer', *The Archaeological Journal*, XV, (1858), 354-62. The inventory is very long and detailed, and only a few items have been selected.

79. R. Williams, 'Early Documents relating to Dolforwyn Castle, Newtown, etc.', *Montgomeryshire Collections*, Vol. 28, (1894), 151-53.

80. E.D. Jones, (1936), 22-25.

Chapter XI Epilogue: Edward IV

1. *An English Chronicle*, J.S. Davies (ed.), (1856), 79-80.

2. *Engl. Chron.*, 64.

3. *Three Fifteenth Century Chronicles*, J. Gairdner (ed.), (Camden Series, 1880), 94.

4. *Engl. Chron.*, 79-80.

5. *Rotuli Parliamentorum*, v, 348 .

6. *Registrum Abbatiae Johannis Whethamstede*, H.T. Riley (ed.), (Rolls Series, 1872), I, 376.

7. *Regist. Abbat.*, 376

8. The point was wittily made by Sir John Harington (1561-1612): 'Treason doth never prosper: what's the reason? For if it prospers, none dare call it treason'.

9. *The Universal Spider, The Memoirs of Philippe de Commynes*, P. Kendall (trans. and ed.), (1973), 117.

10. 'William of Worcester', *Letters and Papers*, J. Stevenson (ed.), (Rolls Series, 1861-64), II, ii, 775. The strengths of the two armies is vastly exaggerated; each probably consisted of 2,000-3,000 men, Geoffrey Hodges, *Ludford Bridge & Mortimer's Cross* (2001), 55.

11. 'William of Worcester', 775.

12. 'William of Worcester', 775.

Index

Page numbers in italics relate to illustrations; listing of consecutive page numbers against an entry in the index indicates that the information on the subject is interrupted by other material

219

Also from Logaston Press

Usk Castle, Priory and Town

edited by Jeremy K. Knight & Andy Johnson

The Norman borough (or town) of Usk was established around its castle and priory and these are at the heart of this book. Through a series of chapters, the contributors explore the life of the town through the history of its inhabitants, and what can be learned about them from the buildings which still make up the town, as well as the archaeology of former times.

Whilst it was the Normans who founded the castle, priory and borough, the Romans preceded them, although the evidence of their presence is now largely below ground. Before them, prehistoric people and then the Celts lived in the surrounding area, and the first chapters of this book look at these phases of Usk's history, the period under Roman rule in some detail.

Subsequent chapters then look at the development of the Norman town and its hospitals and almshouses; the building and life of the priory, with its community of nuns and its shrine to St Radegund; the long history of the construction of the castle and its gradual expansion and strengthening; relations between the Norman incomers and the Welsh over the centuries, and the effect on the region of Owain Glyn Dŵr's uprising, seen through the eyes of one of Usk's most famous sons, Adam Usk, first from a distance and then at firsthand, as he became embroiled in the events that surrounded him.

Later chapters reflect on life in Usk during the period of religious upheaval in the 16th and 17th centuries, telling the story of the town's own martyr, St David Lewis; and chart the development of the medieval town through the Georgian period, as well as the more recent transformation of the castle wards into a remarkable garden. Coming to more recent times, a chapter is devoted to Usk's secret Auxiliary Unit and its operational base, established in preparation for a German invasion in the early 1940s; whilst a final chapter considers current problems and highlights issues on which decisions need to be made to help ensure that Usk has a thriving future.

This book forms a mini series with other Logaston Press publications: *Ludlow Castle: its History and Buildings*; *Tewkesbury Abbey: History, Art and Architecture*; and *Chepstow Castle: its History and Buildings*.

216 pages, with over 120 black and white and 20 colour illustrations

ISBN: 978 1906663 01 8 (hardback)   Price: £17.50
978 1906663 02 5 (paperback)   Price £12.95

Also from Logaston Press

The Fitzalans, Earls of Arundel and Surrey, Lords of the Welsh Marches (1267-1415)

by Michael Burtscher

This book covers the lives and careers of five Fitzalans, earls of Arundel and later of Surrey. They ruled over extensive estates in Sussex, Surrey, and Norfolk but were also powerful lords in the Welsh Marches where in their time they tangled with the Mortimers and Owain Glyn Dŵr. There was scarcely an event or battle at which the earls of Arundel were not present and they were continuously involved in affairs of State at the highest level, serving as royal councillors, military commanders and ambassadors to kings and popes. They lent considerable sums of money to the Crown to finance its wars with France and were, therefore, instrumental in the conduct of the Hundred Years war.

Two of the earls were dramatically beheaded for treason: Earl Edmund, a staunch supporter of King Edward II, was executed at the hands of Queen Isabella and Roger Mortimer when they invaded England in 1326; while Earl Richard III, who became embroiled with King Richard II for his role as one of the Lords Appellant in the 1380s, was similarly condemned in 1397. The family then constructed a crafty piece of propaganda promoting the two earls as martyrs. After 1397, the Fitzalans became powerful supporters of Henry Bolingbroke, duke of Lancaster, and assisted him in the coup d'état against King Richard II.

The career of each of these five earls on the national stage is considered here, along with the management and administration of their estates and their financial dealings with some of the leading merchants and bankers of the day – for it was on this wealth that the power of the Fitzalans rested. One gains not only a feeling for the characters of the earls but also a sense of the life of those beyond the royal and noble circles in which they moved. Many of the castles built by the Fitzalans can still be seen today, not least Arundel Castle and its gothic Fitzalan Chapel, but also many of the castles of their Marcher lordships, including those at Chirk, Oswestry, Clun and the ruins of Holt and Shrawardine. The family is also associated with Haughmond Abbey near Shrewsbury and with what is believed to be the tomb of Earl Richard II and his wife Eleanor of Lancaster at Chichester Cathedral, the inspiration for Philip Larkin's celebrated poem 'An Arundel Tomb'.

Michael Burtscher was raised in Bellinzona, Switzerland, and holds degrees in medieval history from the Sorbonne and Oxford University. In preparing his doctoral thesis, he has undertaken a significant amount of research on the largely unstudied original documents relating to the Fitzalan family. He is a founding member and former editor of the Journal of the Oxford University History Society.

192 pages, with 52 black and white illustrations
ISBN: 978 1904396 94 9   PRICE: £12.95